THE OWNED MEDIA DOCTRINE

THE OWNED MEDIA DOCTRINE

Marketing operations theory, strategy, and execution for the 21st century real-time brand

TAULBEE JACKSON + ERIK DECKERS

WITH FOREWORD BY JAY BAER

ARCHWAY
PUBLISHING

Archway Publishing books may be ordered through booksellers or by contacting:

Archway Publishing
1663 Liberty Drive
Bloomington, IN 47403
www.archwaypublishing.com
1 –(888) –242 –5904

Because of the dynamic nature of the Internet, any web addresses or links contained in this book may have changed since publication and may no longer be valid. The views expressed in this work are solely those of the author and do not necessarily reflect the views of the publisher, and the publisher hereby disclaims any responsibility for them.

ISBN: 978 –1 –4808 –0119 –6 (sc)
ISBN: 978 –1 –4808 –0120 –2 (hc)
ISBN: 978 –1 –4808 –0121 –9 (e)

Library of Congress Control Number: 2013911029

Printed in the United States of America

Archway Publishing rev. date: 7/1/2013

VICTORIA OMNI MOMENTUM.

(Win Every Moment)

Table of Contents

Who Should Read This Book?

A Foreword by JAY BAER

Companies today are competing for attention not just against other companies selling the same products and services. They are competing against everyone and everything.

Look at your Facebook feed. Or your Twitter feed. Or your email inbox. What you'll find is a confluence of messages from people to whom you're tied personally, and companies to which you're tied commercially. Thus, companies must compete line by line, and pixel for pixel against your actual friends, family members and loved ones.

This creates enormous challenges for businesses, that for decades have relied upon various forms of paid media to target messages and garner attention. Paid media struggles in these environments, because it is rightly viewed as an interruption, the marketing equivalent of fingernails on the chalkboard. You're just minding your own business on Twitter, and along comes an advertisement out of left field, reminding you that, at least at times, it's all about commerce not kismet.

To succeed in these new hybrid personal/professional online spaces, companies must use content as the conduit for attention. Owned media – interesting, useful, timely information that appeals to consumers on a level that transcends the linear and transactional – is the online marketing success path in this hyper –competitive age.

I'm particularly fond of owned media of the useful sort, and I believe that if brands can be truly and inherently useful, if they can create content that is so innately valuable that customers would pay for it (if asked), customers will reward those companies with attention and loyalty. In this book, my friends Taulbee Jackson and Erik Deckers provide the recipe for creating useful content, but also detailed prescriptions for doing even more with your owned media.

Joe Pulizzi, founder of the Content Marketing Institute has said, "You are in two businesses now. The business that you're in, and the media business." This becomes more and more true every day, as companies of every size, shape and description recognize that yesterday's playbook of paid, interruption marketing is yielding diminishing returns, online and off.

The challenge is that while companies are increasingly embracing the principles of owned media and content marketing, the detailed playbook for how to DO IT in practice has been missing, resulting in a lot of trial, error and operational inefficiencies.

In this remarkable – and remarkably useful – book, Jackson and Deckers provide the granular, step –by –step instructions and advice that senior digital marketers have craved for years. This is the book you'll keep on your desk forever (or at least until they have time to write the 2nd edition). I especially like the sections on process and staffing, as those are incredibly crucial elements of effective owned media, and often become stumbling blocks on the path to true scalability.

I've had the pleasure of working closely with both of these guys, and they know how the sausage is made in the owned media world, and I couldn't be happier that they were convinced to share their secrets in these pages.

If you're not a noticeably better digital marketer by the time you finish this book, let me know and I'll refund your money. If I have one taker, I'll be shocked.

Enjoy the Owned Media Doctrine. This is the book you've always needed.

Note from the Authors

It used to be that all of the marketing tactics existed to support the TV spot. Agencies created the advertisement and placed it, and then any digital and public relations efforts were there to support that ad in order to drive sales.

We think that's backward. Companies should be spending money and effort on developing their own audiences, using the advertisements, news stories and articles they pitch to drive audience back to the company's content – using their advertising dollars to build their own audience, instead of renting eyeballs from someone else. There's no point in lining the pockets of media companies with your money. Use that money to build your own audience rather than relying on the mercy (and fair pricing) of the media companies.

This is the point of our book. As marketers, we have not all yet realized the obvious need to treat owned media with the same respect we do earned and paid media. In fact, many of us probably don't even think of it that way or even call it that. But this is the most obvious, sane, logical way to approach integrated marketing in today's media environment. Owned media is the missing piece of the puzzle that we've all been struggling to define and deal with for more than a decade. We've been looking through the wrong end of the telescope.

The problem kind of sneaked up on us poor, unsuspecting marketers. We have been dazzled and blinded by buzzwords and bright, shiny objects (Email! Flash! Content management systems! HOLY KAW SOCIAL MEDIA!!!). For years, we have been focused on everything but the one thing that matters. With this book, we hope to remedy that situation, help you retool your team and refocus your efforts, and ultimately help you clarify what the concept of "owned media" really means for you and your team.

Most importantly, we hope at the conclusion of this book you will understand why owned media should be the primary area of focus for your brand, your primary spend, and your primary means of communicating with customers. This is the new hierarchy of enterprise brand marketing.

It's not just another new buzzword. In fact, it is the most head –slappingly obvious idea anyone has probably ever written a book about. At the same time, we have all missed it somehow.

We never said "so what?" when Bill Gates told us "content is king" in 1996. We never really followed that statement through to its logical conclusion, but the full implications of this one simple idea are enormous.

Marketing success doesn't come from paid media alone... or earned media, or owned media, for that matter. It comes from all three working together. But as we will outline in the coming pages, there needs to be a drastic refocusing of how your brand approaches marketing, and a new definition and structure for how brands interact with customers. It all starts with the concept of owned media, and it all ends with content.

Introduction

This isn't a basic "you should be monitoring your brand" or "you should be on social media" book. We assume you already have some experience with online marketing. You're in the trenches, using the tools, and you roll your eyes when you see yet one more blog post or white paper that tells you "first, set up a blog and get on Twitter."

This book is for the advanced, senior –level marketer who wants to leapfrog her competitors. You want to know how to reach more people, leverage all of your digital channels and spend your dollars more effectively.

What you'll get out of this book:

- You'll learn the solution to integrating your marketing efforts
- You'll gain an understanding of how to apply your resources to paid, earned and owned media
- You'll discover how to structure and staff an internal team and an external group of partners for owned media
- You will learn how to reorganize your internal and external teams to fully leverage every marketing dollar
- You will understand why you need to refocus your approach to strategy
- You will learn how to develop an enterprise digital marketing strategy that is both effective and future –proof
- You will be able to implement a strategic framework for your entire company that accounts for the real –time, always –on socialized nature of today's media environment across the entire enterprise
- You will understand how to consistently create content and manage dialogue on an ongoing basis to grow an engaged audience of consumer advocates
- You'll learn how to manage governance and distribution of your content, while keeping your brand both safe and engaged

- You'll understand how to measure the effectiveness of your efforts, and how to leverage that data to impact your business goals in real –time
- You will understand how to easily communicate and position owned media to your C –suite and internal and external partners, and how to merchandise your success
- You will learn about what's around the corner in this fast –moving space, and who to watch to know what's coming next

Keep in mind, everything you read in this book is based on real –world experience with more than 50 marketers over five years. Starting in 2007, this approach has been tested and optimized in a traditional ad agency setting, a digital agency setting, and at Raidious – the first marketing services firm specifically designed for owned media. Raidious was founded on and operates on the principals you will read in this book and has for more than three years. These concepts and approaches have been tested, broken, tested again, optimized, broken, tested, optimized some more, and at this point have evolved to be both effective and scalable in retail, health care, consumer packaged goods, services and many other categories. From the smallest brands to literally the largest brand on the planet, from the most beginner –level brands to the most mature and advanced digital marketers. Regardless of your brand's scenario. This. Stuff. Works.

This book is for the advanced marketer who needs to know the subtle ins and outs of content marketing. You want to know how to reach more people with owned media, and spend less money on less effective channels like paid advertising and public relations. This book will show you how to create content that will reach exactly the people you want to reach, and not an advertising audience filled with the 97 percent of people who aren't interested in your product in the first place.

We believe that, eventually, owned media will eclipse paid media and earned media in terms of where people put their money and resources. We're already seeing this happen in terms of people's content consumption. According to the Pew Research Center's Project for Excellence in Journalism ("2011 State of the News Media"):

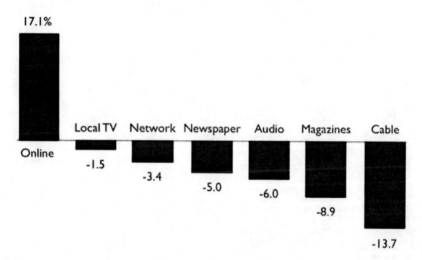

Figure A. The only source of news that has seen increased consumption is online news. All other sources have seen a significant decline from 2010 to 2011.

Some suggested books to read/concepts to understand before you read this one:

Beginners:
- "Permission Marketing" – Seth Godin
- "Tribes" – Seth Godin
- "The Long Tail" – Chris Anderson
- "Email Marketing: An Hour a Day" – Jeanniey Mullen, David Daniels, David Gilmour
- "Google Analytics" – Justin Cutroni
- "No Bullshit Social Media Marketing" – Jason Falls and Erik Deckers (yes, this Erik Deckers)

Intermediate:
- "Content Strategy for the Web" – Kristina Halvorson
- "Inbound Marketing" – David Meerman Scott
- "Don't make me Think" – Steve Krug
- "Marketing in the Age of Google" – Vanessa Fox

Advanced:
- "Information Architecture" – Morville/Rosenfeld
- "The Hero and the Outlaw" – Carol S. Pearson
- "The CRM Handbook" – Jill Dyche

Part I: Applied Theory of Owned Media

1. DEFINING OWNED MEDIA

We wrote this book to help marketers understand and frame the *right* problems and opportunities in today's media environment and to help them actually do something about it. With all of the recent changes that have happened in media and in consumers' media –consumption habits over the last couple of decades, almost everyone in marketing has made an attempt to understand and define the current and future state of affairs in media, particularly online. We want to share a different (more sane, logical, obvious) point of view about how to approach marketing in general, specifically in the online space.

Much of the discussion today is tactical in nature. Marketers talk about social media marketing, mobile marketing, search, digital PR and lots of other emerging online tactics. Is it web marketing? Is it digital marketing? Is it interactive marketing? Who's in charge of that? What does success look like? What should we be measuring? How does it all work together?

There have also been some movements toward coming up with a better, more broad definition of all of those tactics. Is it inbound marketing? Is it content marketing? Is it social media marketing? All of these points of view do a great job of communicating specific areas of tactical best practices, and they seem to be maturing and starting to get to the point. But they don't necessarily contextualize these tactics in a meaningful way that marketers can clearly understand, relate to or build a useful integrated strategy around.

We see a need to rethink this. We see a need to look at the problem at a much higher level and follow it through to its logical conclusion. We see a need to understand the operational implications and to redefine the problem because, as marketers, most of us have been looking through the wrong end of the telescope. It's nobody's fault. We were paying so much attention to the fast –moving, shiny stuff that we forgot to think about the slower –moving, more obvious stuff in a new way that lines up with what media has become. No harm, no foul. But let's fix it, yes?

1

The concept of owned media is designed to tie together all of the fast –changing tactics and platforms you've been struggling with and to bring clarity to how brands should think about, staff for, strategize, execute and generally approach what has always been a confusing mess of disparate, disconnected online tactics. In short, the concept is not only to be more successful at marketing, but to change the very idea of what marketing should be about.

It destroys the old "Above The Line/Below The Line" thinking of typical marketing operations. It gives direction to how brands and marketing services firms must staff and execute. It gives focus and clarity to how brands should be investing their marketing dollars. It moves the focus of marketing from shilling product to truly establishing and owning the direct relationship with the customer. It is a future –proof concept. It (finally) enables a truly holistic approach to marketing. It is an elegant, simple way to think and talk about marketing, and more importantly, how to develop a responsive, real –time strategy around the right things, and how to execute it.

Here is the entire concept of this book, explained in a beautifully simple Venn diagram:

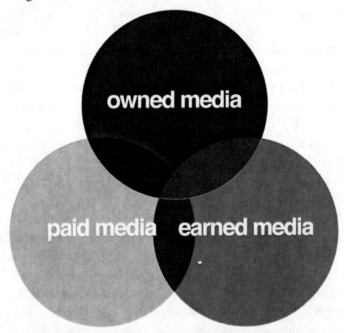

Figure 1A: The Relationship of Owned, Earned and Paid Media

1.1. Overview of owned media

It's a brutally simple concept. In fact, it's about a single word: control. Owned media is the area of marketing dedicated to the platforms or channels your brand owns or controls. This is not a tactical statement; this is a strategic philosophy with major implications for the future of marketing. It's not about Facebook, or email, or blogging, or websites, or inbound marketing or content marketing. It is a content –driven, audience –centric, platform –agnostic point of view on how to grow and leverage your audience, activate your marketing efforts and turn marketing dollars into a true investment in an asset (an audience). If your brand owns or controls the content, and owns or controls the platform, it is owned media.

Most importantly, owned media has always been an afterthought, instead of the central focus of marketing strategy. Millions of dollars are poured into paid media and earned media, and some of those have been allocated to "digital" or "interactive" or "social" components of those two things. Instead, we think owned media should, at the very least, play an equal and integrated role in marketing strategy, and because of the differences in how it must be approached, it requires an entirely different operational and strategic methodology than what has existed in the past.

There are some big differences between paid, owned and earned media:

Owned media is not like paid media, where someone else controls both the content and platform, and you have to pay to rent the audience's eyeballs 30 seconds at a time.

Owned media is not like earned media, where someone else controls both the content and the platform, and you have to pray that the content creator will create content about your brand in a positive way.

It's your content. It's your platform. It's your audience. That means it's your responsibility as a marketer to engage, entertain and grow that audience, so you can turn them into customers and advocates. That is the biggest challenge with owned media – and that is the problem this book will help you solve.

Whether it is owned media, paid media or earned media, there has to be an audience in place before you can convert it to paying customers. You wouldn't speak to an empty room, you wouldn't advertise on a TV channel with no viewers, and you wouldn't pitch a story to a magazine with no readers. The audience is where the value exists in all three approaches to media – paid, owned or earned.

As a company or a brand, does it make sense to continuously pay to deliver your message to someone else's audience that is most likely not interested, or are those dollars better spent on audience development, so that you can identify and reach those consumers who <u>are</u> interested whenever you like?

This book is about how to establish, grow and leverage your own audience, instead of relying on other organizations to do it for you. Once you get the hang of building and growing your own audience, you won't have to rent eyeballs anymore, and you won't have to pray to the PR gods to get a story placed to deliver a message. Smart marketers will use their advertising and public relations budgets to grow their own audiences.

1.2. The unique benefits of owning your audience

It's a land grab, folks. Everyone is fighting for attention, and that is causing audience share to decrease across every channel as more and more media options proliferate. Owned media is about your brand getting its piece of the pie.

When you use paid and earned media, you're putting your message in front of a large percentage of people who are not necessarily interested. The audience you own has already shown they're interested in your brand. It's a more affordable, more efficient approach that has tons of upside, like owning the audience data and owning the direct relationship with the customer. Instead of investing in gross rating points, you can invest in something that literally should show up on your books as a physical company asset … just like CNN, ESPN or The New York Times – the only value they provide to their shareholders is their audience, by far their biggest asset.

Gone are the days when media owners were the people who owned the newspapers and printing presses, and bought ink by the barrel. Gone are the days when few people owned the microphones and broadcast towers, the studios and satellites.

Thanks to technology, anyone can create content and build an audience. Anyone who has a laptop and a basic ability to express themselves can be a publisher, a journalist or a marketer. These people own their media, and they own their content. If they can reach a large and/or influential audience, then they can own their own success too. As can you, as a marketer and a steward of your brand. Brands are no longer at the mercy of the media. In fact, they are now empowered like never before with channels the brand owns and controls.

1.3. Solving the right problem

Marketers have spent so much time focusing on the technology, focusing on the tactics and the newest bright and shiny object, and trying to figure out online marketing that they can't see the forest for the trees. People in online marketing have said for years, "Content Is King!" But no one followed that thread to its logical conclusion. In fact, the deeper into the rabbit hole you go, the more obvious it is that "content is king" is an enormous understatement – but it's not the only place marketers should be focused.

Owned media is about more than content. It is about solving the right problem. Owned media is more about understanding where audiences come from, how to grow and manage them, and the unique benefits of owning your platforms, your own content and your own audience, and how that works with all the other areas of your organization to move the needle in your business. The implications from a marketing operations perspective – and a budgetary perspective – are immense.

1.4. The name game – what's the difference?

This sounds just like content marketing. Or inbound marketing. Or social media marketing. Or interactive/online/Internet/digital/web marketing. Do we really need another buzzword?

No. We need a new doctrine – a new way of thinking, a new set of principles about how these tactics work together, and what we have to change strategically and operationally as marketers to take advantage of this relatively new situation. Owned media is the "unifying theory" of all those tactical things we just mentioned. It is a philosophical approach and framework that is content driven, audience centric, and platform agnostic. It exists in complete and total harmony with paid and earned media. In fact, all three approaches work best when they work together.

Owned media can include lots of different tactical approaches, and some of the buzzwords above are how marketers tend to communicate about them, and define and discuss the problems and opportunities they face. It's important to understand the very subtle, but very important differences between them and how they function within owned media. For instance:

1.4.1. Inbound marketing

This is a set of interactive marketing tactical best practices designed to deliver sales leads. It uses search engine optimization (SEO) to bring people to your content. It uses the latest and greatest SEO research to get your content to rise to the top of the search ranks. Inbound marketers tend to be driven by research and numbers more so than content marketers and social media marketers. Inbound marketing is also beginning to use social media marketing, not only to build relationships, but to help with SEO as well. Business –to –business companies are successful with this lead –generation approach. However, while it's great for sales organizations, it does not really address listening and response, being able to account for so –called "soft" metrics such as preference and awareness, or audience development beyond the basics.

1.4.2. Content marketing

This is about content, with very little focus on audience development or integration with paid and earned media strategy. Close, but not broad enough. Content marketing is a single tactic: Create good stuff. You write good blog posts and articles; you shoot appealing videos; you record interesting podcasts. You create the content that makes people take interest in what you're doing, enough interest not only to read/watch/listen, but enough interest to take further action. Maybe it's to sign up for your newsletter, to download something from your website or even to buy something from your store. But again, the focus here is only about content, which is only half the battle in today's media environment. Content just sits there. To build an audience, we have to get the content in front of the people we want in our audience, and we have to be able to listen and respond to them in real –time. Media today and in the future is a two –way street. Content marketing does not really account for that.

1.4.3. Social media marketing

This is a misnomer. All media are social. Social media marketing is also a single tactic, even if it's done on a multitude of platforms: form relationships with people, get them to trust you and steer them toward your content. You do this on Twitter by sharing good stuff. You do it on Facebook by engaging your audience, or you do it on LinkedIn by connecting with fellow industry professionals. And you try out every new tool that shows any promise, just so you don't miss the next Facebook or Twitter. After all, if people trust you, they're more willing to consume your content, and act on your calls to action. What if you never had to worry about the next new social network? When you build a social media strategy, you are constantly playing catch up. When you build an owned media strategy, focused around content and engagement on a platform –agnostic and channel –agnostic basis, the digital media world evolves around you, not the other way around.

1.4.4. Digital / Interactive / Web / Online / Internet marketing

We still don't really know what we mean when we are using these mostly interchangeable phrases. But this is how a lot of marketers still see and discuss this area of the marketing world. If it happens on the Internet, it is Internet marketing. It's about websites, microsites and templates and banner ads and Flash and HTML5 and maybe email. There tends to be little focus on either content or audience when this is the topic of conversation – it is an afterthought, not the central focus, as it should be.

1.5. Where do audiences come from?

Customers only come from audiences, and there are only three ways to get access to an audience:

- You can buy it. (paid media)
- You can borrow it. (earned media)
- You can build it. (owned media)

Paid media. Earned media. Owned media.

In the past, the marketing world has been focused on buying access to audience through paid media (advertising) or borrowing access to audience through earned media (public relations).

Over the last couple of decades, as the media universe exploded with new channels, marketers tackled these new opportunities in many different ways. Depending on the organization, the responsibility for these areas could fall within different parts of an organization. Unfortunately, most organizations have been focused on the technology and the tactics, instead of on actually developing their own audience – which is the biggest benefit of almost every online tactic.

Owned media is about building your own audience – leveraging the channels a brand owns or controls, and using those channels to build your own audience – in order to turn that audience member into a customer, and eventually, an advocate for your brand.

1.6. History of the owned media concept

What if there was a TV channel that was only about your brand? Something pretty amazing has happened in the last few years, thanks to the Internet. Now, companies can produce their own content and become their own media outlets. The Internet has democratized news and mass communication so much, people (and therefore, brands) are able to reach the same audiences as the news media, be read by the bloggers' readers, and even host their own web TV shows and podcasts.

It actually happened a few years before this. While companies were still focused on traditional media, it was people – citizen journalists, diarists, entrepreneurs – who started using the Internet as a way to communicate with other people. As this got more and more popular, brands started embracing the Internet, but they still thought in old –media terms. They tried to earn media, and they tried to buy media, but they soon figured out they could own their media.

In 2008, we wrote the original business plan for Raidious, designed specifically to deal with owned media and real –time marketing via the brand newsroom concept. The company opened its doors on July 15, 2009. We first publicly defined the idea of "owned media" and its relationship to paid and earned media, as it exists today, on Sept. 28, 2009[1]:

The question about how to think about all this stuff was raised publicly in a David Armano post on Feb. 8, 2009[2].

The earliest appearance we can find of something closer to the current iteration of this concept is March 2, 2009, via Daniel Goodall on his blog "All That Is Good[3]." Goodall's team at Nokia had been using their version of this model internally for about a year at the time, according to his post.

The breakthrough moment for owned media came four months after Raidious opened its doors, on Dec. 16, 2009, when Sean Corcoran, with Forrester Research at the time, released his study on earned, owned and paid media[4].

---

1   http://raidious.com/earned–media–vs–paid–media–vs–owned media/

2   http://darmano.typepad.com/logic_emotion/2009/02/thoughts–on–bought–earned.html

3   http://danielgoodall.com/2009/03/02/owned–bought–and–earned–media/

4   http://blogs.forrester.com/interactive_marketing/2009/12/defining–earned–owned–and–paid–media.html

Corcoran credits R/GA, Critical Mass, Sapient and Isobar as employing the model to help their clients define their marketing initiatives. Since the release of the Forrester research, the term has gained popularity, spawning discussions online, as well as at least one other (highly recommended) book by Nick Burcher.

2. THE NEW HIERARCHY

Owned media is the biggest opportunity for brands in the last hundred years. Marketers have known this for awhile, but many have not been able to fully contextualize it. Its evolution has been an ongoing science experiment in a rapidly shifting media world. Lots of people still call it "new media." It has been relegated to a mostly "experimental" area of marketing because people don't fully understand its ramifications. And even though brands spend a little more every year on interactive marketing, it is still a paltry 10 to 15 percent of many budgets.

Furthermore, the way those dollars are being invested is all over the board. Some to SEO, some to email, and a small bit to social with the rest being spent on design, code and other platform –centric work. What's your audience development budget? What's your content budget? What's your engagement budget? Almost no one spends money like this. They're trying to solve the wrong problems.

2.1. Refocusing your resources

What if your budgets were divided into earned, owned and paid? Where would most of the money be spent? On renting eyeballs or sending press releases? Or would money be budgeted on developing your own audience and your own relationships with your potential customers, instead of financing media companies to compete with you for the attention of your customers?

Owned media is important enough that it needs to not just be included in a marketing plan – it should be the foundation of it. All roads in marketing lead to owned media. It can't be an afterthought. It needs to be part of your strategic planning at the earliest stages, at the same time you are developing your approach to research, campaign concepts, which networks to buy and which media outlets to pursue.

Owned media is by no means free, but you can pursue this for a fraction of the cost of your other marketing channels. Audiences cost money to create and develop, but very few brands spend enough in this area. The ones who do are the ones that are destroying their competitors ... Coke. Nike. Red Bull. Starbucks. Those specific brands are some of the most recognized and valuable in the world, and all are considered marketing thought leaders. All of them have invested heavily in owned media.

2.2. Rethinking your priorities

Instead of spending millions on advertising and public relations, what would happen if you put that same time, energy, money and resources into creating content and developing your own audience on the channels your brand already owns or controls?

Your first priority as a marketer should be to develop more customer relationships so you can sell more stuff. You have an opportunity now to do that with owned media – to have a little bit more control over your own destiny instead of relying on others to deliver an audience. So shouldn't that be the first priority of your spending as well? Your audience should not be an afterthought. Why would you spend 80 percent of your budget to reach an audience that considers your message an interruption? The core of your marketing investment should be in owned media, with paid and earned media supporting it – not the other way around.

2.3. Past tense: media isn't changing

Lots of marketers talk about how quickly the media world is changing. It is not changing – it has changed. Past tense. It's all real –time. It's all two –way. It's all social. Radio, TV, print and out of home – the advertising outlets most people think of as "traditional" – have changed forever. The way people interact with these channels has changed forever, too.

This is not a future state. It has already happened. This is a great opportunity – and mandate – for brands to reconsider their approach to integrated planning and execution. The way things have evolved, almost all media, to a greater or lesser degree, can essentially be treated in the same way. Brands should be taking a truly platform –agnostic point of view to media, with different tactical approaches (paid, owned or earned) to each medium/channel/platform.

2.4. Integration with earned media

With earned media, your story placement is made at the discretion of the editors, publishers, producers and even the bloggers and podcasters. Your placement is based on the publication's needs at that moment, whether the decision maker thought you were the right fit for the story, and the relationship your PR person has with the decision makers. PR strategy is critical for brands, but in the end, you are not serving your audience, you are serving someone else's audience.

Earned media tactics can bring a lot to the table to help you grow your audience. What if your PR team was pitching stories about a remarkable piece of content living on your owned media platforms, instead of a new product announcement? Now as a brand, you have the opportunity to have a direct relationship with the portion of the audience that's actually interested in you or something relevant to your brand.

Owned media can extend and activate your PR efforts in lots of ways that will grow your audience and benefit your brand, but it is critical that your earned media strategy is in line with what is happening on the owned media front, and the paid media front. It all works best when it's working together.

2.5. Integration with paid media

The unfortunate thing for marketers is that they spend millions of dollars to develop and execute advertising campaigns, yet people are trying everything they can to avoid commercials. So marketers are spending even more money and coming up with even more ideas about how to break through the clutter in order to reach people who don't want to be reached. Every day, it becomes more difficult to reach the right people with paid media. That doesn't mean it can't be used effectively – it works. While many see it as a critical way to deliver a marketing message, we see it as a critical tool to establishing and growing your own audience.

Using paid media often means spending more money than you should to reach people who don't want to hear what you have to say. You're being told you're reaching thousands, maybe even millions, of potential customers, but the truth is, they don't always want to hear from you. The truth is, they aren't always ready to buy.

A well –executed owned media presence enables brands to bridge the gap and offer consumers relevant content and relevant direct relationships.

It can activate and extend your paid –media campaign or even form the basis of it. Paid media is a great way to activate owned media, and owned media is a great source for creative use of paid media. Once again – it all works best when it is working together.

3. CONTENT DRIVEN. AUDIENCE CENTRIC. PLATFORM AGNOSTIC.

3.1. Digital marketing doesn't work without content.

Every single interaction that happens online starts and ends with content. Think about the implications of that. Websites are pretty boxes meant to hold content. A blog is a way to publish content proactively and to enable others to post their content and share their point of view. Email isn't successful because it's email. It's successful because of the content it delivers.

What if no one created videos for YouTube? Would we still be trying to figure out how to make a commercial "go viral" there? What if no one posted anything to Facebook? What if no one ever tweeted on Twitter? What if there were no pins on Pinterest? Would we be talking about the success of social media? No, we wouldn't. Even search is successful because of content. Google search results pages are simply a listing of content.

What about earned media and owned media? Same thing. Almost every paid online ad eventually leads to an online interaction with content of some kind ... a landing page, a video, something. Smart public relations efforts are extended online through content. Literally, every single thing that happens online is driven ultimately by content.

Content is the fuel that powers the engine of the Internet. Yet, many marketers are not investing a single dollar into content. They are buying lots of tools to deliver content. They are building lots of platforms to deliver content. They are designing pretty websites to hold content. They are making banner ads that lead to content. They are spending millions and millions of dollars on search engine optimization companies to game Google so it will display specific content. Almost none of the dollars invested in digital are invested in content or in audience development. Yet this is the sole thing that moves the needle for literally every online tactic.

So ... what is your content budget?

3.2. What do we mean by "content"?

Content is an awful word. It's not sexy. It means something different to everyone you ask. In the context of owned media, content is any media a brand creates with the intention of serving an audience. We really can boil it down to some form of text, video, audio, images or interactions.

Lots of marketers get hung up here. They get interested in exactly how they should create a 140 –character tweet or the video that is perfectly imperfect so it "looks like a consumer shot it" or a myriad of other things. Remember, think platform agnostic. The question we should be asking is: "What is the most engaging, compelling way I can tell my story?" Once we know that, the specific platforms become obvious. If we can tell a story better with images, maybe Pinterest is the best place to do that. If it is a shorter story arc, maybe we need to use Twitter for immediacy. If we need to demonstrate a concept, maybe a video. If we need to share complex, perhaps an infographic?

If we focus on the content – the best way to tell the story, not the best platform to tell the story on – it makes the decision about how, when and which platforms easy. The platform should not dictate how you tell the story or what kind of content you create. Content driven. Platform agnostic.

3.3. There is an audience for everything: The Long Tail

But what if I have a "boring" brand or a highly specialized or a technical brand? What if we don't have any interesting content to create? This is a question we get a lot, and the answer is, your brand is not boring to people who have done business with you, are about to do business with you or might someday do business with you. Your brand is relevant to an audience, somewhere, and content about it will be interesting to them, or you wouldn't be able to stay in business.

No matter how boring or specialized your product or service is, there is an audience out there that is interested in it, for whom it is relevant. We have actually tested this idea with a company that makes cardboard boxes. Yes – cardboard boxes. That's what they do. They make packaging – highly technical, highly specialized, and to most of us, highly boring. But it's interesting to their community, to their audience. In fact, using their owned media channels, we were able to completely destroy their marketing key performance indicators and generated a relatively small (but huge for the category), highly engaged audience for this company.

This has to do with the long tail economic theory posited by Chris Anderson a few years back. If you are not familiar, put this book down and Google it, or better yet go buy his book and read it first. Everything else in this book will make a ton more sense.

Here's a personal example of the long tail: Taulbee plays drums. So he is connected to people in music, more specifically in the drumming community. Pretty broad group of people. But let's keep going. He only plays drum set. He is not really a "percussionist." He only plays American drums with Jasper shells. Now we are getting a little further down the tail.

He also collects vintage drums. Vintage Gretsch drums. Vintage Gretsch drums with square badges. Vintage Gretsch drums with square badges from the early '80s. Vintage Gretsch drums with square badges from the early '80s in one color, burnt orange gloss. Now that is a pretty specific community, right?

There can't really be an audience for something like this. It is so personal and specific.

But believe it or not, there is a community of people out there who collect vintage Gretsch drums with square badges from the early '80s in burnt orange gloss.

Taulbee said while we were writing this book, "There are five of us. I know this community exists because these people kept out bidding me on eBay, and we have struck up a couple of conversations over the years. We love this specific thing, and that connects us – it makes us a unique, addressable community. And believe me, while most of the rest of the world would find content about vintage Gretsch drums with square badges from the early '80s in burnt orange gloss completely boring and useless, the five people in my community would absolutely devour any video, text, images, any kind of content, anything you could tell us about it."

THAT is the long tail. There is an addressable audience for absolutely everything, including what your business is about. But they can't find you if you're not producing any content.

3.4. Real –time audience feedback

One thing all online channels and platforms have in common – besides the fact that content is the only thing that makes them work – is the ability to see your audience's reaction to content in real –time and respond to the situation. Good or bad, opportunistic or protectionist, when your brand opts to participate in owned media, it is absolutely critical to understand how the audience is reacting to the content you're publishing. We are not talking just about responding via comments or replying to tweets. We are talking about the feedback every member of the audience provides every day, with their behaviors – analytics. They are telling us everything we want to know about our content, every day.

Most marketers use analytics to understand how their audience is re-acting to content on all of these channels. It is critically important, as you are reviewing channel analytics, to understand that you are actually mea-suring the effect of content on audience, not the effectiveness of the chan-nel. Every measurement online is a measurement of content. Open rate? Measurement of the headline content. Click through rate? Measurement of the content. Time on site? Unique Visitors? Shares? Likes? Clicks? Content. Content. Content. You get the picture.

It is also important to understand how those metrics play together. Think of it as one big audience. It is likely your email subscribers follow you on Facebook or Twitter. It is likely your blog readers also subscribe to email. If a person is really engaged with a brand, it is likely that they are getting content from you in multiple channels. We'll talk more about this in the Measurement section, but it is critical to understand.

What is also critical to understand is the impact of these implications on your ability to respond and react in real –time. Digital is always on, and opportunities have a short shelf life. Keep this in mind as you are thinking through how to holistically approach content strategy in a truly platform agnostic way.

3.5. Platform agnosticism

An owned media strategy has a lot of tactical implications for other parts of your marketing strategy, both online and offline. It's not just a standalone campaign or a single tool to be used all by itself. A successful owned media strategy affects different aspects of the entire spectrum of marketing tactics. What you do with your owned media strategy can drive what you do in paid media and earned media, and vice versa. In fact, it should. It all works best when it's working together. For the practical purposes of keeping this book under 1,000 pages, we will stick to the implications for online channels only.

The clever marketer understands marketing as a web, and much like Sir Arthur Conan Doyle said of Professor James Moriarty, you'll "sit motionless, like a spider in the center of its web, but that web has a thousand radiations, and you know well every quiver of each of them." Pull on, strengthen or cut one thread, and you'll see it affect the surrounding threads, sometimes for the good, sometimes not.

Your content is the primary driver of every effect on your marketing "web." If you take a content –centric approach to your marketing, you'll see it affects every aspect of your online marketing. In fact, it is the one thing that drives its success, and the signals from your audience are the only thing that will make that web vibrate.

4. NONE OF YOUR DIGITAL PLATFORMS WORK.

It is likely that your organization has evolved around tactics and platforms, which is okay. You probably have an "email guy", a "social media manager", maybe even a "webmaster" … new platforms present themselves, and we try to put a smart person in charge of making sure that platform does what it is supposed to do. Except, that will never work as well as the brand newsroom approach, because those people are focused on technology – not content.

Here's what we mean when we say "digital marketing doesn't work", on a platform by platform basis:

4.1. Websites

Websites and microsites (and other similar online user experiences) have changed drastically in the 20 –plus years since we first started creating them for brands. The technology we use today wouldn't even be recognizable to the web guys we were back then, and we wouldn't have even been able to take advantage of it.

Back in the late 1990s and early 2000s, search engine optimization was still new because there were so few websites. You could put up a website, get it listed on Yahoo and count on being found by dozens, if not hundreds, of people who needed exactly what you were offering, because you were one of a handful of people who were offering it online.

> Websites are,
> have always been,
> and will always be,
> a delivery method
> for content.

First Flash was hot stuff because you could create movable, interactive screens. In the late '90s, you would spend two or three minutes waiting for a photo to load on a website over dialup modems. Now you can watch an entire movie on your mobile phone over a cell signal. These kinds of technological innovations are where almost all the focus has been in digital marketing. Now we are at a point where the technology is incredibly easy to use and deploy, and the cost of implementing much of it is zero dollars and a few minutes of your time. Ten years ago, the marketing services world was full of web shops making custom content management systems they could charge $20,000, $50,000 or more for the privilege of using. Now tools like WordPress and other content management systems have evolved to a point where almost anyone with any level of Internet experience can install the same CMS used by companies like CNN and NYTimes.com in one click.

But one thing has not changed in all that time: the need for well –crafted, well –written, well –produced content. Websites are, have always been, and will always be, a delivery method for content.

How many times have you redesigned a website? How many times have you started with the site map, layout, user interface, navigation and color scheme? So many web projects leave content as the last thing they think about because it's hard to deal with. However, that content is the singular reason the user is at your site. Sure, there are going to maybe be some functional things they are there for, if it's a website that delivers a service or an ecommerce website. But for the large majority of websites and microsites, it is about content.

The implication here is that from an owned media perspective, your website is most likely going to be the "center of your universe." It is the "official property." The real deal. It's going to be where your audience goes for verification of anything else they see or hear online or offline about your brand. It is the source of truth for all your communications efforts. This means your site should be built around your content, not the other way around.

This is one of the reasons the blog format became so popular – it is easy to create fresh, timely content. Most websites have functional requirements that will include evergreen content that doesn't need to be updated frequently, but it is also critical to understand which content the audience is most interested in and find a way to make it as easily accessible and findable as possible.

There have been volumes written about content for websites. We highly recommend Kristina Halvorson's "Content Strategy for the World Wide Web," as well as Rachael Lovinger's book "Letting Go of the Words" for a more in –depth guide to developing a user –centric, content –rich website that doesn't suck. It is a lot harder than it sounds, usually because the voice of the audience can't be heard over all the competing departments who "have to have XYZ on the home page" or in the navigation. Don't let your marketing team create your next website. Instead, let your audience tell you which content is most important to them through analytics and what they want to accomplish there through usability testing. Then build a site around that content and that functionality. Your site is there for them, not for you or for your marketing team or agency's awards portfolio. And for the love of all that is good in the world, do not blindly transfer your old content to your new site. If it didn't get you what you needed before, it is probably not going to do much better, even in a shiny new package. Websites don't work. Content works.

4.2. Email

Everything you do and measure in email is about content. People don't just want to be flooded with email. Despite what the spammers think, you can't trick most people into reading and responding to poorly written messages. And if you're in a business, or at least the type of person whose image is important and doesn't want to be known as a no –good spammer, you won't even try any of those methods.

However, many email marketers don't think about content. They're worried about the list, the layout, and the analytics, but they figure what they put in the email isn't as important. If they did, they would think about what the people on their list want to read, how the content affects the layout (and not the other way around), and whether their readers are even paying attention to the content.

In a content –centric email strategy, the content comes first. Figuring out what to write comes before deciding the layout, compiling the list, and reading the analytics. Without good content, your layout is nothing but a pretty, empty shell. Your list will abandon you and put your emails on their spam lists.

This means that you need to focus on content to be successful. You need to concern yourself more with the headline, body copy and images. You'll write headlines that draw in more readers, create copy they enjoy reading and choose the images that resonate with your readers.

Having said that, we believe that the list, the layout and the analytics are still important. But you need to worry about them after you develop your content strategy, not before.

A small, high –quality list will always outperform a large, dubious –quality list. We would much rather send an email newsletter to a list of 1,000 people who love our brand than to a list of 500,000 people who have never heard of us and probably don't care. *Never buy or rent an email list from a list broker.*

You will have to pay attention to the layout because you know that good design affects readability too. But make sure that the content drives the design of the layout, rather than trying to make the content fit the layout.

And of course, the analytics will inform your headlines and body copy. You can run an A/B test to see that the headline, "5 Secrets to Brewing Great Coffee," outperforms "Brew Your Own Coffee and Make it Taste Great." You learn that copy that uses bullet points and is written in an easy –to –read style greatly outperforms the novella that you let your English major intern write about the parallels between Emily Dickinson and a cup of freshly brewed coffee. After finding which types of headlines and body copy perform best, you can then use the analytics to tweak future versions until you reach optimal performance.

Remember – email is just another channel. If content is performing well in social, try it in email. If your blog post is blowing up the analytics numbers, try it in email. YouTube video going viral? Email it.

Conversely, many brands have more experience and a longer track record – and sometimes a bigger audience – with email. It is an older (but still very effective) medium, so in a lot of cases, brands have been able to grow their email audience significantly, sometimes beyond their monthly website audience. If you have a strong, responsive email audience, this could be a great place to co –promote your other channels. I don't mean including Twitter and Facebook logos on your email, I mean a concentrated effort to promote content on those channels via email. Taking a more omni –channel approach and using email as the catalyst for growth in developing platforms has been, in our experience, highly effective.

But what is email, really? Well, it is a way to deliver content. Nothing more, nothing less. Every open, every click, every forward is driven by the content you're delivering, not because "email works." Email doesn't work. Content works.

4.3. Blogs

A blog is a great "hub" for a content strategy. A blog, unlike any printed material, can be created in minutes, not days and weeks. If you find an error, a fix can take minutes, and nothing has been wasted; find a typo on a brochure, and that's 10,000 copies and several thousand dollars down the toilet. Or you can just hope no one sees it when they pick it up.

A blog, unlike a website, doesn't require any special programming knowledge to create, edit or fix the content. In some cases, you can even just email in a blog post or upload it with your mobile phone and have it automatically publish within a few minutes.

You can also easily publish rich media, such as photos, videos and audio files, to your blog. Record a video on a smartphone, or take some photos with a digital camera or mobile phone, and publish them straight to your blog.

Of course, you may end up writing fewer or shorter blog posts because of rich media, but that's OK. Not only do people prefer shorter posts (100 words will fit on a typical smartphone screen), but Google loves photos and videos (especially ones that are uploaded to Picasa and YouTube, both Google –owned properties).

If you're able to focus on a content –centric strategy on a blog, you'll engage customers by giving them the information they want. If it's well –written and interesting, they'll return to you as a trusted source of information.

And if it's optimized for search engines correctly, they'll be able to find you more easily by people who need what you have to offer.

We especially like blogs for content –centric strategy because Google also focuses on a website's frequency and recency. That is, how often do you publish, and when was the last time you did it. Between a website and a blog, the blog is going to be much easier to update and add new content to than the website. Updating a website on a daily basis can be time consuming and expensive, if you're not equipped to do it yourself, or have someone on staff who can handle it.

Also, the way a blog organizes its content – typically with categories and tags – is much more search engine friendly (and user friendly) than how that content is organized on a typical corporate website.

But what is a blog, really? It's just another method of publishing content. Just like a website. Just like email. Just like every other online tactic. All that really matters is the content. Blogging doesn't work. Content works.

4.4. Social

Social media is also driven completely by content. Some would say it is a conversational medium, and it is about the ability to have a one –to –one discussion or one –to –many conversations and dialogue in real –time. True, but what that really boils down to is … you guessed it … content! It is one entity –creating content, another entity (a brand, a person, a company) responding to that content (via comments, tweets, likes, shares, and other actions). How you manage social is completely a content management function – managing the proactive content you create, dealing with content others create related to your brand and managing reactive content.

If you think about it, it's no different than what happens in email, websites and blogs. You proactively publish content you think your audience would find interesting or engaging. That audience responds. You then have to create more content to deal with that response. In email, it happens with the Reply and Forward buttons. On a website or microsite, it happens with your online forms and maybe other technology like live chat.

On a blog, it usually happens in the comments section for each post. In every case there is a **proactive** and **reactive** need for content, as well as a need to make, manage, monitor, moderate and measure that content.

Don't get overwhelmed by the buzz. Social is not a big, new scary thing. It's just another digital platform that delivers content. Are you starting to see a trend here?

Content is the one and only thing that matters in social – proactive content you're creating or curating, and reactive content in response to the content others are making about your brand. If you're only advertising, pitching product or spamming people through social media, they'll learn to ignore you very quickly. If you announce your sales and promote your products, but don't create and share anything important for your audience and their needs, no one will want to see what you have to say when it's actually important to your brand's needs.

Once you've written your outstanding content, you need a way to get people there, besides search engines and email newsletters. Social, along with email, is a great way to do this. This is how you meet people, share content and establish relationships. It's these relationships that make them willing to read your content. By earning friends, followers and fans, you are getting their implied permission to deliver content to them.

But it's not only your content you should be sharing. You should find other people who share your vision and values and share their material as well. That should also be a part of your brand: not only sharing information that supports your marketing campaign, but also your vision and values. This is content curation, and it can be a key part of a content strategy. Again, this is content that someone else has made, but if it is relevant to your audience (and isn't from a competitor!) – why not share it? By sharing it, you're turning someone else's owned media into a potential asset for you. Be sure you understand the legal ramifications of content curation – we go over this in the Risk section of our strategic planning process.

So after all the hoopla and the buzz, what is social, really? Just another channel your brand owns or controls that only works with content. Social media doesn't work. Content works.

4.5. Mobile

If you don't have a mobile marketing strategy, then you're behind the curve. Or at least that is what "they" say. The thing is, you are probably already reaching customers via mobile whether you meant to or not.

Does your brand use a website or social media or email? Then you are already using mobile marketing – your customers are using their mobile devices to interact with you on all those platforms. It's not just about text messaging, apps and location –based services.

So congratulations, you are "doing" mobile marketing! Now you need a 360 –degree strategy!

Where most brands miss it in mobile is understanding how to optimize content for the mobile space and how to ensure a seamless experience from one platform to the next. Many brands were not thinking about a four –inch screen when they designed their website, email and social programs. Now we need to approach everything we do online with mobile as one of many components. Does it work on a four –inch smartphone screen? A 10 –inch tablet or a 17 –inch laptop? A 30 –inch, high –resolution monitor or a 50 –inch TV? Here is a quick checklist to help you optimize the mobile marketing you're already doing BEFORE you invest in that fancy mobile app or near –field text messaging program:

4.5.1. Optimizing email for mobile

Let's dive in to what this means and why it is so important. According to the U.S. Census Bureau, two out of three Americans are considered to be part of "mobile America." It is estimated that 50 percent of mobile users have smartphones. Nearly half of those are using mobile for email.

If you're not thinking about your mobile user when you send an email blast, you may have a serious problem. Screens are small, and data can be heavy. Emails have to be quick and easy to read. Did you know most mobile devices cut your subject line by 15 –25 characters? You can end up with a subject line that makes no sense because you planned for 85 and only got 70. How often do you delete an email without even reading it? Now think about why and keep it in mind the next time you do an email send.

4.5.2. Optimizing social for mobile

Optimizing for mobile goes beyond just email. On average, Americans spend 2.7 hours per day socializing on their mobile devices. If you aren't optimizing your social posts for mobile, you aren't thinking like a mobile marketer. What does that mean?

- Links need to go to a mobile –optimized site or landing page.
- Shorten your links with a link shortener like Bit.ly.
- Images should be standard sizes for each network so the apps and mobile sites they already have will automatically optimize your posts for you.

4.5.3. Mobile landing pages

Does your website have some key pages that relate to your email, social, search or paid advertising programs? If your site is not mobile optimized, you should make sure those key landing pages render properly on mobile devices. When a user clicks a link in an email, a social post, or an ad, they are not going to put down their phone and run to a computer to view it in Internet Explorer. I promise.

4.5.4. Responsive design

If you've redesigned your site recently, maybe you utilized responsive design. If you did a site design in the last year and did not use responsive design – you should go get your money back! Responsive design basically allows for your entire website to display the same way regardless of screen size and device. It is a tough design challenge, but one well worth investing in.

Still considering doing a mobile app or a text program?

Ask yourself these questions before you start investing dollars in your mobile marketing plan:

- Have we optimized our email program for mobile users?
- Have we optimized our social pages for mobile users?
- Have we optimized our social posts for mobile users?
- Have we optimized our website for mobile users?
- Do we have mobile landing pages in place for key pages?

If you answered "no" to any of those questions, you might want to revisit your mobile marketing plans and put these things at the top of the list. Nothing is worse than a broken, incomplete or dysfunctional mobile experience.

If you don't make it easy to interact with your brand when your customers are on the go, they will simply interact with someone else, such as your competitors. Before you launch that awesome mobile app, start with the basics, and give your audience a complete, easy –to –use mobile experience.

What have we learned about mobile? That's right – it is driven by content. Almost all of the other channels you use are going to be working on multiple devices. Not just smartphones with four –inch screens, tablets of every shape and size, laptops with 11 to 17 –inch monitors and desktops with 17 – to 30 –inch monitors (sometimes several monitors), even with 50 –inch HDTVs. The device doesn't matter much (or it shouldn't if you're creating awesome content).

It doesn't matter if you're talking text, apps, mobile sites or any other form of mobile marketing … mobile doesn't work. Content does.

4.6. Search

The winning of organic search rank is a side effect of quality content and engagement. Let's put that in bold to really drive home the point because you're probably spending a ton of money to win organic rank:

> Winning search is a side effect of quality content and engagement.

Thanks to Google's Panda and Penguin updates to their search algorithms – really every update made in the last three years – Google is starting to pay more attention to content quality and engagement. Things such as Click –Through, Time On Site and Bounce Rate determine whether a blog or website is a quality one. Low click –throughs, time on site and bounce rates tell Google the site is not very good and is not something it wants to share with its users.

But sites that are frequently clicked through from Google, sites that have people reading it for more than 30 seconds and sites that have more than one page view per visit are higher –performing sites that it would love to share with its users.

After all, Google believes if its users like what it shared with them this time, they'll like what it shares with them next time.

Google's focus is on providing good search results so users will be back.

Another good one to understand that we like to say, a lot: Winning rank is not a business objective. Say it out loud:

Winning rank is not a business objective.

Everybody wants to be the No. 1 result on Google. It could mean millions or even billions in revenue for some companies whose lives depend on referral traffic from Google. That doesn't mean rank shouldn't be a key performance indicator or something you should watch closely. But if that is the only thing you're measured on, you should re –examine your business case because winning rank is not winning search. Winning *rank* just puts you at the starting line along with all of your competitors. How does that make you money? Well, it doesn't. Winning search does.

Winning *search* happens after the click. Winning search means the user discovered the content she was looking for on your website or whichever digital property showed up in Google's search engine results page. Winning search means converting the user. Winning search means the user did not bounce or hit the back button on her browser.

All those things are driven by the content they find at the conclusion of their search. If the content is good and people engage with it, Google will rank it. But it gets ranked only if your brand really deserves it. You have to earn it – not once, but every day – if you want to keep it. There are no short cuts that Google won't eventually address, regardless of what your shady search engine optimization rep says. This brings us to our next point we want to make in big bold letters (last one, we promise):

Nobody can outsmart Google.

There are a lot of companies out there that offer to help improve your SEO. But be careful. While some companies like ours focus on driving rank through quality content and engagement, other companies only focus on "onsite SEO," or fully optimizing the code on your site or building links. Still others resort to trickery and "black hat" techniques, which only work for just a short time and will often get you banned by Google.

"Bad" SEO firms will probably want to talk to you about your link graph and your on –page optimization, and all kinds of other stuff. Don't buy it. They can't outsmart Google, and neither can you.

All the search optimization you need to do should happen as part of the process you develop in the distribution part of your strategy. Optimizing for search isn't something you do as a project. It it is something you have to do as a part of creating great content your audience will love.

Reputable search companies will spend the majority of their time talking to you about content and engagement strategy across all your platforms – i.e. your owned media strategy: to create great content, and build an engaged audience of consumer advocates. The good search companies know that content and engagement strategies are the only approach that Google is not trying to defend against. Google wants you to do one thing: Earn. Your. Rank. It even says so in its guidelines[5].

It's possible to game the search engines to build rank for a blog or website in the short term, but you can't game quality. Google's algorithms are already too smart for that. The only way to get quality stuff is to create it. There are no shortcuts. You'll either pay for the quality in time or money (or both). The important thing is to avoid shady strategies that don't do anything for you in the long run, and focus more on how to use a content –centric strategy to help you win search.

In fact, after the recent changes to Google's algorithm, there are companies springing up to un –do what SEO firms have done because Google is now smart enough to identify shoddy links, bad content and other nefarious practices that have gone unchecked until recently. It now penalizes websites that use those tactics. To see all of the changes Google has made to help deliver high –quality content to its users – and to keep SEOs from gaming their system – we recommend reading history of the algorithm from SEOMoz[6].

---

5   http://www.google.com/competition/howgooglesearchworks.html

6   http://www.seomoz.org/google–algorithm–change

It's amazing how much time and effort Google has spent to deliver quality content (which someone else is paying to develop) to its users. So what is search, really? It's a list of the best content with the most engagement around the subject in the search query. That's right. Search is about content. Search doesn't work. Content works.

5. WHO OWNS OWNED MEDIA?

One of the biggest operational problems in enterprise brand marketing is the problem of ownership. Over the last 100 years or so, two main functions emerged – advertising and public relations.

In some cases, those functions report up to a chief marketing officer. In other cases, there is a C –suite representative for both functions. We have seen all kinds of scenarios for how brands organize the marketing function internally. Almost all of them boil down to either a single marketing function that oversees both paid and earned media or a dual function where there is a marketing department responsible for things like advertising and merchandising, and a public relations department that handles corporate affairs, media relations and other related publicity functions. Considering the need for a dedicated owned media function, how should that look now? Let's find out!

5.1. Marketing operations – past, present, future

Over the last 15 to 20 years, many brands have struggled with who should be in charge of things like websites, email, as well as social, mobile and digital channels. Early on, many brands put these functions under their information technology departments because the problems they were trying to solve were technical in nature. It wasn't about how to get traffic to a website; it was about how to even build and maintain a website at all.

Entering from stage left: **the web shop**. The web shop helped brands build websites. They worked with IT and marketing to get your site to "go live."

As digital channels proliferated, most sane companies moved this function to their marketing department. We've got this technical stuff figured out. Now we need to figure out how to monetize our web properties and leverage all this technology for marketing. Enter from stage right: **the digital agency.**

Smart marketers who knew a thing or two about building a website – and how to get traffic to it – started breaking off from traditional agencies and figuring this stuff out. They even started breaking off into specialities such as search, online media buying, flash shops and other kinds of deep vertical expertise.

Traditional agencies and holding companies saw budgets starting to shift, and they immediately hired vice presidents of interactive marketing, or they simply bought a digital shop or two. "We can do this stuff," they said. And some could.

Almost out of nowhere, social media entered the picture, giving public relations a place online to call its own. PR people and PR agencies all over the world attempted to claim this turf. But internally, most are still in a tug of war with marketing, as well as with web shops, SEOs, digital agencies, and just about anyone else with a Twitter handle, to "own social."

All these digital functions have been shoehorned into places they shouldn't be. Your marketing team and your ad agency are not in the business of creating content in a real –time, two –way media environment, and they have zero knowledge or experience building audience. They know marketing. They know how to create great ads. They "get" paid media, and they are good at it. They can reach audiences and speak to audiences, but that is much different than building an audience. They simply don't have the training, experience, skill sets or structure they need to grow an audience because they were never designed to.

Your PR team is in the same boat. They are great at pitching stories, managing crisis communications, employee relations and all those other functions of public relations they have been trained to do. None of them have ever built an audience. They are not good at it. And that, in the words of Stuart Smally, is OK. They were never designed to build audiences, any more than agencies were.

Your marketing services partners – all structured to solve specific problems in paid media and earned media – are all having the same problem. They were not built for media as it exists today. They aren't staffed for it. They aren't structured for it. They don't have the strategic acumen or the real –world experience to create an audience. And that is what every digital tactic is about.

So what is a brand to do?

You have the answer right here in your hands. The missing piece of the puzzle – the thing everyone has been trying to solve for about 10 or 15 years – is this simple, logical, obvious concept of "owned media."

Marketers need to establish a new internal function for all their owned media properties and put someone in charge of it who understands the space and understands how to build an audience. Not a marketing person. Not a PR person.

Hire an audience development person, with a staff of storytellers – content people, engagement people, audience analysts, producers, maybe some developers and designers. Take all of the owned media responsibilities away from PR and marketing and park them with the audience development person. This means the website, all the microsites and all your other digital properties. Email. Blogs. Mobile. Social. All of it.

Give the audience development person the same resources you would give to your marketing and PR teams – staff, budget, tools, external partners, executive –level support and internal buy –in. Give them equal opportunity and standing with their colleagues in the paid and earned media.

This doesn't mean the paid media folks are out of the "digital" business. Someone has to create and buy online paid media, such as banner ads, adwords, sponsorships and all the other paid media that happens online. The earned media team still needs to be pitching stories to online sources, including bloggers and online publishers, and they need to be developing relationships with influential content creators. But neither of these functions should be responsible for your owned media properties.

The rationale is that, beyond their functional inability to do the job, your teams need to focus on their areas of expertise. If you have a marketing department placing an $8 million media buy, do you really want them worried about what they are going to post to Twitter today? If your PR team is pitching a story to The Wall Street Journal, do you want them also creating a web video for your blog? Most brands are asking too much of their paid and earned media functions.

The division shouldn't be around "digital" or "web" or "social." It's all digital. It's all social. The division should be around the three possible ways to access potential customers, and the diverse skill sets and strategies needed to make them all work – paid, owned and earned media. This does not mean we are working in silos. Remember how the circles overlapped each other in the Venn diagram? This should be a holistic, integrated effort at the brand strategy level – a marketing effort supported by separate functions in paid, owned and earned media, not traditional and digital, not just PR and advertising. Those models are broken and missing some very big pieces.

The team responsible for your owned media channels should be built to make them work for your business. If you want any of these channels to work, the only answer is great content and audience development. Remember, customers only come from audiences, and audiences only come from three places: You can buy them (paid), you can borrow them (earned), or you can build them (owned). Nobody in your company has been truly enabled to "own" owned media. When you think about it, it is an almost painfully, embarrassingly obvious path forward.

The idea is not to create silos. In a perfect world, paid, earned and owned media functions still report up to a single chief marketing officer, whose job it is (as it is today) to keep these people working together in an integrated, holistic fashion that moves the needle for your business.

This is not a bold idea, it's a logical one. It's not change for the sake of some trendy buzzword. It's an obvious, common –sense solution that enables you to apply the right tools to the right problems in a focused way that will lead to success for everyone. It is a game changer that should have happened years ago, but we have all been so transfixed by code and technology, buzzwords and social media "experts" that we missed the most obvious thing. We were all singing "content is king" with the chorus so loudly, we missed our cue. Now is your opportunity to go fix that.

5.2. Implications outside of marketing

With this new owned media position in your company, what happens to the other areas of your brand that are impacted by today's media environment? This new function should guide and develop how your owned media channels work within other areas of the enterprise, in much the same way marketing and public relations do. Here are some examples.

5.2.1. Customer service

If you have a customer service function, you have to get them dialed in to your owned media channels. Not just social, but email, blog ... anywhere a user can interact with your brand. . . which is essentially everywhere online. This book is limited in scope to focus on marketing, and there are a ton of great resources out there that address how customer service works online in the 21st century.

What we will address here is primarily how your strategy will impact customer service, particularly tone and manner. Your tone and manner will go a long way in affecting the response you get from your users, especially when you're dealing with a complaint. If your tone and manner are dismissive or insulting, or you give off the impression that you don't actually care about your customers, you can pretty much guarantee that you'll anger the person, and they'll stop being your customer.

Don't believe us? Google "bad customer service," or visit sites like Randy Cassingham's CrankyCustomer.com.

There are plenty of people who are angry enough to go to great lengths to express their displeasure to as many people as possible if they feel slighted or insulted by a company. These efforts go far beyond the "you guys suck" comments left on a blog post. They are concerted efforts that these people take to show just how badly those companies do suck. (Randy Cassingham's "This Is True" weird news site has more than 1 million readers worldwide, so people pay attention when he mentions he has a new CrankyCustomer story.)

But a friendly tone and manner – such as @ComcastCare's friendly "How can I help?" question to every angry tweet that crosses their desk – goes a long way in defusing an angry customer and making a tense situation a relaxed one. The smart move is to respond to every customer comment, question and complaint in the same friendly manner. Your willingness to take the high road in aggravating situations will win more points (and customers) in the end.

5.2.2. Other areas of the enterprise

Marketing/PR and customer service typically are the most affected areas of the enterprise. But there are implications for lots of other parts of the company.

There has been a recent movement, which we are in full agreement with, toward what some call "social enterprise." A lot of the focus here has been on how the social media component affects different areas of your company and how to take advantage of the new opportunities a socialized media environment can deliver, while still managing risk. Of course, we know that social media is a misnomer – it's all social. What brands should be trying to do is leverage all of their owned media across the enterprise.

Why stop at social? Here are a a few areas to consider in your owned media strategy.

Product development – Product development can benefit greatly from owned media audiences and from the monitoring function of owned media. Product dev teams can now hear customers in real –time in ways they never could before. Not only can product development team members hear what customers are saying online about their products, but they can also look for things like negative sentiment in the audience to understand what problems their customers might be having that are going unsolved. Some brands have even gone as far as crowd –sourcing product development (which is an exercise in ... content!). With a centralized owned media function, your product development team has an experienced, trusted resource to help them innovate and produce better products.

Research – Like product development, research on owned media channels can provide incredible insights for any number of different questions. Not sure which direction to go? Ask your customers via email. Need some ideas on customer service? Send out a tweet and ask. You can get as granular or as broad as you like with combinations of social, email, and online polling research. Formstack is a great application for this – just create the questions in an easy –to –use form, and not only can you embed it anywhere, you can easily tie it to your other data sources, such as your email database or Salesforce.com. In many cases, the answers are already out there being discussed everyday. You just have to be listening.

Human resources – A big factor we deal with in a lot of large enterprises is human resources and related employee engagement functions. If you have a company with a lot of employees, it is crucial to have your owned media function involved with HR, not only from a policy and risk management standpoint, but from an opportunistic point of view. In a lot of cases, employees are customers, too. This is especially true in retail. Why not leverage this internal audience's unique understanding of your brand to create content, and maybe even manage dialogue for the brand? It has worked great for companies like Dell and Best Buy.

5.3. Executive buy-in

There are lots of things your organization should have in place but given what we've just outlined, the most important is probably executive level buy in. This is an adjustment that will shake up the org chart, and the overall philosophy of the entire marketing function. This is not to be taken lightly, and your C –Suite should support you philosophically as well as with budget, staff and other resources.

It will be a political challenge to reorganize, and sell that in to your leadership, but reorganize you must. It is the most logical, sane thing for any brand to do. It will enable the brand to fully leverage its owned media across every aspect of the enterprise. Not reorganizing will lead to continued turf battles, inefficient spending, and middle –of –the –road results.

5.4. Budget

The big question: How much is this going to cost us? How much time do I have to spend on this? What's the minimum amount of time I can spend on this?

This is one of the most cost –effective, far –reaching marketing channels you could have ever gotten your hands on. We're living in an amazing time as marketers. Unless you have millions of dollars to spend on a Super Bowl commercial or World Cup sponsorship, there will never be another way to reach so many people with so many different free or very cheap tools.

This doesn't mean growing your owned media audience is free.

As two business owners who make their living doing this for brands, we need to point out that while the tools themselves are sometimes free, and access to many platforms you can own or control is free, it takes dollars and highly skilled, experienced people to make them work, just like paid and earned media. If you're a small business owner, you have opportunity costs associated with social media. If you have a marketing department, there are the salaries of your employees to consider. And if you outsource your work because you don't have the time or employees to do it yourself, there are fees associated with that. Only humans can make content, and only content makes digital marketing work.

There is also the effectiveness issue.

Study after study shows the source of information is critical to establishing trust with consumers. Your customers and potential customers do everything they can to avoid being advertised to. Things like "banner blindness," the iPod and Pandora, the DVR and the long, slow death of print media have made it harder and harder to get the same results with the same advertising spend.

Dollars follow audience. At this time, Facebook has over 1.06 *billion* users worldwide, and Twitter has well over 500 million. More than 75 percent of all Internet users read blogs. And smartphones – iPhones and Androids – have penetrated more than 40 percent of the American cell phone market.

Figure 3 Consumers Spend Less Time With Traditional Media

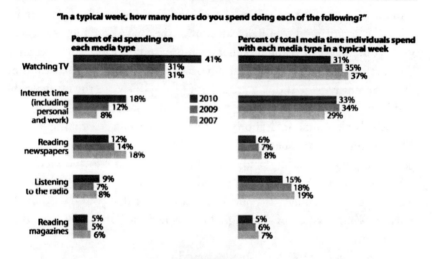

"In a typical week, how many hours do you spend doing each of the following?"

Base: US adults
(percentages may not total 100 because of rounding)

Source: North American Technographics® Benchmark Survey, 2007; North American Technographics® Benchmark Survey, 2009; and North American Technographics® Benchmark Survey, 2010; Forrester Research Online Display Advertising Forecast, 2011 To 2016 (US)

59379   Source: Forrester Research, Inc.

In Forrester Research's most recent marketing spending forecasts, the majority of marketers are continuing to shift their budgets to content –driven owned media like social, email, search and mobile. Yet, not all of them are investing those dollars where it counts – into content and audience engagement, and investing in building their own audience.

This is why asking "How much do I have to spend?" and "What is the minimum amount of time I can spend?" are the wrong questions to ask. As our friend Douglas Karr says, it's like owning a race car and then asking how slow you can drive it. Owned media has a relatively low cost, low barrier to entry, and is relatively easy to use. The question is not "how little," but "how much is right for my brand?"

Don't budget by channel. Most marketers line item by tactic – so much to search, so much to email, so much for retargeting, so much for PR. Instead, budget by owned, paid and earned. Put your dollars where they count and where they keep paying dividends over time – into content and audience development.

Once you rent someone's eyeballs with paid media, you have to pay to do it again later. Every time you reach out to someone, it costs you money. Not so when you develop your own audience. There is cost involved in acquiring the audience, but once they have opted in or engaged with you, they can actually generate more audience on your behalf if they are truly engaged consumer advocates. This is, of course, assuming your content is great and you are able to be responsive to the needs of the audience.

We think you should approach this as a percentage of your budget. Many companies are spending between 30 and 40 percent of their budget on "digital," including paid, earned and owned, and including design, development, programming and outside help from an agency partner. We would get rid of "digital" as a budget line and make that your owned media bucket. We think half of that digital (or owned media) budget should go to content.

Here is an example for a smaller brand:

- Total annual marketing spend: $3 million
- 40 percent to digital: $1,200,000
- 50 percent of digital budget to content: $600,000

The dollars spent on content will make everything else you do more effective. At this point, most brands have the basics – a website with a content management system, an email service provider like ExactTarget or Delivra, and many have a social media monitoring or management tool in place, like Hootsuite, or in larger and more mature brands, Spredfast or Sprinklr. The investment in content – videos, articles, white papers, website content refreshes, presentations, infographics, photo galleries – can be leveraged across all of your digital channels.

You already *have* a budget for owned media, it is just being divided up across your other departments. Rethink your spend, and prioritize content in your marketing budget. This is the new hierarchy of owned, paid, and earned media. Don't make the one thing that makes it all work an afterthought. Mark it the centerpiece of your strategy and your budget.

Here are some benchmarks from a 2010 Altimeter Research report. The average spend for "social business" alone is more than $800,000. This is just what is being spent on a single channel of owned media.

Average Annual Social Business Budget Per Corporation by Company Revenue

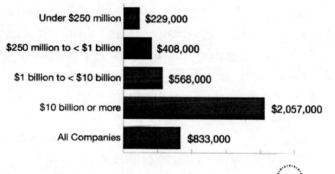

Under $250 million	$229,000
$250 million to < $1 billion	$408,000
$1 billion to < $10 billion	$568,000
$10 billion or more	$2,057,000
All Companies	$833,000

Base: 140 Global Corporate Social Strategists (Oct. 2010)

ALTIMETER

5.5. Staff

This is not a one –person job, even for a smaller brand. For very small businesses, it can sometimes work, but to take advantage of owned media for most brands, it means rethinking how you're staffed internally and what your external partner mix looks like.

There has been a lot of experimentation with how to staff internally for owned media and social media. We've gone from "webmasters" (yes, that actually used to be a job title) to interactive marketing managers to social media managers and everything in between. Rarely has a company actually staffed up with content people. In some cases, particularly in large complicated enterprises like health care, there is a "content person" who is in charge of making updates to the website. That is typically as far as it goes.

Except, the largest and most admired (and most valuable) brands on earth are doing exactly that. They have reorganized marketing internally around content and audience building.

Red Bull

Red Bull invests the majority of its spend on an internal audience development team called Red Bull Studios. Please visit
its site at RedBullUSA.com for an example of a brand doing
owned media right. From Fast Company: "In 2011 alone,
it filmed movies, signed a partnership deal with NBC for a
show called Red Bull Signature Series, developed reality TV
ideas with big–time producer Bunim/Murray, honed its own
web and mobile outlets, and became a partner in YouTube's
new plan to publish original content. Pushing go –juice to
Generation Y is still important, of course, and the company
did that to the tune of $471 million in U.S. sales in 2011, an
increase of 11.9 percent from 2010 with a 44 percent market
share of energy drinks, according to SymphonyIRI."

Nike

Nike invested more than $200 million and hired more than
200 employees dedicated to creating content and growing
audience on their owned media channels last year alone.
From Fortune: "Nike's spending on TV and print advertising in the U.S. has dropped by 40 percent in just three years,
even as its total marketing budget has steadily climbed upward to hit a record $2.4 billion last year. 'There's barely any
media advertising these days for Nike,' says Brian Collins, a
brand consultant." The company's stock has returned 120
percent over the past five years as the S&P 500 index (SPX)
has returned just 2.5 percent.

Starbucks

In 2010, Starbucks launched a major content marketing effort, the Starbucks Digital Network. News, Entertainment, Business, Careers and My Neighborhood are just a few of the categories of content Starbucks produces daily, on a localized level. Also, Starbucks spends almost no paid or earned media dollars, nor has it ever. Starbucks stock hit an all –time high about two years after implementing Starbucks Digital Network.

Apple

Apple not only markets itself with amazing, helpful, well –designed content – it controls most of yours. Your music? In iTunes. Your movies? Apple TV. Your documents? iCloud. Everything else? On your iPhone. Apple is a content play, not a technology play. They make devices that help you create and access content. Period. Apple recently became the most valuable company in history.

So what's right for your brand? There are lots of different approaches. Before we talk about what we think works best, let's make sure we cover what we know will not work.

5.6. What won't work

Using students or interns will not work. Just because you can use a phone does not mean you can run a call center. Why on earth anyone would trust the voice of their brand to an intern is beyond unbelievable. It is flat —out irresponsible to the stakeholders of your company. We still see this happening in very large brands.

Adding duties to your current staff's job descriptions will not work. They already have another job that still needs to be done, and done well. It is a job they are qualified for, a job they are experienced in. It is not growing your audience, or making content; it is marketing or public relations or advertising or design. Let them do their thing, and don't ask them to wear yet another hat that doesn't even fit their head.

Also, the odds are good that your current staff is not in the content business or the audience development business. That doesn't mean they shouldn't contribute, but you should not hold them accountable for success, and you should lower your expectations of the quality of work you expect to get.

Asking your ad agency or public relations firm or web design shop to help you will not work. They were not designed to do this. They will say they can do it, and maybe some can, albeit in a "functionally capable" way. But very few marketing services firms were ever designed to build audience and generate content for brands on a real —time basis.

6. THE "BRAND NEWSROOM" MARKETING OPERATIONS MODEL

You're probably asking yourself about now that if your current staff can't help with this, and your agency partners can't do it, who can? Who is really good at this stuff?

Glad you asked. Let's step outside of the marketing department, and the public relations department. Let's move beyond the typical staff you would put in place for paid media and earned media. Move beyond the partners you use today. Now ask: Which organizations are in the business of audience building that are really good at it, that make their living by it? Which ones operate in real –time? Which ones really have to be always –on? The answer is pretty obvious:

CNN. ESPN. NPR. NYTimes.com. Turner Sports. Broadcast news operations have been doing this for years, and they have been leaders in leveraging audience feedback to create content centrally and deploy it across multiple platforms in real –time. Their operating structure is purpose built to generate large, engaged audiences. They rent their audience's eyeballs out to marketers like you. Their editors are constantly being pitched story ideas from your public relations departments. They are in the business of building and monetizing audience.

This is the way to structure your team. Raidious first pioneered this approach in 2009, and several other in –house brands and marketing services firms have since restructured to a similar model, including GolinHarris in 2011, as covered in Ad Age magazine as its "G4" initiative.[7]

There are four key functions you will need to account for:

6.1. The producer function

In a news operation, this is the person ultimately responsible for leading all the content development efforts, getting high –quality content produced and distributed on time and on budget, and who is ultimately responsible for the audience numbers. If the ratings are down, the anchors don't get fired; the producer does. This is the key leadership role in your owned media efforts. This person needs to understand what stories work, how to get them produced and distributed, and how to measure their success to inform the next stories.

This is the day –to –day leadership function in an owned media program. This person leads strategy development and manages the resources of the team to deliver the metrics goals you outlined in your strategy. This is the central point of contact and ultimate decision maker on all things related to content for all your owned media properties.

6.2. The writer/reporter function

This person is the actual content creator. He or she produces stories assigned by the producer or assignment editor, going out and gathering information and actually producing content. Writer/reporters are usually teamed up

---

7   http://adage.com/article/agency–news/golinharris–restructure–begins–paying/238370/

with a video production specialist in TV news, but many today write, shoot and edit video or take photos, and produce "omnichannel packages," or stories that can easily be used and distributed not just on TV but on websites, blogs, in email, in mobile apps, in social media and other digital channels. Other specialists you might see in this category are graphics production people. They are making visual content to support the story – a chart or a graph, an animation or other visual content. But the core story –gathering and writing component will always be the most important piece of the puzzle. The actual production of the story is the easy part.

This function is responsible for actually producing content for your owned media properties. It is important that the person in this function is "wired" like a reporter. The key issue here is expertise. While a traditional PR person has deep subject matter expertise, they don't really "scale" very broadly. Your brand will need to create content about many different subjects that are relevant to your brand, but not necessarily "about" your brand. It is important to have someone in this role who can create a story – quickly, and at a high level of quality – with nothing but a subject and source, just like a real reporter. Depending on the size and scope of your operation, and your budget, you could augment your content creator with specialists in video, graphics and other specialty production functions.

6.3. The assignment editor function

This is the "eyes and ears" of a news operation. The assignment editor performs the "listening" function. He or she monitors trends, watching competitors, getting story leads, monitoring police radios, and helping to inform the producer about developing situations and story opportunities.

This is the typical "social media manager" function at most companies. This function should be focused on monitoring in the context of finding opportunistic situations for your brand that your audience would find entertaining and engaging. They should be in close contact with your writer/reporter function and your producer function to keep them informed about what is happening with your audience and in the world at large. This function should also be a good content creator, but focused on proactive, short –form content (like sharing and distributing what your content team is creating) and reactive, short –form content (like responding to content others are making about your brand). Depending on the needs of the brand, you might want to augment this role with the customer service component of your marketing efforts. These are two distinct and separate roles – one is about building audience, and one is about customer service. Keep this in mind as you are determining how to staff your team. You could also add specialists in data analysis, analytics reporting and other similar roles to augment your assignment editor function.

6.4. The engineering function

In a news room, the engineering team is responsible for making sure all the technical facets of the operation are working the way they are supposed to. They buy the right technology and tools; they implement the technology and train the news team to use it; and when necessary, they build custom technology when an off –the –shelf solution isn't readily available.

This is your traditional in –house digital/web development team, or in some cases IT/IS depending on how your brand is structured. This is where you want someone with relatively deep expertise in a development role, typically a "front end" developer, to lead this function. Again, depending on the scope of your brand and your specific needs, you could augment this role with programmers, user interface designers and other technical and code –oriented functions. This team's role is to support the rest of the team from a functional perspective.

This is how the team at Raidious is structured. There are four divisions, which we call strategy, content, engagement and platforms.

- **Strategy:** Producers, augmented by directors, strategists and analysts
- **Content:** Content correspondents, augmented by editors, video and graphics specialists
- **Engagement:** Audience engagement specialists, handling monitoring, moderation, reporting and alerts
- **Platforms:** Developers, augmented by programmers and user interface designers

We organized our four functions into "pods" lead by a producer. Each function is represented in each pod (at least one team member to represent each function: strategy, content, engagement and platforms). Depending on the clients each producer is responsible for, her "pod" could include additional team members from any of our four functions. For instance, if a producer has a group of clients very focused on the social component, we may have three or four engagement team members in that producer's pod. We have found this to be a great way to scale. For instance, if you are a large enterprise brand marketer such as Proctor & Gamble, you might need a separate team (or "pod") for each individual brand or a category of brands.

The GolinHarris G4 model was based on its experience with its Nintendo account and divides its employees into a flat structure including similar roles. Their model includes Strategists, which is a support function including group –driven strategy and analytics that we roll into our Producer function; Catalyst, which is the main thrust of our producer role; Connector, which is the function of the assignment editor, our Engagement role; and Creator, which is the writer/reporter role we call Content Correspondent. Notably absent in the GolinHarris model is the engineering function, which we think is critical to support the other three functions and can contribute in more technical areas that are necessary for online marketing.

As we mentioned earlier, brands like Nike, Red Bull, Starbucks, Apple and many other global brands have also taken a version of this approach to their internal structure. Many of the brands that Raidious has worked with have also restructured their internal teams to better equip themselves to deal with the requirements of real –time, always –on owned, earned and paid media.

It is important to note that, in our experience, it is incredibly difficult if not impossible to find any one person who can do all of this, and all of these roles are critical to making your owned media program work. That doesn't mean you have to hire more full –time employees for this. These these functions could be covered by reorganizing existing resources. Also, you can always augment and scale these functions with outside partners. But without having someone in your company responsible for and accountable to each of these four distinct areas, your owned media efforts will fail.

6.5. Hiring the right people.

Someone has to own and implement strategy and understand the story that the audience metrics are telling about your success (or failure) to produce great content.

Someone has to be responsible for actually producing content – lots of different kinds at high –quality levels.

Someone has to be responsible for the listening and response function in your organization. And all of those people – none of whom are going to be necessarily technical in nature – are going to need technical support.

You might also be surprised to learn that the people you might expect to be the best fit for these types of roles are not always "wired" to do them well. One might assume that if a person is very active personally on social, that they would make a great social media manager. This is actually the opposite of what we've found. At Raidious, we take each of our hires through psychographic analysis to ensure that they will be able to function productively in their role long –term.

One of the dirty little secrets of owned media is that it is not glamorous. Not even a little bit. It is a grind. It is mentally very challenging and exhausting, and the work itself can become repetitive over time. It takes a lot of "sitability" and high tolerance for repetition and attention to detail to do many of these jobs well.

Raidious worked with BJ McKay and his company, Advisa, to implement Predictive Index for all of our hires early in the company's history. What we learned was completely counter –intuitive to the direction we were originally heading with our approach to staffing. BJ McKay and his team at Advisa and Predictive Index saved us untold time, money and stress by helping us understand what kind of person we needed in each of these roles. I would highly recommend contacting them before you hire anyone. Through our work with BJ, Raidious has achieved a 90 percent employee –retention rate for three years running.

If content is king, then the people who create it are the kingmakers. Hire accordingly.

6.6. Agencies, PR Firms, Digital Shops

The first American advertising agency was opened in 1850 by Volney Palmer in Philadelphia. They placed ads created by their clients into different newspapers. In fact, for the next nearly 30 years, ad agencies only bought space; it was the clients themselves who were the creators of those ads.

That began to change in 1877. James Walter Thompson bought out William James Carlton's advertising firm, and began producing content for their clients as a way to sell more space. He hired artists and writers and created the first creative department in an ad agency.

Nothing else changed until DDB paired art directors and writers in the '60s. Essentially, the operational structure has remained the same since. Creative Department. Account Service Department. Media Department. You've seen Mad Men, right? Today, it is essentially that with computers instead of typewriters – and a lot less formal. Some agencies added a digital department of some kind in the early to mid 2000s, but most of them still outsource all the production.

While the media environment has changed – drastically, and almost every day over the last decade – not much has changed with agencies. It's the same operational model we've had since James Walter hired his first creatives, and not much else has really changed about it since then. Ad agencies are fantastic at making advertising and buying ads. They are great at paid media.

There is a similar story in the public relations world. Again, not much has really changed in PR agency operations. They still pitch stories and make their living by their Rolodex. The borrow interest for brands, and do earned media at a very high level. They should. That is what they were designed to do.

Digital agencies and web shops are in a similar place. They were originally designed, operationally, to build platforms – websites, microsites, apps. And they are better at creating an online user experience platform than any other marketing services group. They should be – that is exactly what they were designed to do.

As you search for partners to help you with owned media, keep these things in mind. Agencies, PR firms and digital shops will tell you that "they can do this stuff." Many of them even believe it. But the fact of the matter is they were never designed to deal with owned media as it exists today. Can they buy ads on digital? Yes. They rock at that. Can they pitch stories to bloggers? Absolutely, without question. Can a digital shop make you a kick –ass website? No doubt. Can any of these companies effectively create content and manage dialogue across multiple digital platforms in real –time? Hell, no. Not even close.

You are going to have to find highly specialized outside help for the owned media space because very few companies exist out there right now that were actually designed to help you in this space. Most companies cobble together a group of partners to represent the functions they need – a content company to help with content, a social media agency to help with the engagement function, maybe a video project shop to help with the web video piece of the puzzle, a search shop to do analytics reporting and optimization. While many agencies are moving toward a better solution for owned media, they have a long way to go. Of course, we should mention Raidious was the first marketing services firm purpose –built specifically to address real –time owned media using the brand newsroom approach, and almost everything you're reading here is a direct result of their real –world experience.

7. A HOLISTIC APPROACH TO PAID, EARNED, AND OWNED MEDIA

We want to be clear that we are not advocating for owned media as a stand-alone approach. We believe there is a place for paid, earned, and owned media. We just think it is logical and rational to give owned media as much or more resources than paid or earned media because it supports them both. In a perfect world, all three facets of marketing work together, and your brand strategy is what keeps them all on course.

7.1. Activating and extending earned media with owned media

Even though you can't control your own destiny in public relations, you can still use it to a great benefit. In fact, there are several ways you can and should use earned media.

One way to use it is to support your owned media. If you have invested in great content, PR is a great way to expose that content to new audiences and grow your audience. Also, when you use earned media to support your owned media efforts, it allows you the opportunity to essentially capture the part of the audience that is most interested in your brand.

Create content that people want to share via earned media – news stories on TV and in the newspapers, blog posts by fans and industry influencers – but do it to drive people back to your own online properties or real –world locations.

You're going to have a tougher time getting your buying message through these channels in the first place. Not only do news outlets refuse to allow purchased messages to go out over their airwaves without you paying for them, but they're going to spin down your message however they want. Remember – they own the platform. They control the content. Not you. So all your messaging in earned media runs the risk of being "colored" by someone other than you.

In this case, your content really can't be about buying stuff. It has to be relevant to the audience for anyone to bite on the story and run it. For example, a travel destination might want to entice people to its site with new videos and photos or a contest for two lucky travelers or even a special celebration. But it needs to be something that other people think is important and newsworthy enough to tell their own viewers, readers and listeners about. It has to be, literally, remarkable. If you want to get your brand in the news, the best way to do that is to do something newsworthy.

7.2. Activating and extending owned media with earned media

Conversely, your owned media efforts can help activate and extend your earned media efforts. Get a great hit in Wired magazine? Esquire including a quote from your CEO in this month's issue? CEO appearing on CNN? Leverage and extend these earned media wins online by creating content about them for your audience.

One of the interesting things about social media is that it gives people a chance to tell their friends, "Hey, look at this! This is something I made/saw/liked/ate/took a picture of/laughed at/gasped at." And their friends will react appropriately, telling the sender that they like it, saw it too, are hungry, thought the picture was cool, laughed too, or made an "eww" face. They will even share that with their own networks.

As part of an owned media campaign, you are going to earn "friends" on your social networks. Hopefully these friends will be customers who are turning into raving fans and telling their own friends about you.

Because of this, it makes sense to share any earned media to your network via your owned media campaign. Whether another blogger wrote about your company or latest product offering, or someone retweeted one of your messages, or shared a video of your last conference talk, you should thank them. This encourages people to continue to do more of the same, helping them continue to share your message via word –of –mouth marketing. Get enough people to be your raving fans, and they'll evangelize on your behalf, driving sales and marketing dollars to your website, stores or locations.

Earned media is about borrowing the interest of the reader/viewer/listener in channels you don't own or control. It is never a predictable "given." But it's about more than newspaper, TV and radio. It's also about blogs, websites, and online magazines/journals, online TV and podcasts. Almost all so –called "traditional" media have extended their properties online, and their audience is there sometimes more than in the traditional channels where the media was originally established. I don't watch much CNN on cable, but I get text alerts and I'm in their mobile app multiple times a day. Additionally, online –only media like Mashable, Huffington Post and many other digital publishers have become as influential and have as big an audience as more established media properties. Some individuals are highly influential and have massive audiences as well. All of these channels should be considered as part of your earned media strategy.

7.3. Understanding earned media in the online space

Earning online attention from other publishers follows the same basic public relations principles people have practiced for years. It is just another channel for the PR team. But there are some subtleties to consider in online PR.

If "we'll send a press release, of course" is the standard answer your PR department gives whenever you have a new product or service offering, this will not help you at all. A lot of influential social media people have grown to a finicky, almost spoiled bunch – and we say this as influential social media people – who expect special, personalized treatment. They don't want to be blanketed with the same old press release everyone else is getting. They want to feel like you are paying special attention to them.

To be fair, many print and broadcast journalists are now feeling the same way. The smart ones aren't too picky because they're always on the lookout for a good story. But you'll meet a lot of traditional media people who are becoming prima donnas too.

This means personalized pitches to the different journalists. It means reading a couple of their blog posts or articles, and then mentioning that fact in the email you send only to them. It means explaining why you think they would be interested in the particular story you're pitching.

> *"Dear Taulbee,*
>
> *"I was recently reading your blog about creating a social media command center during Super Bowl XLVI. I had also read several articles of your success on Mashable and on CNN. I can imagine that must have been very difficult to manage since social media played such a big part of the Super Bowl coverage this year.*
>
> *"My company, DotComStat, is a social media monitoring solution geared toward large –scale operations like the Super Bowl, auto races, political conventions, or even*

large –scale disasters. I wanted to see if you would be
interested in testing our new software solution, FasTweet,
for your blog, and discussing how you think it could be
used in other events similar to the Super Bowl."

When a social media person receives a pitch like this, they're more likely to respond positively, giving the product a fair consideration, and then giving it an honest review.

This last part is important because brands can have some negative things said about them. While regular earned media in the traditional outlets will usually be positive and say nice things about a product or service (because in many cases those same brands are funding their company through paid advertising), bloggers and online reviewers will not always do the same. They can be just as critical as their book –and –movie reviewing colleagues.

This fact should also be a reminder about why you need a personalized pitch. An offended blogger who's stuck for a topic may just as easily bash your impersonal mass –mailed pitch and write about that for 500 words. And if they're influential enough, some of their fellow bloggers could do the same, drawing more attention to an awful PR pitch. Read the Bad Pitch Blog at badpitch.blogspot.com for some examples of what some bloggers will do to bad PR pitches.

And if you don't think some of these pitches don't gain some serious attention, read The Bloggess' post, "And then the PR guy called me 'a fucking bitch'" on TheBloggess.com[8]. Basically, she tweeted about the unprofessionalism of a PR professional to his employer, and "many, many of my 164,000 followers replied and retweeted in the most clever and hysterically awesome ways imaginable." For a brand, this is a nightmare. For that PR guy, it was a set of walking papers. You can't even make this stuff up.

The moral of the story? Don't screw around with social media influencers. Many of them are snarky and angry enough to rain down holy hell on an unsuspecting PR professional. Please just take our advice: Research every blogger you're going to pitch to, and make sure you personalize that pitch to their blog focus, content preference, and even their quirky style.

For anyone who's a fan of the book "Crush It" by Gary Vaynerchuk, an obvious tactic might be to leave a series of comments on other people's blogs. This is a good strategy, especially if you can take the time and effort

---

8   http://bit.ly/AozRQS

to do it. Make sure these are intelligent, well –written comments that are done in response to a blog post, and not just "nice post!" responses.

However, you need to know that this is an owned media tactic, not earned media. Public relations and earned media is about borrowing the interest of the reader. A comment strategy is more about building relationships and managing dialogue. We mention this only if you are considering making a commenting strategy a part of your earned media campaign. It needs to be a part of the owned media function, unless you're pitching a story in the comments section. In which case, you missed everything we just said.

7.4. Understanding paid media in the online space

One of the reasons advertising on today's digital media is so effective is that is allows advertisers to escape the traditional advertising and marketing model to a certain extent. At the very least, it helps us move beyond "mass marketing," which is helpful because the mass market no longer exists (see Chris Anderson's The Long Tail for more on this reality). The broadcast –and –blast model. The spray –and –pray model. There is no mass market left to. . . uh, spray on. But now you can target in every way imaginable because of all the data we leave behind and share as users of these platforms. There's an old saying in the online publishing business: "When something online is free, you're not the customer, you're the product." That's pretty important to understand.

Whatever you want to call it – hypertargeting, social targeting, whether it is based on behaviors, demographics, or social graphs – it is still the same old idea that marketers send out messages in the form of advertisements. This is all a more fine –grained form of what is called interruption marketing. For more on this concept, read Seth Godin's timeless "Permission Marketing" – the foundation of owned media marketing.

TV and radio commercials interrupt what you're viewing or listening to. Billboards interrupt your scenic views along the highway. Newspaper ads interrupt the stories you're reading. People use social media because they are looking for relevant content. They are not there to see your advertising, any more than they do when they are watching the news or reading a magazine article. In fact, the last thing they want to see is your advertising.

That's why the companies that treat social media like it's just another advertising channel will often fail. It's also why campaigns that point to your ad on YouTube or your website will not produce the results you were hoping for. Posting your 30 –second TV spot to YouTube is not a social media strategy. Sorry, but if that is all you're doing, that's just lazy.

7.5. Activating and extending owned media with paid media

Instead of using paid media to deliver a product's message, why not use those same tactics to build your own audience of paying customers and raving fans? Rather than trying to buy views for your commercials, why not buy an opportunity to capture the audience instead? Then you don't have to rent their eyeballs anymore.

Many brands have been doing this with their websites. Whenever you see a TV commercial or read a magazine ad that says, "visit www.mycoolwebsite.com for more information," that's what we mean.

But that is just the tip of the iceberg. Instead of just tagging the ad, why not make it about how awesome your online community is? Or why not brag about some amazing content you've created? Why not give yourself a chance to add that consumer to your audience by drawing them into the community?

While some people love GoDaddy and other people hate the brand, you can't argue against its effectiveness. Its ads featuring Danica Patrick, Jillian Michaels, and the "GoDaddy Girls" are geared toward driving people toward its website where they can see more content – the not –safe –for –TV content – and, by the way, tell people about their low –cost domain names in more depth with more information available to customize the message. The brand's strategy of starting little movies on TV with paid media that have to be continued on the website is an ideal strategy for driving traffic to its owned media.

Here's another early (and ground –breaking) example of leveraging paid media to drive audience development in owned media.

In 2001, BMW Films created several short films about "The Driver," played by Clive Owen and directed by several different movie directors such as Ang Lee, Guy Ritchie and John Woo. The idea was that these short movies would be released online and showcase "The Driver" traveling from place to place, being hired by different people to be a transport for whatever they needed.

After the series began, BMW's 2001 sales number went up. The movies were viewed 11 million times in four months, and 2 million people registered on BMW Films' website, and many of them shared movie links with family and friends.

Keep in mind that this all happened before broadband was as accessible as it is now, 12 years later. Let's reiterate a key point here: This wasn't an ad for BMW. This was a product integration video that didn't have anything to do with having people buy cars. It was just cool content that people found interesting and remarkable.

This is a great example of paid media driving people back to the owned media property, BMW's website, where BMW was able to capture more audience and ultimately move that audience to purchase. It was text-book –perfect owned media strategy before anyone was even using the phrase "owned media."

7.6. Activating and extending paid media with owned media

Another thing to think about is activating your paid media with your owned media. What kind of campaign could your creative team come up with if they were not limited to 30 seconds or full –page ads? How could you use your owned media properties to help activate and extend your paid media campaigns? (Don't say, "Put my ad on YouTube!")

What if it all worked together? What if, instead of talking about features and benefits in your advertising, you were to tell people about the amazing content on your Facebook page or Twitter handle or blog? What if you showed people part of a longer video that they could only see on your website or on your YouTube channel? What if you serialized an ongoing story told in two –minute videos and told people they could see it via a magazine ad?

Now instead of advertising your product in 30 seconds, what if you could spend that time getting people to experience your content in any channel they want online, where they can interact with longer messaging, and make their own decisions about what information they are interested in? Or better yet, where you could determine what they are most likely interested in based on their profile data? What if you could build an audience of people who truly want to learn and understand more about your brand and product?

The cost of sharing a two –minute video online is a whole lot less than the air time to run it on TV. The cost of getting the right people to see it on TV is also drastically high because not everyone is a potential customer. You're paying for that TV commercial (or radio commercial or magazine ad) to go out to people who: 1) Are probably not your potential customers, but who knows because there's no reliable data. 2) Are going to tune it out anyway because they are on that channel to see content, not your ad.

If your customer base is 2 percent of the total viewership, why did you just waste that much money on the other 98 percent?

But if you could put the most important information online where you can track views and visits, where you can collect their information, and where you can ultimately see who became a paying customer, you'll get the biggest bang out of your paid media dollars by building an audience of people who actually want to see and hear what you have to say.

Part II: Developing an Owned Media Strategy

8. KEY SHIFTS IN ENTERPRISE MARKETING STRATEGY

The great thing about the socialization of media, from the consumer point of view, is that it has caused companies to change how they interact with them. Just 20 years ago, even 10 years ago, you only had to launch a marketing campaign, and see whether it led to any sales or an increase in name recognition. You held focus groups to see what people liked, and when the campaign was all over, you took the lessons learned and applied them to the new campaign.

Today, customers expect you to listen to them. They're already talking *about* you – now they want to talk *with* you. And with tools like Facebook, Twitter and blogs, they're able to talk with (and about) you in a very public manner. As a result, there are three key paradigm shifts in the way brands have to approach marketing, now and in the future: the need to listen, the need to respond in real –time and the need to plan for what you can't plan for.

8.1. Real –Time

The level of expectation of consumers today compared to where they were several years ago is consumers expect their brands to respond. You need to be able to react if something good or bad happens. It's more than a matter of shifting budgets, adding additional tactics or tools, or making other plans and arrangements on the fly. It requires a fundamental shift in how the marketing function operates.

The requirement to engage directly in public, real –time, online dialogue is very important. It changes what marketing people need to do in terms of budget, resources and content. They need to have a different set of resources that enable them able to react to people immediately, and they need to have both the understanding of how it impacts the rest of the brand's tactical efforts and the ability to take action on those threats or opportunities.

Also, from a content perspective, timeliness equals relevancy. If an opportunity arises, and it takes you five days to respond, you're no longer relevant. You're last week's news. Your consumers are operating in real –time, so you have to, too, if you want any input on how your brand dialogue is shaped.

The impact on opportunity is best showcased by Proctor & Gamble's near real –time response to a crash at a NASCAR race where their Tide brand was a major sponsor.[9]

This not only underlines the importance of a real –time marketing effort, but it also shows the impact of a real –time media environment on crisis response. While we want to leverage opportunity in real –time, we also must be aware of threat in real –time, so we are in a position to manage and guide dialogue in the event of a crisis, or better yet, suppress a crisis situation before it becomes a major issue. This leads us to the second key paradigm shift in marketing planning: the ability to listen.

8.2. Ability to listen

In the past, listening was done by focus groups and other market research tools. Listening was never really done in real –time. The typical approach has always been to listen via research, but it was typically only done once a quarter, or even once a year – or worse, not at all.

Now it's happening online, and you can gather intelligence by listening to your customers who are engaging with you. We call this **on –channel monitoring** – all the dialogue happening on the channels you own and control. You can also gather intelligence by listening to the world at large. We call this **off –channel monitoring**, which would include all the dialogue around a given keyword set on any channel on the Internet, whether you own it or not.

Brands today must have the ability to gather data more quickly, assess that data and determine if there are any opportunities or threats, and then be agile in response to that new data. It's the 24/7 focus group, and it is happening right now while you're reading this.

Let's imagine a restaurant that's monitoring its customer experiences, and it wants to pay better attention to what its customers are saying. In the past, customers would have filled out comment cards, leaving messages that their dinner was cold or the service was poor. They would have told a couple of friends, and that would have been the end of it. If the manager

---

9   http://www.bizjournals.com/cincinnati/blog/2012/02/tide–got–about–8m–in–free–
    media–from.html?page=all

heard about the problem, it was too late to fix it, but it wasn't such a big deal that they had to make it right for the customer.

Today, however, a customer can complain online, sending a message out on Twitter or Facebook. More importantly, they can complain while they're still in the restaurant. And they can complain to their 3,000 Twitter followers and 1,200 Facebook friends, many of whom are in the same city.

Just a couple years ago, when brands weren't using social media, those complaints would go unheard by restaurant management, and the complaints could grow and fester, turning into a serious brand crisis without management ever hearing about what was going on.

Today, smart restaurant managers are paying attention to Twitter, Facebook and other social networking channels. They see those complaints and respond immediately. "We're sorry your food was not up to your expectation. I'll send someone to take care of this immediately." Better yet, the manager will leap into action, find the patron and fix it herself.

We both love Scotty's Brewhouse, a small restaurant chain in Indianapolis, which does exactly this. We have tweeted, or privately messaged, restaurant owner Scott Wise, who has fixed problems while we were sitting in the restaurant, and he was in a different location.

Now let's expand this vision to a large national brand. Brand managers are able to use social media as a 24/7 focus group, using social media monitoring tools to keep an eye on mentions for the brand, and its competitors, as a way to keep customers happy.

Rather than seeing a comment from one customer who is unhappy because his food was cold, a brand manager can watch dozens, hundreds or even thousands of comments and complaints from unhappy customers as they unfold. They're responding to complaints immediately, putting out fires before they have a chance to go viral and do serious harm. No brand manager wants to get a call from a traditional media journalist asking about an international uproar over a situation they knew nothing about. If anything: 1) They want to know about it beforehand. 2) They don't want it to become an incident in the first place. Yet, that kind of thing still happens to a lot of companies because they're caught unaware.

By now, everyone has heard of the famous United Breaks Guitars debacle. If you haven't, Google it. You can even start searching for "United breaks guitars" on Google, and the results – 5.15 million of them – will start popping up before you start typing the second word. This story turned into an international uproar with a music video about the issue reaching millions of views before United's corporate executives ever heard about the problem in the first place.

This is not a simple matter of going out and buying a social media monitoring tool. This shift in thinking impacts not just marketing, but every area of the enterprise. Listening has become mission –critical because of all the tactical uses of listening – research, product development, customer service, recruiting, human resources and all of the other things you can use it for across the enterprise, in addition to its requirement in marketing and public relations. Can social media really cause enterprises to change their product development? You bet. By listening, they are able to come up with new product ideas and bring them to market faster. Or you could just do focus groups once a year. Many companies still are.

That's because brands and marketers still aren't used to listening. They have never had to in the past the way they do today. They're used to talking and not being talked back to. That's what makes this a huge paradigm shift, not just from a functional capability perspective – but for the entire strategic approach to how a brand markets itself.

8.3. Planning for the unplannable

In the past, everything was very linear in a branding campaign. We're going to start at A, end at B. Now there are all kinds of things that can fall outside of your control, such as how consumers react to your campaign and what they think of your brand. You have to be flexible enough in your planning to allow for what has become a non –linear approach in brand planning. A lot of marketing people will plan out the whole calendar for an entire year. Even worse, they will take their budget and commit it to a long –term, linear campaign with no ability to course correct because traditional media is so expensive on the production side. If you just spent $2 million on a new TV commercial, and another $500,000 testing it, it is a lot harder to be flexible and responsive with that asset. You have to plug it in to your linear campaign and live with it and hope what you projected to happen actually happens. But if you are able to listen and react in real –time, this means you can use real –time signals to understand what is working and what is not, and adjust on the fly. So how do you plan for that?

The short answer is you don't. You have to plan for what you can't plan for. This is a huge shift in how marketers have approached their strategic planning in the past, but it is a requirement driven by inarguable logic: If the media environment is always –on, socialized and real –time, the brand's strategy must account for an always –on, socialized real –time environment. If the brand wants to be able to respond in real –time, the brand must take into account how listening – and what we learn from listening – will affect strategy and tactics. Since we don't know what we are going to hear when we listen, we have to build a strategy that can pivot and shift and respond on the fly, without really knowing what future variables could manifest.

Keep in mind, we are still just talking about the strategic approach, not functional capability. The approach to strategy has to change. Brands going out and hiring people and buying tools and checking these things off the list solves a functional requirement, not a strategic requirement. A Radian6 license doesn't solve a problem. You just bought a tool. Hiring a social media team means you now have the resources to actually use the tool. It does not mean your marketing strategy has changed. So many brands work backwards into the strategy component by throwing money at tactics and functional capability. Then they wonder why "it's not working." If it's not working, it's because your entire approach to marketing has to be refocused and account for these three key shifts. Otherwise, you're putting lipstick on a pig, as my farmer friend likes to say (yes, he is a pig farmer).

8.4. Framework vs. campaigns

In the past, marketing was linear. A campaign had a start and a stop. But owned media and branding are ongoing cycles. Marketers are still thinking linearly – I'm going to start with A and end with Z. But this doesn't account for the rest of the world moving around you.

A proper owned media strategy has a "guardrails" approach. On one side, these are the things we want to accomplish, and on the other these are the things we want to avoid or protect against. What's left in the middle are the tactics that we can employ throughout the framework, and not just a single campaign. The framework is an ongoing process and is something that a campaign can sit on top of.

So when Brand X says "we want to do a social media campaign," there are systematic pieces of the puzzle that have to already be put in place to do that – our framework has to be there for us to run a campaign on top of.

A framework allows brands to read and react. In football, when you run a play, the defense reacts. If you're in a third –and –long situation, and you see the defense is in deep –zone coverage, you have to audible to a different play. In the world of 21st century media, your brand has to be able to do the same thing – react quickly and adapt to any changes in the marketplace. In a linear campaign, you're committed to it, because you have to be. You've spent all this time and money on developing it. But a more agile strategy – the "guardrails" approach to strategic planning – and more agile production and execution methodology allows your brand to be more flexible.

8.5. The big idea vs. 1,000 little ideas

Campaign –style thinking has led marketers to cherish and worship "the big idea." The big idea is a central campaign concept, or in strategy, the actual brand promise. For instance, with Nike, the big idea is athletic endeavor. Everything they do as a brand ties back to this concept. An example of a big idea for a Nike campaign is its current "Find Your Greatness" campaign, one of the best campaigns we have seen. "Find Your Greatness" ties the concept of athletic endeavor to everyday non –athletes. The execution on the broadcast front has been flawless. It is an amazing way to sell running shoes to people like us who wouldn't run unless they were being chased.

How does that big idea get delivered online in Nike's owned media? Thematically, there are tons of ways that could be leveraged from a content perspective. This is where the need for 1,000 little ideas comes into play in today's real –time media environment. Nike activated "Find Your Greatness" with its sponsorship of the 2012 London Olympics, releasing a new TV spot every day with a different story. Every story came from a different London, such as London, Ohio. The brand covered baseball, gymnastics, soccer, and running, showing everyday people overcoming adversity. Amazing, touching stories. Not commercials about shoes.

All of these stories were extended on YouTube, with one story about Nathan Sorrell going viral to the tune of more than 1 million views. Twitter exploded with the #findgreatness hashtag. While there was some criticism about Nike supposedly "exploiting" an obese child to sell shoes, generally the sentiment was positive. Nike teamed up with celebrities and athletes to further promote the hashtag and to share its stories of finding greatness at gameon.nike.com. The brand also used Nike+ and its FuelBand product (both products that generate online content for the brand and drive audience engagement) to make Aug. 12 the most active day in the history of Nike+ with their extension, "Greatness Is Ours." All of this lead to more than 400,000 Facebook mentions a day, according to AppData. com. Throughout the campaign, Nike had more than 200 in –house employees making content, managing its distribution, monitoring, moderating dialogue and measuring results – creating thousands of little ideas, managing thousands of little interactions in real –time.

Nike's Global Digital Brand and Innovation Director Jesse Stollak was quoted in a 2010 Mashable article:

> "Ultimately, we are about connecting
> with the consumer where they are.
> We started with notion that this was about
> publishing to them with the right message
> and at the right time. We've quickly
> evolved to a focus on conversations and
> engaging them to participate as opposed to
> using new media in traditional ways."

Nike began experimenting with digital audience development in 1996. Apparently when Bill Gates said, "Content is king," someone at Nike heard him.

8.5.1. The continued importance of the big idea

The big idea – the essence of a brand, the core promise, the thing that your brand stands for – will always, always play the "lodestar" role in marketing strategy. This is what guides all things across the entire brand experience, at every touchpoint, at every interaction. This is the promise the brand must fulfill. This is the concept you have to check down to regardless of the marketing tactic in paid, owned or earned media – does it ladder up to the big idea? But because of the way people consume media today, and the speed at which it is consumed, and the type of media being consumed, and the real –time nature of it, and the ability for the consumer to have a voice, and their ultimate control of that brand idea, and for 1,000 other reasons – brands have to also deliver not just one big idea, but 1,000 little ideas.

8.5.2. A thousand little ideas

What do we mean by 1,000 little ideas? This has to do with the concept of story arcs. This is something we will talk about in more detail later in the book, but essentially, what we are saying is that the conversation online moves fast, and not every idea is going to have a long enough shelf life to invest in it as you would in a big idea. This means from an operational standpoint, brands have to generate – and execute – a lot more little ideas to keep audiences engaged in real –time. They have to be topical and relevant for what is happening in the world right now, and those ideas have to be executed much more rapidly than the typical production cycle allows for. These are ideas that can't wait weeks or months for script approvals, casting, location scouting and all the other things you would typically do in the production of campaign –style content. And because the story arc for these ideas is typically shorter – weeks, days, maybe hours or minutes – it does not make sense to invest in them or produce them the way you might for a campaign.

So who is good at producing lots of content with short –term story arcs, at a reasonably high level of quality in near real –time? News organizations. ENG (electronic news gathering) style production methodology is far superior to what you would find for a Hollywood film, an agency TV spot, print ad, or other creative.

ENG style production is about speed and efficiency and telling the story in the most high –quality, compelling way possible given the constraints of time and relevance. This is the production model necessary to produce 1,000 little ideas. It can't be done in a typical creative production environment. The speed and flexibility are not there. The type of staff required is very different, and the systems, methodology, tool sets, and other operational parameters required for this level of responsiveness and agility don't typically exist in today's internal marketing departments and external agencies.

In the case of external partners, it is almost impossible for them to be profitable with this kind of production because they were never designed to do this financially, either. We'll go into more detail on team structure and operational methodology later in the book, but understand the strategic approach we will be outlining is ultimately designed to deliver 1,000 little ideas that integrate with a big idea.

8.6. Strategic implications for real –time owned media

We know we need a strategy that accounts for a real –time, socialized –media environment. We know we have to account for listening in our strategic approach. We know that we need an agile, responsive plan that allows the brand to pivot and shift and be opportunistic, as well as manage risk. We know we need a framework for the strategy that is always –on, and can deliver 1,000 little ideas, not just one big idea.

How do we change our approach to strategy to account for all of this?

First, we have to build a strategy that is focused on the audience. Without an audience, owned media is worthless.

Second, that strategy must be built around content, not platforms. The platforms will always change (anyone remember Geocities, or MySpace?). The only constant is content. This will allow media to evolve around our strategy, not the other way around. Finally, we need a strategy that will enable the brand to generate 1,000 little ideas that activate the brand promise.

Over the last five years, we identified eight key areas that must be addressed in a specific order to enable a brand to put the necessary strategic framework in place to create a successful owned media strategy. Like most strategic approaches, this borrows from many areas including traditional brand development, web design, content strategy, library science, search, risk management, broadcast programming, and incorporates many other cross –disciplinary best –practices. You can adopt this process and make it your own, and it has been designed to scale to the needs of any business.

But each of these areas has to be addressed to the appropriate depths of inquiry for what is at stake for your brand, or your strategy will fail. We learned this through several years of sometimes painful and sometimes pleasurable experience with real brands in the real world. This is not just theory, it is experience –based. While this process continues to evolve, every problem we have encountered over the last five years falls into one of the following areas of focus, and can be addressed with this methodology. It's awesome. And it works great. Let's dive in.

9. DISCOVERY

The discovery phase is where the background research happens. This is the foundation of a solid owned media strategy, and it is different than typical marketing discovery. In fact, it relies on already having a solid brand strategy in place and well –documented. We want to understand the brand, but we also want to see not only the content that exists, but who makes it, how the audience responds to it, and how the brand takes real –time listening and response into account (or how it doesn't).

Most importantly, we want to discover what the audience finds compelling, interesting and remarkable. This is more than just a content audit – marketers need to know where the content lives in the organization, what resources are already available, which areas of the organization need to provide input and what their specific communications goals are. Most importantly, we want to know what the audience is all about. We do this with monitoring, existing documentation, interviews, and research.

9.1. Monitoring

Anyone in digital media, content marketing, social –media marketing or any other form of online marketing, will tell you: Listen first. This is what discovery is all about. The most important thing we can do in discovery is learn about the audience. Before you do anything else, invest in a monitoring effort. Don't just buy a tool or run a report. Dig in to the audience. Unless you already have a relatively sophisticated and robust monitoring function in place, you will probably want to call in an expert on this. This is something Raidious does before we even have an introductory conversation with a client, before we ever agree to work with them.

Monitoring will tell you all kinds of useful things about a brand and its customers. Most of all, it will tell you how the audience feels about the brand. Are there any issues with its product or services? Are people proactively bashing the brand or singing its praises? Are they talking about the category, but not the brand? Are the brand's competitors actively pursuing this audience? Or – worst case scenario – is the audience not talking about the brand at all?

9.2. Documentation

In order to develop a fully integrated owned media strategy, it is necessary to know what is happening with the rest of the organization's marketing plans. The first thing to do in discovery is to get a handle on what will happen in advertising, merchandising, publicity, promotion, product development and all other communications functions in the enterprise. This could even include recruiting plans from human resources or customer service initiatives.

The goal is to understand what activity is already happening, so we know how to structure our strategy to support, activate and enhance everything else the brand is doing on the marketing and communications front. Every interaction – every touchpoint – will ultimately end with online digital content, or content will play a role in some form, with almost every tactic. So it is important to understand both the full picture of the overall marketing and communications strategy, as well as having an in –depth view of each of the individual building blocks.

Here, in order of priority, are some ideas for documentation to gather for your strategy team to review as they are beginning the development process for your owned media efforts:

Consumer research – This might include a summary or overview of a recent survey, focus group or similar research. Website usability profiles or personae would fall into this category. If you have any channel strategy or segmentation research, this will be critical for your owned media team to have access to in order to fully understand the audience and develop the appropriate personae.

Strategic marketing documentation – This could include something like a high –level overview of your brand strategy, marketing strategy or the actual documentation from your strategy partner. This is not your corporate identity standards; this is the core, DNA –level documentation of your brand. Most likely produced in partnership with your agency of record, brand strategy firm or research partner.

Sample creative brief – This is usually a brief drafted by your agency for advertising production. The team will want to know and understand the thinking, rationale and approach for each campaign you have planned. Creative briefs are a great way to get a high –level overview of the point of a campaign.

Sample creative – This could be print ads, TV spots, brochures or any other form of advertising creative your marketing team produces for each campaign. This is helpful in defining and fully understanding the voice of the brand, and how these campaigns can be fully activated in owned media channels.

Paid media/advertising plan – Knowing how the advertising buy is set up will be important for your owned media team, particularly with regard to proactive content development. Knowing when you have advertising running is also critical from a monitoring perspective. This is usually available as an Excel spreadsheet and is available from your agency or in –house media buyer.

Sales/merchandising/promotions/event marketing plan – Merchandising calendars, promotions, special sales, sponsorships, special events, trade shows, community support events, guerilla efforts, off –premise events – all of these are opportunities for your owned media team to contribute strategic thinking, content and engagement support and other execution resources to extend and activate these kinds of programs and campaigns.

Public relations plan – This would be your "earned –media" plans – press release subjects and dates, etc. If the company is planning on making a big announcement, or even has a schedule for the release of more common things like key hires, it is important both for monitoring and proactive engagement for your owned media team to be aware of what is happening so it can help activate it.

Search – Search, as we will discuss later in the book, is simply a side effect of great content and great engagement. In order to understand the language of the consumer and the brand, and your goals from a search perspective, as well as the kinds of terms the team should be monitoring for, you should share any research and results on organic/paid search efforts, including all keywords that are being targeted and any related metrics and reporting from a search perspective.

Email marketing – Your team should have access directly to your email marketing analytics tool, recent reports, and examples of emails. Knowing what lists exist and what the rationale is behind them would be good to know as well. This includes transactional email (eCommerce), triggered campaigns or automated campaigns, marketing email systems, CRM email systems, sales, human resources, and all other email efforts.

Social analytics – Access to any social media reporting that might currently be available is critical. If this is not already in place in your organization, this should be the first thing you implement. We cover this in more detail below, in Research. Your team will want to know about dialogue volume, sentiment, any influencers you watch in your category, past online crisis –oriented situations, and any other available data on your social media audience.

Web analytics data – Your team will need access to your website/blog/microsite analytics to understand audience motivations and how people are interacting directly with your brand online.

Mobile analytics data – If you have a separate mobile marketing initiative or campaign in place – text, mobile apps, separate mobile sites – this will be critical information as well.

Corporate identity – This includes PMS colors, typography, graphic elements, tone and style guides, and any other relevant corporate image governance materials. Your team will use these elements to guide your look and feel from a design perspective in your owned media channels, and these will help the team develop a similar style guide for your owned channels. For instance, what are the hexadecimal equivalents of your PMS colors? How will the brand be represented in icons and avatars in social channels? What are the web –safe font equivalents?

9.3. Interviews

It's more than just a conversation with the marketing team. It's understanding the implications from human resources, legal, finance, the stakeholders and other areas of the enterprise affected by the changes in today's media environment.

For example, HR might want to talk about different career opportunities in the hopes of recruiting top talent. Finance might need to share financial news for shareholders as part of their legally –mandated financial disclosure. And the legal department might need to address pending legal action being taken on behalf of the company. All of this has implications for how you structure your owned media efforts.

Discovery is also about getting a full understanding about how the organization works and learning where the gaps are in order to build the entire planning process. It's important to know whether legal's statements will affect HR's efforts. It's important to know whether a major new product launch is going to affect what finance says in its upcoming disclosure. It's important to know how to unify messaging across those disparate departments, as well as unifying the monitoring and response effort, and how to make it all function in real –time.

We also want to discover which content management systems are in use, identify whether there is any risk management documentation in place, what HR policies say about social media usage, and how the brand will leverage and respond to user –generated content, like blog comments and tweets about the company.

This is different from what you would typically look for in a strategic brand development / planning process. Ultimately, everything is about branding because any mention that can be made of a company online is going to be one more piece of content that will impact the brand. But owned media strategy is not brand strategy. Owned Media strategy is about growing an audience and putting the guardrails and framework in place – systems, resources, processes – to create the content and manage the dialogue that enables that audience growth. Owned media strategy allows you to manage all those online touch points with the brand.

But these questions might also lead to discussions with other departments. For example: "Is there a call center within the organization? How much leeway do they have to solve a customer's problem?" Answers to these questions can help them better understand how each department fits and works within the organization, and how (and if) they are integrated into the communication.

The reason brands should be asking these questions is because all of it has some implication for decision making about the framework for how the brand is going to listen and respond in real –time. This establishes and influences everything else in the strategy. It gives the brand the ability to establish a framework and the necessary processes required to execute in real –time.

This is a far cry from the kind of discovery work that informs typical marketing planning. In the past, discovery has only focused on developing the marketing message and what marketing needs to accomplish from a business perspective. Because so many other areas of the enterprise are impacted by today's real –time, socialized media environment, marketing has to take their input into account when developing an audience –centric, owned media strategy.

9.4. Research

In addition to materials your brand probably already has in place, it is likely your strategy team will want to do some additional research as part of the discovery process in order to fill in the gaps and get a better understanding of the brand's owned media properties and audience. In order of priority, are some examples of more specific discovery activity you may want to perform:

Online research – It will most likely be necessary to do some additional off –channel monitoring to understand the current dialogue around the brand. In –depth online research is fast and inexpensive compared to most traditional forms of research and can give the team very good directional insights, fast.

Human resources – Only humans can make content, and only content grows audiences. We need to know what resources already exist that we can leverage. Who internally has been dealing with your owned media properties? What other internal resources exist that we could leverage as we develop strategy? What external partners do we currently work with, what is the scope of their assignments, and how can they help us? Agencies, public relations firms, web shops, design shops – any external strategic contributors that you think could contribute some strategic thinking – should be included in the interview process and can be helpful in sourcing and providing documentation.

Content resources – Many brands have tons of content that already exists, they just don't see it. There is content in your brochures. There is content in old emails you've sent. There are probably some blog posts that could be repurposed. While an in –depth traditional content audit may not always be necessary, it is important for your team to know what content exists today. This could include:

- **Consumer generated** – This is not just blog comments. What about reviews, customer interviews, testimonials and other content that your customers have generated about your company? Could that be used or repurposed?
- **Aggregated** – Is the brand curating, or sharing, content from other third –party sources? For instance, if your brand is in health care, are you selectively curating content from WebMD or another source? Are we aggregating content from multiple, outside sources? Which ones, why and how?
- **Licensed** – Does the brand subscribe to a content library of some sort?
- **Original** – Does the brand use internal or external resources to produce original content? Who are those resources, how are they performing and what is their current scope of work?
- **Usability** – Many brands do not understand or implement user –centered design on their web properties, which can often be a huge success factor, particularly as it relates to conversion and readability. If the brand has not performed any recent usability work, this would be the time to take a look at how usable your web properties are. This can be done with lots of analytics tools, again fairly affordably and pretty quickly. Our favorite tool is Feng –Gui, which lets you see how your users experience your website. For larger properties,

particularly in ecommerce, we recommend physical user testing and investing in a proper usability audit with a reputable user interface firm.

- **Additional web analytics** – Depending on your web analytics platform and how it has been implemented, it may be necessary to employ additional external analytics tools to get to more specific answers or baseline intelligence.
- **Competitor intelligence** – Competitor analysis can be helpful, particularly if the brand is early in the process and does not have a good idea of what its baselines should be. An analysis of a competitor can give the brand some idea of what a realistic baseline metric should look like for each of its owned media channels.
- **Audience research/segmentation** – The audience drives all owned media activity. Therefore, it's critical to understand your target audience and how it might be segmented, both from a content development perspective as well as in other areas – such as how to structure voices, accounts and your brand's distribution methodology. If your answer is "everybody" when asked who your target is, you need to do some more research to refine this in order to realistically address your potential audience. You don't have the resources to target "everybody".
- **Content audit** – An in –depth content audit is a key part of developing a multi –channel strategy. What do we already have that can be repurposed in other channels? A good content audit will include both quantitative (What do we have, and where is it?) and qualitative (Is it any good, and can it be repurposed?) of pre –existing source content on all of your owned media channels. Kristina Halvorson's "Content Strategy for the Web" has some great in –depth perspective on how to structure a traditional content audit. It's highly recommended reading.
- **Outcome: Initiative statement** – The outcome of the discovery process should be an initiative statement that gives a recap of all the materials reviewed and an overview of any insights uncovered that will inform the rest of the strategy process. The team will be referring back to all these materials throughout the process, and new insights will be made along the way. We recommend making this initiative statement one of the last things your team does before presenting it to management or the C –suite.

10. RISK

There is a basic checklist of "must –know" things that are important to learn during the discovery phase and then keep in mind throughout the rest of the process. These are company legal procedures, processes, industry requirements, safety regulations and special rules regarding company communication.

There are specific risks every business has to deal with, so this stage of the process is critical. You need to know what's OK and what's not OK to talk about, what known issues exist and how they are being dealt with, what the current governance structure is for sensitive communications, and what the current crisis response plans are. If your brand is going to engage with people in real –time, in a public forum, the brand absolutely has to play defense first. We see the risk function of strategic planning as setting up a "defensive perimeter" around the brand to protect it against as many known and unknown risks as possible.

While we don't want to scare marketers, this is a critically important step. Too many brands have lost millions in value because they did not address risk in their owned media strategy. That being said, we don't want brands to handcuff themselves, either. It is just as important to be able to engage in dialogue in real –time without 20 lawyers approving every tweet (however, if you need corporate approval to send even a single tweet, then your company is not ready for this). It's important for companies to be human – something many companies are just now learning (read Jay Baer's and Amber Naslund's "The NOW Revolution" for more about being human).

While it's important for employees to follow the pre –approved steps in the response flow chart, we also need to be able to humanize the information. There may be scenarios where customer service people have never faced a specific issue, but it's still important to have a system in place to be able to respond to the situation. Again – planning for what we can't plan for and being agile and responsive, not legislating silence to manage risk. Being silent and not responding is a far more risky proposition in many cases, specifically in a crisis.

While this might not seem like it should be part of an owned media strategy, keep in mind that in a perfect world, customer service is part of marketing, which means that word of mouth and customer loyalty should be a component of the strategy. Also keep in mind that what your audience says your brand is, is what it is. You no longer get to control that. You can influence it, but you have to play defense first and understand the dialogue – and be able to respond to it – before you can influence it.

10.1. Key risk areas to consider

Because many brands have not adjusted to the need to listen and respond in real –time – and the fairly recent empowerment of the consumer voice online – the next step after discovery in strategic planning should be a thorough risk assessment to understand any threats that currently exist or could exist in the future and any risk –oriented constraints around content and audience development. This is an absolutely crucial exercise for brands to go through in order to protect the brand, its employees, and its shareholders. Far too many brands have just "jumped in" to social media efforts or ignored social media dialogue. The Internet is littered with stories of brands that did not take the proper steps to protect themselves and lost millions in brand equity or, at the very least, took a big reputational hit due to negative dialogue that went unchecked, publishing content that wasn't properly vetted, and for scores of other reasons. These are painful lessons to learn and can be avoided by examining potential risk factors, including:

Compliance – Is your brand regulated in any way, shape or form? If it is, your owned media team needs to know this so the proper compliance steps can be accounted for in distribution and engagement. For instance: Is there a federal, state or local government entity that has oversight of your industry?

Legal – Are there any legal approval requirements for publishing content? For instance – do you have to have anything cleared by legal before it gets published to the web?

Technology – Are the properties you are hosting technically capable of 90 –percent –plus uptime? Can they scale to handle large traffic spikes? The last thing you want when an event or piece of content draws a lot of traffic is a server failure. Prepare for success here.

Online crisis response planning – Do you have any crisis management plans in place? Your public relations counsel should have this in place already, and this can be a good running start for an online response plan. We typically would recommend centralizing crisis response with your earned –media function and allowing your owned media team to become additional eyes, ears and voices to be leveraged by the earned –media team in crisis scenarios. Right tool for the right job.

FAQs and escalation path – How do we respond to situations we already know about, and how do we escalate situations we can't plan for? Who does the information go to, in what order, and how does that happen systematically? Knowing about any existing situations or issues and developing pre –approved "canned" responses is an important piece of the puzzle here that allows the brand to plan for the known, as well as the unknown.

IP protection – Does the company have any licensing in place to protect its intellectual property? This pertains to all published content. Are your blog posts or emails or web videos copyright protected in some way? If not, this is something you should consider as part of your editorial and optimization process (unless you are OK with competitors or others reusing, remixing, curating and otherwise "borrowing" your content). This is still a very gray area from a legal and intellectual property perspective. Consult your legal counsel. At a minimum, we recommend Creative Commons licensing for all your content. This is a free, easy way to protect your content, while still being flexible about how it can be reused and remixed online. Visit CreativeCommons.org for more information on this evolving subject.

Terms and conditions – Have you recently reviewed your website's terms of service? This is usually located at the bottom of your website and is usually only updated during a website redesign. Terms of service should be as broad as your legal team thinks is reasonable to include the ability to use any content a user creates on a brand –owned channel, as well as to establish ownership of that content. Depending on the brand, there are most likely a number of other issues that need to be addressed and updated here to account for the way media works today, versus when the terms and conditions were originally created (probably several years ago at a minimum). Consult your legal team on this.

Privacy policy – Have you recently reviewed your website's privacy policy? This is also usually a link at the bottom of your site. Privacy policies typically need to be updated more regularly than terms and conditions because of the ever –shifting nature of how personal information gets shared online. This has been a big issue for Facebook, and something your brand should be aware of. Are you using cookies in browser sessions to track behaviors? You should disclose that. Using Facebook Connect to personalize a website experience? That should also be disclosed. Any time you gather personal information from a user, knowingly or unknowingly, in a logged –in state or not, no matter where the information is coming from, that should be disclosed in the privacy policy. Again, consult your legal team on this.

Employee –use policy – Do you have an acceptable –use policy governing Internet and/or social media use by employees? Check with human resources, your legal department, or in your employee handbook. This is one document that should be reviewed and updated regularly, at least every six months. If there is not a policy in place, one needs to be created. Employees represent the brand online, whether a company likes it or not, and regardless of the degree to which a brand should influence personal online behaviors "off the clock," expectations for which behaviors are considered acceptable and not acceptable should be communicated to your employees. This is typically a big area of internal debate, as well as legal debate, and it is not an easy policy to implement. Involve your HR team, as well as legal, on this to ensure you are both protecting the brand and protecting the rights and the privacy of your employees.

Security/permissions – How are you handling credentials security for your platforms? Are user names and passwords protected, updated and changed with regularity? If this is something you have not considered – or if more than one or two senior, trusted people have administration –level access to your accounts (for instance, direct access Twitter, Facebook or other social accounts, or access to email tools) – you should put this book on pause, and address that situation as soon as possible. There are plenty of tools to manage access and mitigate risk, and these are typically very easy fixes to implement. This is a simple and somewhat obvious, but often overlooked, way to manage risk for your brand. Ungoverned access to publish on behalf of a brand can lead to all kinds of usually unintended problems, and there is no reason not to put some sort of governance and approval controls in place immediately if not sooner.

Internet law – How familiar are you with the following laws and policies, and do you follow them? Internet law is always changing, and it is difficult to stay on top of those changes. Your legal team typically has its hands full, and it is important for your owned media team to understand the inherent legal risks associated with publishing content, so they can work within the legal constraints. If you're a company that operates internationally, it becomes an even more complicated problem. Here are just a few laws your team should understand and be aware of:

- Can Spam Act of 2003
- Data Protection Act of 1998
- Digital Millennium Copyright Act of 1998
- Children's Internet Protection Act of 2000

Platform usage terms and conditions – Know the terms of use and privacy policies for publishing platforms like YouTube, Flickr, Facebook, Twitter, Google and any other platform your brand intends to use for content distribution. You might be surprised at what you find in some of these policies, and it is important for you to consider the long –term implications of these policies as you create your strategy.

Monitoring – Do you currently use any specific metrics to identify negative sentiment about your brand? If not, this is something that should be implemented now to identify and understand any potential threats or risks that you might not already be aware of. This information can be invaluable in a number of ways, but most importantly, it is invaluable as a defensive measure to protect the brand.

Archiving – Did you know that every day a large chunk of the Internet disappears? Not only that, but in many instances, once your content has been published, it is out of your control and can be deleted for a number of reasons depending on the platform. From a legal perspective, particularly in highly regulated industry, archiving both the content you're publishing and dialogue around the brand from external sources can be important safety measures to take. There are several tools available to archive published content and dialogue. Putting an archiving system in place can help protect the brand in the case of future litigation, as well as offer a great content resource for future platforms.

Outcomes – Examining these areas where brands could be at risk will help inform your strategy in a number of different ways. It will give you a set of "guardrails" to work with and will help your team understand what its legal boundaries are, as well as how to create a governance and approval structure that mitigates risk, develops FAQs and response flowcharts around known issues, and develops monitoring and crisis response plans.

The primary outcome of risk assessment should be an action items list with due dates for addressing any risks identified in this process. This important piece of the puzzle is one of the pillars of creating a strategy that allows you to "plan for what you can't plan for." You might not be able to see the future, but you can develop risk identification and response systems that can deal with just about any scenario that develops. Documenting the right processes and procedures to manage your brand in a real –time crisis scenario – and mitigating the development of one in the first place – will also give your team, your management and your C –Suite the confidence to execute responsively and in real –time because so much of the thinking will have already been completed and approved in advance.

10.2. The social media threat matrix

For many companies, we have found it's helpful to develop a social media threat matrix, to determine how and where to respond to certain types and levels of crises based on online dialogue. Especially when a brand is dealing with multiple issues at once, a threat matrix helps provide an easy, high –level, prioritized view of each situation in context with the "norm." A threat matrix basically plots dialogue volume, influence or sentiment and damage potential on an X/Y axis, and plots each situation according to the recommended responses – monitor, respond, escalate or alert. You can combine this with comparative norms to give your communications team or executive team a clear idea of the situation and recommended path forward in one easy chart. Here is an example:

Brand X Norms:
- Volume: 100,000/day
- Sentiment: 57%+, 4%=, 39% –
- Influence: 30% influential

Situation One
- Volume: 20,000 (20% of norm)
- Sentiment: 30%+, 6%=, 64% –
- Influence: 45% influential_

Situation Two
- Volume: 10,000 (10% of norm)
- Sentiment: 50%+, 5%=, 45% –
- Influence: 15% influential

Situation Three
- Volume: 45,000 (45% of norm)
- Sentiment: 10%+, 7%=, 83% –
- Influence: 74% influential

10.3. Real –time communications and predictive analytics

Anyone who has ever dealt with real –time communication, especially if they face company crises and emergencies on a regular basis, understands that risk management is more like crisis communication planning than a strengths, weaknesses, opportunities and threats analysis.

For example, a company has a problem with a product that threatens to raise the ire of a large and vocal customer base. With the number of tools that are currently available, it's possible for a company to examine things that are happening, but usually after the fact. A user can see what did happen but can't be sure if a situation will escalate or die down as time passes.

With today's technology, it is possible to use predictive analysis to get a pretty good idea of whether or not a situation is going to escalate into a problem in the future. This enables brands to look at the volume of negative and positive dialogue and determine when and where a company is going to need to engage with their customers to defuse the situation. This is different than just looking that the numbers your social media monitoring tool spits out. Most tools do not have that predictive factor, and knowing what is likely to happen next based on past trends will help companies jump on negative issues before they spiral out of control. As we outlined earlier, this means having access to an analyst to understand and find insights in the analytics, not just buying a tool.

11. BUSINESS CASE

This is where companies make the business case for their strategy. It's just straight –ahead business planning – opportunities, goals, metrics, baselines, how success will be measured – but in the context of audience development. We are looking for business outcomes here.

The business case can't be developed until companies have gone through their discovery and risk management exercise. That way, they will know what resources and staff exist, what the constraints and dependencies are from a risk perspective, and anything else that can impact the goals and measurement of the business case that might or might not be in marketing's sphere of influence in the company.

The business case is about advanced decision making and collaboratively developing a set of reasonable expectations for your owned media program. We mentioned earlier in the book about the importance of setting goals and being able to measure them. This is the part of the process where companies set those goals, decide how they will be measured, and determine the methods by which they will measure those goals. There are lots of books that deal with how to establish and measure goals and metrics, so we will keep this section short. But keep in mind that all of this is in the context of developing an audience around your owned media properties – not your overall marketing objectives. You should already know what those are, and they should inform your business case. Marketing goals and audience development goals are two very different things that require very different tactics and resources to accomplish.

11.1. Definitions of success

This exercise paints an aspirational picture of what the brand would consider success over a given time period. It might be a quarterly vision, or annual, or much longer –term. This is "where we are going" with the strategy – what it is that we are ultimately trying to accomplish. Remember – this is not about marketing. It is about audience development. Do we want a larger audience? A more engaged audience? Are there internal functional capabilities we want to establish? Do we want to be more responsive to our audience? Do we want to make better content? Those are the kinds of things we want to focus on.

11.2. Metrics of success

Establishing metrics of success allows us to tie hard, empirical numbers back to our successes. If it's not worth measuring, it's not worth doing. So find a metric for every single success you want to achieve. Sometimes this is more difficult with some goals than others or more expensive or difficult to measure. If it is truly important, your company will find a way to measure it. For instance, if we want a more engaged audience, we need to determine which metrics on which platform we are going to use to measure engagement. If we want to create better content, we have to determine how to measure "better." Is it views? Time spent? Bounce rate? Open rate? Here is where this is determined and agreed upon.

11.3. Baseline

Depending on how far along your owned media program is, establishing baselines can be difficult – particularly for new areas. If your brand is moving into a new platform you've never used before (for instance, many brands right now are experimenting with Instagram and Pinterest), how can you establish a baseline? We typically recommend a month –over –month percentage metric (increase or decrease) as a baseline for new platforms and channels.

11.4. Goal

Setting realistic goals can also be a challenge for new programs. We recommend looking at industry averages and competitive intelligence whenever it is available – but keep in mind, others in your industry might be investing more resources or might have a more mature program in place. If your competitor is spending $5 million a year and has 20 in –house staff and two outside firms helping them with their owned media effort, don't expect the $200,000 you're investing and the intern you hired to produce similar results. Set reasonable, meaningful goals you are confident you can achieve based on the resources you have.

11.5. Percentage of change

Looking at the desired percentage of change, or movement, in a given metric goal is a great way to determine how realistic your goals are. If you want to increase your email open rate to 20 percent, but currently you're at 5 percent, that is a 300 percent increase in open rates. Based on your past investment in resources and your current planned investment in resources (tools, staff, outside help) – is this a realistic expectation? Are you increasing your investment by 300 percent? It's not always necessary or realistic to expect to increase your investment at the same rate that you want to grow your metrics. In many cases, small changes in what you're currently doing can get you to your goals with little to no additional investment. It really depends on your unique situation. We are not suggesting there should be a one –to –one correlation here, but there should be some correlation between the goals you set for your owned media, and the investment you are making in it to get to those goals. Understanding the percentage of change between baseline and goal will help you understand if you're being realistic and honest with yourself about what you can expect to achieve.

11.6. Business case outcomes

At the conclusion of developing your business case, your team should be able to clearly communicate, internally and externally, up and down the ladder, the following things:

- Why are we doing this? What is the business reason driving our efforts?
- In order to be successful, this program must (fill in the blank). What does success look like?

Specifically, the team must know these answers:

- What are our key performance indicators – the metrics we use to measure success?
- What is the current baseline for those key performance indicators?
- What are the changes we want to accomplish in relation to those key performance indicators to be successful?

How do we define conversion?

If your team can understand, buy into, and consistently verbalize, present and defend these questions and answers, you are now ready for the next step in your strategic planning process.

12. PERSONAE

In this critical strategy exercise, we want to move you from thinking about a demographic target to thinking about the people in your audience – not the consumers, not the users – the people. We want to literally personify your target audience. It's how you define the voice of your content – defining you target personae, potentially identifying negative personae and establishing the brand voice.

Personae are critical to drive content creation and manage dialogue. It's hard to tell someone to create content for women ages 25 to 44. For one thing, it's too vague. Are the women single or married? Mothers or not? Do they have a career, or are they stay –at –home moms? What makes them tick emotionally?

The hot –button issues and important keywords for each of those groups are completely different. The working, single mother is going to be different from the non –working wife, and she will have different needs, wants and goals.

By creating a representative persona of the target audience, it makes it easier for content creators to "speak to" a specific person, and create content that will resonate specifically with that persona. It also helps companies developing their owned media strategy to make sure everyone is "singing from the same songbook." Most importantly, it keeps the focus where it should be – on the audience, not the brand.

Personae enable content creators to serve the audience with content that is relevant and compelling to them. We want the brand to feel like a helpful, engaging or entertaining resource – not sound like marketers typically do when they are pushing product. We are interested in creating content that goes beyond price point, features and benefits. There is a place for that kind of messaging – it's called advertising.

Using personae also lets creators identify and add key communication points to the strategy. They can ask themselves: "What do we want this person to know versus that person?"

For example, Steve is a 20 –year –old college student and Stephanie is a 37 –year –old mom. Steve doesn't care that his new TV remote is safe for use around children, but Stephanie does. But both Steve and Stephanie may want to know that the remote is water –tight against errant liquid spills.

It's important to create personae based on the research you have done and keep it data driven. These are not stereotypical assumptions, but should be based on as much data as possible to create these personae. The best place to find nuggets and insights to bring a persona to life is with qualitative research. If your brand has done any psychographic segmentation work, that is a great place to start. If you're not sure, or you don't have data available, you can always take an educated guess. As a marketer, you probably have a pretty good idea of who your customer is, even without fresh research. The more you guess, the bigger the risk is that your content will be off target, and your engagement methodology will not resonate. Research – any research – is better than a guess. But an educated guess is better than doing nothing.

12.1. What's in a persona?

A persona typically includes more qualitative, interpretive information to present an "at –a –glance" picture of the target audience. You should be able to put your persona in front of any content creator anywhere, and get content back that is at least 70 or 80 percent "on target" for the audience without any further background information. The following elements are good to include in a persona:

Name – This is a person. Not a user, not a consumer, not just "the audience." We will be using the persona to shape all kinds of communications, and it is helpful as a content creator to think in terms of how they would present content to a specific person. So let's give that person a memorable, easy –to –recall name. Be creative here. If it's a politician, maybe his name is Government Glen. If it's a female investor audience, maybe it's Wall Street Wendy. Give them a full name too. Maybe Glen's last name is Johnson, and maybe Wendy uses a hyphenated last name like Witmer –Scott. This helps humanize the persona.

Photograph – This is by far the most important piece of the puzzle. Spend time on this. Use an actual, representative customer or target customer if you can. This photo should give the content creator a good idea of who they are talking to just by glancing at the picture. The stakeholders in your strategic planning group should see this picture and unanimously say, "Oh yeah, I have seen that person in our stores or using our product." It should be very obvious and easy to identify as your target.

Demographic/qualitative basics – Age. Education. Job title. Family status. Transportation. Hobbies. Media. Neighborhood. This quickly helps paint a lifestyle picture of the persona. Do not go into a lot of detail here.

For instance: "Government Glen is 41 years old. He did his undergrad at NYU and his master's at Princeton. He took the bar exam twice after law school and passed it the second time, but he never practiced law formally. Currently making $280,000 a year working as an advisor to a political action committee in D.C. He is on his second marriage, with two kids from the first. He has an 8 –year –old daughter, Clarissa, and a 6 –year –old son, Carlton (named after his grandfather, Carlton Johnson, a prominent New York senator). He leases a Mercedes S –Class convertible, but takes the train to work because he doesn't want to rack up miles on the Benz lease, and it looks good politically for him to use public transport. He plays pickup basketball on the weekends with some of his buddies from college and is an avid concert –goer. He stays glued to CNN on TV, satellite radio, and on the CNN app and is also voracious reader of online news from the Post, Times and Newsweek. He stopped taking the paper two years ago. He lives in a very high –end suburb just outside of D.C. It's not a gated mansion community, but it is pretty close."

While these things might not be true for every single member of your audience, the goal here is to paint a general, representative picture of the target.

Attitudes, perceptions, motivations – This is what a person thinks and does today. What motivates this person? What are his hopes, fears and dreams? What is she afraid of? What is stopping her from taking the action you want her to take? How does he see himself in relation to the brand? How does she feel about the brand or the category? What is the "prime mover" that gets this person to take an action? This should be aimed at the emotional nuts and bolts that are likely to move this person, not just qualitative factoids. This is the information we need as content creators to make people laugh or to make people cry – to create a story that will move them at an emotional level and not just provide functional information. Condense this down to no more than three to five bullet points. Only the most important stuff.

Key communication points – This is about what we want them to think and do. No more than three to five bullet points that boil down, in plain English, what you would like to communicate to this audience. This could include what you would like them to know about the brand, perceptions you would like to influence, how you want them to think and feel about the brand, the actions you would like them to take and the key points you want to make to this audience.

How they use the Internet – As almost all of your owned media efforts will be online, it is important to know how this person uses the Internet. This needs to go beyond "She's on Facebook." You need to know how they actually use the platform. Is this a primary means of communications to high school friends? Is this how she keeps in touch with her kids? Does she use the mobile app? How often is she logged in to Facebook? Or, in the case of Google – is she a Google power user or is she one of those people who still thinks Google "is" the Internet? Does she type in full web addresses to the search field? Does she read her email? How much email does she get? Is she a smartphone user and how advanced? How many apps are on her phone? Depending on the nature of the brand, this could be any number of specific "nuggets" about how the person interacts online with others, but try to keep this to no more than seven to 10 short bullet points.

12.2. Primary, secondary, tertiary, negative

Many brands have extremely broad audiences or extremely segmented audiences. Your owned media will be available to them all. In many cases, it becomes necessary to build more than one persona. We would recommend making the primary persona as broad and universal as possible. The more personae we have to address in strategy, the more we have to segment voices, channels and platforms, and create specific content for each persona. This can be difficult to accomplish, depending on the resources your brand has available – and as we mentioned, most of the content is going to be available to <u>all</u> the personae and audience segments, anyway. Remember, they don't know they're in a segment! They don't see themselves that way. You can't really publish content publicly that is only meant for one specific persona and not another because it is all public. They don't know it's not for them.

Wanting to microtarget content to very specific audiences makes sense. It is just very difficult to accomplish with public owned media. A better approach would be a more "audience of one" approach through customer relationship management and automated content. That is a topic that will require a whole separate book.

We recommend keeping it as simple as possible and focusing your resources on growing overall audience. Let your audience metrics tell you when it is time to establish a new initiative specific to a given audience segment, and use more of an automated customer relationship management/lifecycle marketing approach for individuals. Marketers like to have fine –grained control around messaging to their segments, and automated marketing is the best way to do that. It's still going to require content, but automating the delivery and using the dynamic, data –driven functionality that exists in most automation tools makes it a lot more manageable to target individuals than subsets and segments of a target. That sounds counter –intuitive, but that's a fact.

If your brand chooses a segmented approach, keep it as limited as you can to start. Establish one primary persona. No more than two or three secondary personae. If you have more audience segments, these should be considered tertiary personae. Even though brands like to market to precise audiences, it is important to realize that no matter how big your budget is, applying resources to one small segment takes those resources away from larger segments. It is always a trade off. You can do incredible work for one large segment, or you can take the same resources and do OK work for all of your segments and subsegments. Your business case will help drive the decisions on how to approach this – which segment is most profitable? Which is most likely to share your message and advocate for you? Understand where to apply resources to your personae.

Finally, you might want to consider creating a negative persona. This is a person who represents an audience we do not want to reach or engage with. One we want to avoid. Particularly with highly politicized brands, this can come in handy with reactive content, risk management, FAQs and other similar content.

12.3. The brand voice

The most important persona to spend your time on is the brand voice or brand voices. This is your corporate voice, your personality, the way people think of your company.

For the most part, a friendly, light, human tone and manner is appropriate for most brands. In very few cases is a formal, official tone appropriate or even expected (or appreciated). After all, businesses are just collections of humans. Yes, we have come to expect a very serious, almost clinical tone from the government, law enforcement, or the military. Depending on your brand, that approach may make some sense – but those organizations are not known for their warm and fuzzy customer relations. The whole point of a brand voice persona is to literally humanize the brand. So do that.

Is your brand more technical in nature, like an information technology company? Should you be considered a thought leader with a more academic tone and manner? Is your brand fun and outgoing? Does it deal with sensitive issues and require something more somber? The question we need to answer with this persona is not "what" is the brand, but "who" is the brand?

Create the persona exactly the same way you would a target persona. Find a picture. Give your brand a relatable, human background. This can be a difficult exercise, but it is a crucial one to go through, particularly in regards to reactive content like social media engagement.

There are times, however, when you need to drop your more human, friendly, light tone for a serious, almost clinical one. This is especially true when your company is facing a big problem.

If, for example, your CEO is implicated in a bribery scheme, if you are faced with a giant recall of nearly all of your spring product line, if your stock has dropped 40 percent because of an accounting error by one of the interns, it's time to be serious. Any of these or other crisis –oriented issues mean you need to drop the light tone and be more somber. This tone needs to be carried through your response to these incidents and crises, regardless of when you're writing about them. Whether it's the day it happened, or two years later, if you communicate on your channels about the situation, adjust your tone and manner to match the seriousness of it. This is PR 101. What you say and how you say it on Twitter or in an email are going to be under just as much scrutiny as your press release. Treat your content accordingly in crisis scenarios. That doesn't necessarily mean you need a separate "day –to –day" and "corporate" voice, but for some companies, this is appropriate.

Also, if you decide you are going to a segmented, target –persona approach, it might be necessary to adjust your brand voice accordingly for each segment. This, in our opinion, makes it more difficult and complicated to manage content production and audience engagement, and in many cases, there are not enough major differences from one voice to the next to really make that much of a difference in the tone of the content. We would always lean toward simple and focused over complex and fragmented. But if the resources are available and your team can handle this level of complexity – and it's necessary to accomplish the goals outlined in your business case – then go for it!

13. DISTRIBUTION

Believe it or not, distribution can be the biggest, messiest part of an owned media strategy, not the publishing and social media promotion. That's pretty easy. Publish a blog post to the blog – easy. Upload a video to YouTube and embed it to the blog – piece of cake. Promote them both via social media channels – routine stuff.

No, what's messy about the distribution strategy is the internal working of the company before content ever gets published. Again, this is why the discovery phase is so important. The information we gather there allows your team to take your two –ton elephant of a company and teach it to dance like a prima ballerina.

Distribution includes understanding the governance structure within the company. This means knowing who approves what, which platforms will be used to distribute it, how the brand voice will play out across multiple accounts, how much content will be published, and the roles and responsibilities of your existing content resources. Does legal have a say? Do you have to run everything through public affairs or public relations? Does the vice president of finance insist on editing everything? Who makes which content, and how will it be edited and optimized? How often will we publish and on which platforms? These are all important decisions, informed by our prior steps – discovery, risk, business case and personae. The decisions we made there and what we learned should drive our decisions regarding distribution strategy.

Distribution also can include a publishing schedule and the determination of what happens after content is published. This includes how audience reactions will be monitored and how/when the content metrics and feedback gets cycled back into the publishing workflow.

Once your team has a clear understanding of your resources and plans (discovery), your risk profile and constraints (risk), what business outcome we are looking for (business case) and who the audience is (persona), we are ready to start talking about distribution. This is where many companies start: How many Twitter handles should we have? How many Facebook pages? And so on and so forth. You have probably seen one of the many, many dormant corporate Facebook pages or Twitter accounts (or websites, or blogs) out there. It is because these accounts and platforms have no purpose. The brand did not clearly understand its own resources, risks, business case and audience. Let's see if we can avoid this with a well –considered, realistic distribution strategy.

13.1. Brand maturity / sophistication level

Altimeter Research did a great study in 2010 of how brands handle content distribution. These distribution models are a good starting point for your brand to consider when developing a distribution strategy for your owned media. We consider this the definition of best practices in content distribution, both proactive and reactive. Altimeter identified the following models, in order of maturity:

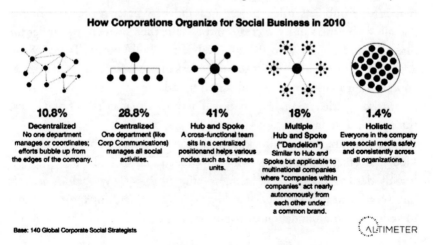

How Corporations Organize for Social Business in 2010

10.8%	28.8%	41%	18%	1.4%
Decentralized	Centralized	Hub and Spoke	Multiple	Holistic
No one department manages or coordinates; efforts bubble up from the edges of the company.	One department (like Corp Communications) manages all social activities.	A cross-functional team sits in a centralized positionand helps various nodes such as business units.	Hub and Spoke ("Dandelion") Similar to Hub and Spoke but applicable to multinational companies where "companies within companies" act nearly autonomously from each other under a common brand.	Everyone in the company uses social media safely and consistently across all organizations.

Base: 140 Global Corporate Social Strategists

ALTIMETER

Decentralized: This is not so much a strategy as it is a description of a state of being. A decentralized approach is one that is essentially ungoverned by any central strategy or approach. There are organic efforts happening in multiple areas of the organization. Employees, for example, experiment with different tactics without any coordination, and while there might be some periodic wins, and some siloed successes in one department or another, it is essentially chaos. This is what to expect in early –stage organizations just starting out in owned media.

Centralized: The next step in a company's maturity is a centralized, "command and control" approach. One department, usually marketing or public relations, takes control of all social media and other owned media efforts. This enables some level of risk management, and at the very least, a consistent tone and manner and centralized approach. The upside to this approach is that it offers some level of protection to the brand, but it is usually very difficult to function in real –time. It also limits the influence of departments outside of marketing and PR, and the brand's voice tends to come off as bland and corporate. This is what we would call a "functionally capable" distribution strategy, meaning the brand has matured to a point where it is capable of publishing proactive and reactive content in some centrally directed way. About one –third of brands take a centralized, command and control approach to their owned media.

Hub and Spoke: As organizations start to understand the operational, strategic and tactical requirements – not to mention the man hours, smarts and creativity – that it takes to operate an owned media function, we see brands moving to the very popular "hub –and –spoke" model. In this model, one hub sets rules, procedures and best practices for the brand, and allows business units to create and execute their own efforts, under the direction and usually with the approval of the "hub" entity. Typically this approach to distribution leads to more marked successes and can be a great approach for many small to mid –sized brands. It can even work for some enterprise –grade regional and national brands. The majority of brands use this approach today.

Dandelion: This is also known as the "multiple hub –and –spoke" model. It takes a hub –and –spoke approach and extends it to multiple brands, departments or other business units. As many larger brands become more confident in their understanding and capabilities, this approach starts to show up. In a dandelion distribution model, you might have multiple hub "owners" with access to the same set of voices and accounts for a brand functioning as an editorial or optimization layer. Or you might also have multiple segmented brand voices with unique associated accounts controlled by many different hub "owners" but governed centrally.

A great way to move to this model is with a "center of excellence" – a cross –functional team representative of all the interests of the enterprise. A center of excellence doesn't execute. It governs. This group is responsible for things such as setting policy, overall strategy, best practices and related principles among all the different hub "owners."

Honeycomb: The honeycomb model might look from the outside to be very similar to what you see in the more organic (some would say chaotic) decentralized model. In a holistic, or honeycomb approach, each individual employee is empowered to make both proactive and reactive content about a brand – on behalf of a brand, as a representative of that brand and on the brands owned media channels. This approach is practiced by only a handful of companies and is still very experimental. Depending on your brand's size, scope and unique circumstance, this might be a very rewarding approach. We have seen Dell, Zappos, Intel and Best Buy use this approach with varying degrees of success. It is important to make sure you understand the company's culture, and the kinds of employees to whom you will be giving the "keys to the car."

In any case, whether you use this model or not, it is important to make sure each employee understands, at a minimum, what your expectations of them are because they represent the brand, regardless of whether you choose to empower them at this level or not.

Using these guideposts and best practices, we will decide on a distribution structure and move on to the nuts and bolts of how content – proactive and reactive – gets published.

13.2. Voices, channels, platforms, accounts, and tools

The concept of voices and how they relate to channels, platforms, tools and accounts is an important one to understand. At the very least, we think it is important to outline a single language for all of these things, so you can have a clear conversation about them with your team.

Voices: Voices are singular sources of content – both proactive and reactive. Remember the personae we built for the brand voice? That is the source from which all content comes, but that content can be distributed through lots of different means. Here is how we talk about that:

Channels: Channels are categories of places you can publish content. Social. Email. Blog. Website. Mobile. These are all channels, much the same way direct mail, broadcast, outdoor and print are channels for publishing with paid media.

Platforms: Platforms are the specific places in each channel where you publish your content. In the social channel, our platforms might include Twitter, Facebook and YouTube. In the blog channel, we might have four or five different blogs. We could have several different approaches to email – newsletters, transactional and CRM, for instance.

Accounts: Accounts are our specific accounts within those platforms. In the social channel, we might decide to use the Twitter platform and have multiple accounts in that platform. We might also have multiple Facebook accounts, multiple "from" addresses in email, multiple short codes in a text program.

Your team will need to identify and make some decisions about the appropriate channels to use for your owned media. It will then need to decide which platforms within those channels make the most sense, and what accounts already exist or need to be created on those platforms, based on the resources you identified in discovery, your risk profile and constraints, your business case and your persona.

Tools: Tools are the third –party applications used to create and distribute content in our owned media channels. We probably have a content management tool for our websites and blogs, and a social media monitoring tool, and a social media management tool, and an email service provider – all of which are used to manage our multiple accounts.

CAUTION:

This is not the point at which to make any decisions regarding what tools your team will use to manage all of this. There is still more for your team to understand before they even begin to evaluate what is the best fit for your organization when it comes to third –party tools and software. It is easy to get swept up in the hype and go buy the latest and greatest piece of software for your team. It will solve every problem, just ask your sales rep! Sorry for the sarcasm, but as you know by now, tools don't solve the problem. They only enable humans to solve the problem.

13.3. Governance and approval path

Governance is understanding how the approval cycle works within your orga-nization, managing multiple versions and revisions of the content you're work-ing on, ensuring that any necessary legal oversight or approval happens.

This is a very important, key point to understand about governance: It applies to both proactive and reactive content. In other words, content is content. Whether you are creating a video to publish on a certain date or you're responding to something someone said about your brand, you are creating content, and that content should go through the same approval cycle regardless of the context, channel, platform or account it is being published to. Even a short Twitter response is still the creation and publica-tion of content, and for the appropriate governance, editorial, optimization and approval, even reactive responses should go through the same process as proactive or pre –scheduled content.

This is sometimes the biggest challenge for brands because in order to par-ticipate in a real –time medium, this approval and governance process has to happen in real –time. Keep this in mind as you are structuring your approval path.

13.4. Roles and responsibilities

Establishing roles and responsibilities for the resources you have on your team is your first step in determining an approval path. Once we under-stand the key governance roles and responsibilities, as well as the production timelines, we can map out how content gets from creation to publication.

Here is a "for instance" scenario: If you want to publish an infographic about a health care issue that requires HIPAA compliance oversight, you have to ensure the compliance department sees it before it goes live. If you're in a high –risk or highly regulated business, you may also have to make sure it's been reviewed by your communication department. At some point, it needs to be edited and optimized to ensure there are no grammati-cal errors and that it has been properly formatted for the web, including search optimization and image optimization.

It requires very different skill sets to perform all these tasks, and in many cases, the same person should not be responsible for multiple gov-ernance functions, even if the person is functionally capable of doing the job. For this reason, it is critically important to define the basic roles in governance.

13.4.1. Creation layer, editorial layer, approval layer

Typically, the basic roles in governance involve at least three separate functions – the content creation layer, the editorial/optimization layer and the approval layer. In some cases, there needs to be additional governance layers as well, but try to limit yourself to these three functions in order to stay agile, responsive and real –time.

There are good reasons why these functions are separate. The approver shouldn't edit or create. The creator shouldn't approve or edit, and the editor shouldn't approve or create without another editor. These are very specific roles for very specific skill sets and responsibilities. The roles need to be limited to these responsibilities – and these responsibilities only – in order to keep things moving in real –time and to keep the right resources focused on the right tasks.

For example, it keeps a lawyer who fancies herself a wordsmith from screwing up the copy with legalese. It keeps the editor from jumping the gun and approving the content when he shouldn't. It also makes sure that people don't create bottlenecks for creation by having too many people with their fingers in the pie.

13.4.2. Passive versus active approval

In many cases, multiple people in various areas of the organization need to be in the loop on content before it gets published. In other cases, these people need to approve things before they go live. It is important to understand the difference between passive and active approval.

Passive approval is great for "keeping someone in the loop". This means you essentially give them the ability to hit the stop button, but you don't have to wait on them to hit the go button.

In large organizations, your team should push hard to limit the number of active approvers. Usually involvement in the process at a passive level is enough for the many people involved in an owned media effort.

Active approvers should only be mission –critical oversight roles, like compliance. Active approvers should also limit themselves to just that – approve or deny. It is best if the approval role does not edit the content. There are a couple of reasons for this. First, this does not allow our system to get smarter because the roles of content creator and editor are not doing the work over again, and might not even be aware of the changes being made or why they are being made. Second, the approver is most likely not qualified to create or edit content and probably does not have the appropriate background on the content to decide how to fix the problem in a way that still accomplishes the goal of the content. Again, this separation in the process keeps things moving and limits the friction in the process.

13.4.3. Approval teams

In enterprise organizations, and especially with more complicated governance structures, there is always one person who is not on top of their notifications or approval requests. He might be busy working in other areas of the company, or maybe she took a vacation. Reliance on single individuals for active approval means when that person is otherwise occupied, everything stops.

One way around this is with approval teams. These are groups of active approvers, all of whom have the same role and responsibility, any of whom can approve content. Let's say instead of picking out one lawyer on your team, Legalese Larry, to approve content on compliance issues, you choose five. Legalese Larry forgets to tell you he is going to Tahiti for three weeks. In a team setting, the content does not sit with Larry for three weeks awaiting approval. Someone else on the approval team can approve the content. Or, in real –time situations, if Larry is at lunch and you need something approved in minutes, you still have a fighting chance of making that happen without waiting on Larry to finish his dessert.

13.5. Production timelines

One of the secrets to being able to operate responsively in real –time is planning ahead for what you know, so you have the flexibility and opportunity to deal with what you can't possibly plan for. Planning for what we can't plan for is going to be a crucial part of the distribution process. By setting up realistic, static, drop –dead deadlines and production timelines, it gives your team something to anchor itself to when it comes to producing proactive content. It is important to have this in place along with roles and responsibilities, so you can set expectations for the people in those roles and hold them accountable to their responsibilities.

When creating your production timelines for your team, you will want to make sure you have consistent deadlines in place for each part of the process where content moves from one step to the next. If your process is going to include an internal team review before it goes to compliance and legal, there needs to be a deadline for the internal review. There also needs to be a deadline for compliance and legal to review and move the content to the next step.

A good place to start is with a two –week production cycle. Producing content any further in advance will lead to a lot of spinning wheels. Remember, this is not brochure content we are going to produce that will be sitting around, evergreen for at least a year before anyone revises it. Some content may be like that, but most will be driven by relevance and timeliness, which means the content you produce today is highly likely to be old news if you wait four weeks to publish it.

Here is an example of what a reasonable two –week production timeline could look like:

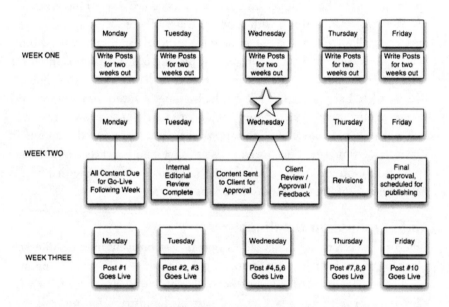

The more steps in your process, the more deadlines you will have and the more compressed everyone's timelines will become. In this example, content creators have a week to produce their content. Everything is due at 8 a.m. Monday for publication the following Monday. That gives us another week for editorial, optimization and approval. Our team gathers and reviews all the content due for next week on Monday. It is due to our editorial and optimization team at 8 a.m. Tuesday, where they have an entire day to work on editorial and optimization. At 8 a.m. Wednesday, the content is sent to the approval teams for review and feedback. They also have a full day to review. Thursday is reserved for any revisions that need to happen, and Friday is reserved for final approval and scheduling.

This is a rolling production timeline with consistent deliverables deadlines that everyone is aware of and accountable to. Everyone in the process has ample time to do the tasks they are responsible for. You will find similar production timelines across every news organization and most publishers, from print to broadcast. Implementing a similar production timeline that works for your team will be a necessary component of your owned media strategy.

13.6. Publishing frequency

Now that we have answered the "how" question, and the "who" question, and the "where" question, as it relates to distribution, invariably the discussion turns to "what," "what kind" and "how much" as it relates to the actual content. We would encourage you to not tackle these questions quite yet. We have more strategy work to do to answer the first two questions, which are about the content itself. The "how much" question should not be answered by your team; it should be answered by your audience.

Every brand we have worked with wants to know "how much." How many blog posts per week is the right amount? How many videos should we make? How many infographics per month? It is important to address this question while we are talking about distribution.

The biggest cause of the loss of your audience is publishing too much, not publishing too little. Very few people have said, "You're not sending me enough stuff, so I'm unsubscribing/unfollowing." Instead, they just forget about you and are pleasantly surprised when your content shows up in their inbox.

Because people engage in multiple channels, the frequency of activity is spread out, and you can inadvertently be pushing content to or interacting with someone 30 times a month, even though you're only publishing content once or twice a week on a handful of accounts.

Here's an example of what many would consider a moderate, typical publishing frequency:

- Blog posts – 5 times a week (daily)
- Videos – 2 times a month (biweekly)
- Twitter – 3 times a day (15 per week)
- Facebook – 2 times a day (10 per week)
- LinkedIn – 1 times a day (5 per week)
- Email (Promotional) – 1 time a week (4 per month)
- Email (Newsletter) – 1 time a month

That's not too much, one would think. But if I am an engaged consumer advocate and I use more than one of these channels, and I have given you permission to interact with me by following, friending or subscribing, this is a lot of content.

If I just subscribed to your email newsletter and your promotion list, followed you on Twitter and Facebook and added your blog to my feed reader, I would be hearing from you as much as 125 times per month. Does anyone need to hear from anyone else four times a day about anything? This is not atypical behavior of your best customers. If you are truly engaged with a brand, it is not out of the norm to be engaged in several channels at once.

Ask yourself this: Is there anyone – not just brands you love, but people in your life – you really <u>need and want</u> to hear from today? Sure, your significant other… your kids… maybe your mom and a couple of close friends here or there. But beyond that? And out of all your other relationships online, which ones do you actually look forward to hearing from? Which ones actually send you things that are compelling, interesting or entertaining?

That once –a –day interaction, which can be a mix of your usual channels, can often be seen as too much, especially if all you're doing is publishing and pushing content. Don't just publish content for the sake of marking it off your list or hitting a quota. Let your audience metrics tell you what is appropriate through the use of baselines and ongoing experimentation.

Remember, people want interaction as well, which means you don't always have to be "on." You can use your resources to talk with them as well. Not only will they respond, they will likely be thrilled with the personal interaction. Try it. Next time you publish a video, check in with commenters and ask them what they thought. Or next time you publish a tweet, @ tag an individual follower and get his reaction. Your resources don't have to be pointed at cranking out content just for the sake of content. Content is only half the battle. Engagement is the other half.

If you don't pay attention to your audience, someone else will do it for you. Google makes decisions for its users based on content quality, not just quantity. Facebook's EdgeRank figures in here too. If you're publishing a lot of stuff on Facebook, and people aren't interacting with it, Facebook will hide it from the users' streams, or it will at least keep the post from appearing in their stream as often. This is why Facebook took status updates out of their platform, and replaced it with the Top Stories setting, putting rich content – shared articles, movies, photos – into their streams. The change was because Facebook was losing user engagement because so many people posted so much bad content so frequently. These companies go to great lengths to acquire users and provide them with a user experience, so they can monetize the audience. That means protecting them against people posting content they are not interested in seeing or posting too much content.

13.7. Distribution strategy outcomes

There are four things that should come out of your distribution strategy discussions:

Voices and Accounts – The first is a chart or graphic that shows the group's decisions regarding which voices, platforms and accounts will be used in your approach to owned media.

Approval Path – The next thing to document is your distribution framework, a chart outlining the approval path of content that shows how content gets from creation to publication.

Production Timelines – As part of your distribution strategy, set up and document a regular timeline for proactive content production. This can be a simple list of deadlines or a calendar format for longer timelines.

Roles and Responsibilities – The last thing to document is a chart or graphic outlining roles and responsibilities for each person on the team that maps to the publishing process established in the distribution chart. This should include a list of all the voices and accounts, the team member(s) responsible for active approval and passive approval of each voice, along with their contact information, and the associated accounts, and that team member's governance role (creator, editor, approver, or other role your team defines). This should include both internal and external team members and resources involved in publishing content, both proactively and reactively.

14. METADATA

If you've been involved with online marketing, you've probably heard the terms search engine optimization and SEO and know what they mean. This is the part of your owned media strategy where it becomes important to understand what makes search work in more detail. Google keeps making major changes to its algorithms to drive up the quality of results it displays to its users. But, Metadata isn't just about search.

Having a solid metadata strategy will solve a lot of problems you don't know you have yet. Metadata essentially means data about data and can be organized into a taxonomy, which is a framework to classify and label different words, topics, and other language that is relevant to your brand – not just for search, but for your entire owned media effort.

This is where you will determine the critical keywords associated with your audience and your brand to help classify your content, and to know what to listen for. Combined with the subject topography (in the next section), this is where the editorial direction for your strategy will come from, as well as the tactical direction for your engagement approach (which comes after we establish the subject topography).

Your keywords are based on a few factors: What is your audience interested in? What do you want to be known for? What terms are you using to describe your products or services, and what terms are people really using when they search for what you offer?

This last point is very important because you might figure out quickly that the terms you want to use are not the terms your customers are using. You may completely dominate the search engines for terms like "bi –folding money case," while your customers are looking for a "wallet." It doesn't matter how loudly or how long you tell people it's a bi –folding money case. You can spend millions of dollars on advertising, go on a national speaking circuit and sponsor event after event. To your audience, it's still a wallet, and it will always be a wallet.

This is important because if you focus your strategy on content about bi –folding money cases, you probably won't see a huge return on your investment. You need to find out what terms people are using and start using those keywords to classify and label your content and the terms you're listening for.

During this phase and the next, you'll establish a list of keywords you want your content creators to use, as well as the keywords and phrases to monitor for. There could be a product taxonomy from the retail department, another from ecommerce and still another from customer service.

This is where these lists are pulled together, so you can come up with the list of words, synonyms, co –occurrences and competitor terms to be used globally, across the enterprise.

14.1. The global taxonomy approach

The concept of a global taxonomy is to normalize and standardize the language structure of your brand and the topics associated with it. In most organizations, there are several taxonomies floating around. There might be one list of keywords your social team is monitoring and another list of categories and tags for your blog. Meanwhile, there might be a totally different navigation taxonomy for your website user interface, and then a whole list of keywords you're buying ads for on search engines, as well as a related but different list of keywords you're going after in organic search, not to mention a product taxonomy you use in merchandising. In many cases, there is duplication across these taxonomies. The problem is that we should all be using the same language, and it should be understandable to our audience. This is rarely the case in most organizations, and most brands don't fully understand the ramifications of this.

If you're in the business of selling widgets, and you're trying to grow the blue widget category, you might have a product page on your website called "Blue Widgets." But on the blog, they're called sky blue widgets and categorized under widgets, but tagged "special widgets."

Your marketing team is buying Google Adwords for azure, periwinkle and 50 other shades of blue. Your search consultant is taking a localized keyword strategy to cover blue widgets in Arkansas, blue widgets in Indiana, and several thousand other long –tail keywords. Meanwhile, the product development team has decided to break out blue widgets into four categories, light blue, powder blue, sky blue and royal blue. Your social team is monitoring for catalina blue, and all your customer wants is a navy blue widget. Every area of your organization is communicating about the product differently.

The way search works today, every different description of the same thing is taken into account and treated uniquely. Social is organized through words. Email is driven by words. The entire Internet is organized – and millions of decisions are made through algorithms and by humans every millisecond – based on words.

Our goal is to come up with one unified, cleanly organized taxonomy that everyone can work from, in order to deliver to both your audience and all the algorithms out there that make decisions about what your brand is (not just Google) a singular idea of what your brand is "about". The goal is a unified understanding, a global taxonomic profile around your brand that realistically represents what is relevant to the brand, using the language of the audience.

14.2. Importance of content labeling and organization

As your friendly neighborhood search consultant probably shared with you, the structure of a website property and the words used to describe that structure – the way it is organized – can have a huge impact on search algorithms and other algorithms. Remember, every content algorithm was built for one reason – to provide better, more relevant content to humans.

Our recommendation is to organize your content for human readers. If you take this approach and execute properly, as well as produce great content that engages your audience, the algorithms will figure the rest out without needing much help from you.

To maximize your impact, you can apply a global taxonomy to organize all your content everywhere, which will have a compounding effect on any algorithm that uses the content and engagement around your brand as a signal to determine rank – which at this point is pretty much every algorithm.

For example: If you want people looking for "13 –inch laptop" to find your brand, or see your content, you will want to use that phrase not just in your webpage metadata, but everywhere. This could also be a tag or category in your blog, a keyword phrase you are talking about frequently on Twitter and Facebook. You could create video and infographic content labeled with "13" laptop" and create a high –level landing page at www.yoursite.com/13 –inch –laptop called "13 inch laptop" that is referenced in all of your other content.

14.3. Implications for monitoring

The global taxonomy goes beyond just search. You can also use this for monitoring by creating a query for off –channel dialogue about 13 –inch laptops. You can use it for identifying influencers and engage with them about 13 –inch laptops. Create a moderation query for on –channel dialogue from your audience, and ask them questions about their 13 –inch laptops. Run a contest to generate content from your audience and make a photo gallery of your audience's 13 –inch laptops.

This is not rocket science. Both humans and algorithms will quickly surmise that your brand is interested in, related to and all about 13 –inch laptops. If people are engaged and interested in your content, they are spending time with it, clicking on it, sharing it with others. If this is happening, your content will start to be shown to more users by the algorithm gatekeepers of Google, Facebook and other platforms. The problem comes when your owned media team is working on 13 –inch laptops and everyone else in your organization is talking about 13 –inch netbooks, but your consumers just want a 13 –inch ultraportable. Or worse, you're someone like Dell trying to sell your XPS 13 ultrabook, and your consumers are only talking about the MacBook Air.

14.4. How to build a global taxonomy

This is by far the most difficult, cumbersome and time –consuming part of building an owned media strategy. Yet it is also the part that tends to yield the most ideas and insights.

Remember way back in discovery where we asked for documentation on paid and organic search keywords? That is probably the best place to start. You will also want to have access to your company's website and microsite analytics, and its social media analytics. Finally, if there is already a product taxonomy in place, you will want that as well as the navigation taxonomy, including categories and tags, from your website, microsites and blogs.

That's a lot of words!

This exercise is not for the faint of heart or for the short of attention span. If it gets too heavy, call in an experienced content strategist. Not only do those folks love this stuff, but they will probably do it faster and better than you or your team will.

Here is a basic approach to generating a running start at a global taxonomy. Create a spreadsheet with these categories to start.

- **Brand** – Include all the broader terms and phrases your brand currently "owns". If you're Nike, you will want to include not just Nike, but Just Do It, Swoosh, etc.
- **Product** – This is where you list actual product names you would be concerned with, such as Air Max, Pegasus and other product names.
- **Competitor** – Here, you list your competing brands – Adidas, Reebok or Puma.
- **People** – This is for actual people associated to your brand. Kobe Bryant, Lebron James, Peyton Manning and Roger Federer.
- **Category** – This is the broader name for the business you're in – running shoes, basketball shoes, athletic wear.

14.4.1. Keyword or phrases

For each category, list what you think are the most commonly used keywords or phrases.

Make it easy on yourself and start with your existing website properties. What words are used in the main navigation? Subnavigation? What are the categories and tags used on the blog or on the site in these categories? This will give you a good running start at documenting the current state of affairs, and it will provide insight into how your content is organized and what language is being used to organize it.

14.4.2. Search volume

You can use Google's keyword research tool to help here, as it will show you related keywords or phrases to the ones you picked and rank them by search volume and competitiveness. This will show you how many searches are happening for your keywords, and it will also highlight where others are focused (most likely competitors). This can reveal interesting opportunities for which keywords you decide to use in your taxonomy.

As you get into this, you will discover lots of new keywords. You will also discover that some of the ones you're using might not be the most high –volume keywords, meaning people are talking about the same thing you are using different language. You might also find that people online are looking for something completely different. For instance, a health care company may use the word "maternity" to describe its services for expecting mothers. However, everyone searching for that term is more interested in bathing suits and dress clothes. It means something totally different to the audience than it does to the brand.

As you go through your keyword research, pick out and rank the best fits and opportunities, and note any disconnects between your language and the language your audience uses.

14.4.3. Site engagement

Next, use your website analytics to see which keywords and phrases are getting the most uptake on your sites. For instance, if you have a page called Running Shoes and another page called Marathon Shoes, which one is getting the most engagement and traffic? Why is that? This is another factor you can use to determine which keywords to ultimately select.

14.4.4. Dialogue volume

Finally, check in with your social media analytics report or tool. Once you have listed all your keywords from your site, and you are reasonably sure you have a good taxonomy in place, test it against what people are saying. Is there more dialogue around Dresses or Skirts? Are those considered two different things, or do people use those terms interchangeably?

14.4.5 Synonyms, derivatives, co –occurrence, and other weird science

This should get you to a more focused place as you refine your keyword categories through search volume, site engagement and dialogue volume. Hopefully you can narrow down the keywords in each category to 15 or 20 ideal keywords or phrases, but depending on the complexity of the brand, you could wind up with hundreds and hundreds of keywords in each category. If this is the case, it is time to create subcategories to make this all more manageable.

Once you have your focused list of core keywords, or keyword categories, we are going to go back and expand on these. It is important to identify your core keywords or categories and associate the next set of keywords to those. The next keywords we are going to deal with are secondary or tertiary in nature to helping humans and algorithms understand what you're talking about. But they need to be processed by both humans and algorithms relative to the core keyword in terms of importance. Think of the first part of this exercise as developing a keyword dictionary. The second part is developing a thesaurus to go along with it. Still with me? Good!

Synonyms – For each keyword we want to focus on, we also need to know synonyms of that keyword, so they also can be used in our content and engagement activities relationally, albeit in lower volumes. If we are Samsung, and we are looking at the mobile device category, and our core keyword is SmartPhone, we also may want to be creating content and listening for derivatives of that keyword, such as mobile phone, telephone, cellular phone, handset, receiver.

Derivative phrases – for each keyword, we may also want to list derivative phrases to help us understand what contexts people are most interested in related to our keyword. Our friends at Samsung might want to check into mobile phone comparisons, mobile phone providers, mobile phone plans, or mobile phone reviews – the most relevant related searches to mobile phone.

Co –occurrences – now we are getting deeper into the taxonomy and some deep –in –the –weed semantic methodology. This is more relevant to brands with a deep interest in or focus on search. Co –occurrences are words that are likely to occur in close proximity to a keyword on a page. This is a factor in how many algorithms make decisions about what content is about, but not one that has much impact on human users. This is only important to include if you are looking into the depths of your on –page content for every advantage. There are several tools out there that can help you generate co –occurrence keywords and phrases for your target keywords, but for most global taxonomies, this can be skipped.

Latent Dirichlet Allocation and other weird science – LDA is a statistical topic model that shows the probability of certain words appearing in content because of their relationship with other words. This is different than a synonym, a derivative phrase, or a co –occurrent keyword. LDA shows contextual relationship.

For instance, if your keyword was "cow," related keywords from an LDA perspective would be things like "milk" and "bell" from a probability standpoint. Highly advanced search practitioners should include LDA and other related categories as new data emerges about the signals algorithms are using to make decisions about how and when content is displayed. But for many brands, this level of detail may not be necessary. For more on LDA, and enough advanced math to make your eyes bleed, check out LDA on Wikipedia.

14.5. Metadata usage in the enterprise

You should, at this stage, have a well –defined group of categories and keywords, and the most relevant derivatives of those keywords. What can you do with it? Just about everything.

This document can and should inform everything from product naming to your next website redesign. It should ground you in how you label and organize your content to the keywords you buy in paid media, as well as what you listen for in monitoring and moderation. It is an excellent, go –to resource for anyone who requires metadata or classification or a taxonomy of any kind.

If it is all working together from the same set of keywords, it should do a couple of things. For for your internal team, it is a great source of topics for content. For your audience, it will help connect them to you using their language, not yours. It will help them find the content they are looking for and participate in conversations they are interested in, relevant to your brand. And as a side effect of all of this, you should see increased rank in the keywords you are targeting over time, assuming you produce great, engaging content that your audience loves.

15. TOPOGRAPHY

Subject topography is where the relevance of the content is connected to the core brand promise. A subject topography is a simple mind –mapping exercise to determine what subjects, at a very high level, are most relevant to the core brand idea. This helps us easily generate "a thousand little ideas" and still stay on strategy. We typically go through this exercise after sifting through all of the metadata and keywords in the metadata section.

Mapping this out visually solves the problem of what to create content about. It eliminates writer's block (or "creator's block" if we want to be agnostic about the content we are creating). It will tell you how to prioritize your subjects, and help you figure out which subjects are most likely to resonate the most with your target personae.

It is important to note here that the objective of developing a subject topography is not to create a content calendar. We have a different solution for that. The topography is meant to function as kind of a "guiding light" for your content creators. It is a quick, at –a –glance reminder of where they should be focusing. It is easy to stray off course and produce content that generates metrics, but the content might be irrelevant to the brand (kitty memes, anyone?). Subject topographies give both the content creator and the person who owns the strategy the same one –page playbook to produce relevant content on a daily basis.

Your subject topography could have multiple variations, according to the number of personae you want to address. The stay –at –home mom might be concerned with back –to –school topics, while the college student may be more concerned with getting ready to graduate, finding a job and moving out into the real world. Keep in mind, developing multiple personae and multiple subject topographies does dilute the focus of your resources. It is always better to do one thing well than lots of things poorly when it comes to owned media.

Now gather up the most creative members of your team, along with your audience data. You will want the global taxonomy you created in the metadata section for this exercise, as well as multiple perspectives from your team. This is about coming up with the subject –level topics you want to create content about – a different challenge than how to classify that content, which is what we addressed in the metadata section. Admittedly, the two are closely related.

15.1. The core brand idea

We start this exercise by putting the core brand idea in a circle. Everything we come up with has to be relevant to this idea. Remember the "thesaurus" part of the global taxonomy? That is what we are looking for here, except we are looking for contextual relevance. Some of the LDA research we mentioned could come in handy here, but we have found we get where we need to be faster with good old human brainstorming. Plus, it is a lot more fun. The team can bond, and everyone can have a thumbprint on the strategy – great for internal buy in.

15.2. Establishing relevance

The next step in this simple exercise is to go around the room and brainstorm topics that are relevant to our core brand idea. Let's go back to our Nike example. Nike means athletic endeavor. That is what the brand is all about. Now using your audience persona, and related research from discovery, based on the risk parameters we have to work within, what are some things related to that core brand idea we could make content about? How about …sports? Work ethic? Health? Competition? Notice we are not as interested in the language component here. We are not looking for keyword –level product topics. We are looking for broader, but related topics. It is definitely more art and interpretation of data than science and optimization of data.

Now, let's go to the next level and do the same thing. What are some topics related to sports? Work ethic? Health? Competition? How about …football, basketball, baseball for sports. Drive, goal setting, and discipline for work ethic. Diet, exercise, and injuries in health. Winning, losing, and stats for competition. We are now two degrees removed from the core brand idea, but we are still talking about topics that have a direct, relevant correlation to that idea.

You could repeat this exercise two, three, four or more degrees away from the core brand idea. It becomes harder and harder to stay relevant as you get farther away, but you can always trace it back to the core idea. The end result is an extremely focused mind map of potential topics your content creators can use any time they need an idea.

15.3. Measuring interest

Once your team has its subject topography mind map in place, the next step is to prioritize it in an easy –to –understand, visual way. We can see how the subjects all connect back to the brand, but which ones should we focus on?

The first part of the exercise answers the "what" question, as in what should we create content about.

"How much" content is answered by measuring interest in these topics. This can be done by cross referencing your subject topography against social media dialogue volume, and search volume, similar to what we did in metadata. Based on what your audience wants, change the size of each circle. For instance, if 500,000 people mentioned "diet" in social channels over the last 12 months, and there were 250,000 queries for it, but "exercise" was mentioned 5 million times, and there were 2 million queries for it, exercise is going to be a bigger circle – a higher priority for your audience (not you or your team or your brand).

Now you have some general, broad answers to "what" content to create and "how much." The only remaining questions are "what kind" and "then what," both of which will be answered shortly. Let's first tackle "then what?" We will cover "what kind" when we get to execution. "What kind" is not a strategy question. It is a tactical one. So be patient, we will get there.

16. ENGAGEMENT

Developing an engagement strategy is one of the hardest things for brands to do. What do I respond to? What do I not respond to? What do I say? Where do I find audience that is interested in engaging with my brand? How do I sort through all the noise to find meaningful conversation with people?

There is no magic bullet to engagement. Managing and moderating audience dialogue in real –time, at scale, is among the newest and most difficult marketing challenges a brand has to solve. But solve it we must. Like everything in digital, we treat our engagement approach like a science experiment – execute, learn, optimize, execute, learn, optimize and on and on. Building a strategy for engagement is like designing a science experiment. We posit a theory, establish some variables to play with and experiment.

Planning your brand's engagement strategy is a lot like flying a plane in a hurricane on instruments alone. You know where you want to go, and you're pretty sure you're heading in the right direction, but you can't really see what's coming, so you can't plan for it. All you can do is trust your gauges, pay close attention to what's happening around you and be responsive when your gauges tell you to make an adjustment. This is the ultimate in planning for the unplannable. Here are a few strategic exercises we have developed that will help a brand of any size get started.

16.1. Rules of Engagement

One of the first things we do in engagement strategy is establish rules of engagement. These are based on the persona we developed earlier. We have identified the audience we are speaking with, and we know how to engage based on the persona we built for the brand.

We know why because our business case tells us this, and we know where and how thanks to our distribution strategy. We know what we can expect to engage about from our risk exercise and our metadata and subject topography.

The next thing we can decide on in advance is who to engage with and when to engage them. Do we want to respond to everyone who mentions the brand? Is that realistic? What conditions have to exist in order for us to engage? We can answer these questions with metrics – the gauges we use to fly our ship in any storm. Our rules of engagement should include the following:

16.2. Query and filter building

Remember that long, boring exercise we went through in the metadata section? This is your basis for query building. Query building is not an exercise you go through once. It is an ongoing science experiment. Input the query; look at the results; try a different variation. Include some words, and exclude others. Change the time frame. Change the geography. Test every possible variable until you weed all of the noise out of the signal – or at least enough to make the query string manageable. Regardless of the monitoring tool you use, it will require a lot of ongoing adjustment to deliver more signal than noise for your brand.

As you build queries for the dialogue, you are interested in participating in off channel. Don't forget to do the same for your on –channel tools for moderation. These will most likely be two completely different sets of queries for two different applications – one for what everyone is saying outside the brand channels, and one for what your specific audience is talking about on the channels you own and control.

Also, once you have found some queries that are delivering the kind of information you want, make sure you document them. This is a time –consuming exercise that takes a lot of practice and ongoing optimization to get right. Don't make yourself start over from scratch when your software fails or when you choose a different technology vendor.

16.3. Alerts, reporting and intelligence

Once your queries are built, expect to get a lot of questions. As your organization becomes more comfortable and familiar with the power of online monitoring as a research tool, you will be getting lots of requests for lots of information. These usually fall into one of these three categories:

Alerts – This type of engagement reporting has to do with the escalation of specifics around a situation based on broader query parameters. For instance, you might be monitoring a very basic query about your brand and find a highly influential person sharing negative and potentially damaging content about your brand. In this case, speed is of the essence, and an alert should go out to the proper person, who is specifically identified in your escalation path. It is impossible to know in advance when you will need to send alerts, but plan some resources for this based on what you think your brand will need. Don't just pass on a link; give the person the appropriate background information and rationale behind why the alert is being sent. It is very helpful to define specific alert parameters, contents, metrics to include, framework and formatting in advance. Remember, you're planning for what you can't plan for.

Reporting – This is a more in –depth look at an emerging or ongoing situation, sometimes on an ad –hoc basis. More general reporting is usually delivered on a regular basis. For instance, a brand sentiment report might be a regularly scheduled deliverable for the team, whereas situational reporting comes up without notice based on what is happening in the world.

You might want to be able to report a broader view of a specific situation and how it is playing out online, along with recommended engagement actions, beyond just an alert. This is something that must be anticipated, and your team will have to be flexible in order to accommodate these scenarios. For instance, in the example above, if this negative and potentially damaging content starts to be republished and the dialogue volume around it spreads, or negative sentiment about the brand starts to increase over time, your team may need to produce more in –depth, predictive information about the situation. That might mean moving around known reporting deliverables in order to accommodate a time –sensitive situational report. Again, based on the unique needs of your brand, you might do very little situational reporting, or you might need to do three or four a day. In any case, you can plan for recurring, broad reporting and dial in situational reports to your operations schedule in advance as situations present themselves, in order to predict any resource shortcomings on the horizon.

Intelligence – Intelligence is a more internal –facing function of engagement and has to do with informing content subject matter and type. This type of reporting happens with your internal team, and it is the connective tissue between your audience and the content your team is producing for them. The goal here is to look at our queries in an opportunistic way, on channel and off channel, to determine what the audience is most interested in, what content is working best and what emerging trends can be capitalized on from a content perspective. Great audience intelligence leads directly to great content. Internal intelligence reporting is a must for real –time content development and responsive levels of engagement. Account for this as you are planning your resources.

16.4. Escalation path

You will need to establish escalation paths for your team in advance. Who do these reports go to, and how do we get them there? This is something best handled with your earned media team from a crisis management point of view, but don't forget to include other areas of the enterprise. Who should you escalate content to for product feedback? Customer service?

Human Resources issues? What about the positive stuff? Who needs to see that beyond the owned media team?

16.5. Setting threshold parameters

Without some guardrails on alerts, reporting and intelligence, you might find yourself drowning quickly in a sea of data. By setting agreed –upon threshold parameters for escalation, you can make it easy on your team to find only the relevant signal and avoid irrelevant noise. Here are some example parameters you can use to help your team filter their escalations:

Volume – How many mentions establish a "situation" based on our baseline dialogue volume? Baseline information is crucial in understanding how to set up thresholds for monitoring, reporting and engagement. For some brands, 100,000 negative mentions is a good day. For others, it is an out –of –control firestorm from hell that could ruin the business forever.

Sentiment – How negative can the sentiment get before we escalate content? Understand your baseline sentiment and reasonable deviations from it to give some context to this number. If normal is 40 percent negative, a 45 percent negative situation might not be worth escalating, but a 55 percent negative situation would be something to escalate if your deviation threshold is only plus or minus 10 percent.

Influence – How influential is the source of the content? Does this entity have a large and active audience, or does this entity have three Twitter followers, including his mom, and two of his three sisters?

Frequency – How many unique stories or mentions have we identified about this situation? How much content is being created about it? Five posts? Ten? Knowing the baseline is important. Five or ten out of fifteen stories is vastly different from five or ten out of a hundred.

Rank – What is the legitimacy of the content source? Is this a top newspaper website with millions of international visitors or someone's blog with no audience? Is it a Top 500 site?

Decay – When was the first known mention of the situation or first appearance of the content? If it is less than a few hours old and has not been reported on, it might make sense to escalate. If it is three months old and it has not shown up anywhere else, the story is probably dead.

Threat – "How bad could this get for us?" That is the question we want to answer here. This is totally subjective but totally necessary. If only one post is made but the situation could irrevocably damage the brand, it is time to send an alert and strap in.

Intensity – Is this a rapidly developing story arc? What is the rate of growth over time? This helps us understand how quickly the story is growing online and allows us to project when it will most likely peak and die off.

Presence – Does the content include any brand content, quotes from employees or other presence? If it does, is that content being used legally? Remember, we protected our content in the risk stage, so if we can leverage that to get potentially damaging content removed, we have won yet another small battle.

Story arc – This is subjective and only learned through experience. How long of a shelf life do we think this story has? Hours? Days? Weeks? Having some idea of how long we think we are going to be dealing with a given situation will help the rest of the team understand what they need to plan for.

Once these parameters have been established, it is easy to determine what to escalate.

16.6 Defining influencers

One thing many brands struggle with is identifying and defining influencers. This is different for every brand, depending on your business case and target persona. To define an influencer, we need to establish key parameters. We typically use minimum network reach, minimum Klout score and a third –party influence measurement to normalize against Klout.

It is important for your team to have a shared definition of what an influencer is. It is not an ambassador or an advocate. It is someone with influence relevant to the brand (see your metadata exercise to determine what subjects a person should be influential about to qualify for your list of influencers).

Influencers are an important audience in the same way that traditional media is an important audience, mainly because of reach, but also because of trust. A trusted influential source will be believed and embraced by your audience far more quickly than traditional media in many cases. Your brand should plan accordingly – identify influencers in your space early on and add them to your watch lists. Engage proactively with them, not just when you need something. If those relationships are managed well, it can be an incredible boon for your brand.

16.7. Identifying external sources and communities

In addition to identifying influencers relevant to your brand, you will also want to look for pre –existing online communities to engage with and external sources of relevant content. Create a watch list of people, organizations, communities, publishers, and other destinations for your monitoring efforts. Not only do we want to be monitoring here for intelligence purposes and content curation purposes, we will want to be able to proactively participate with these people or in these communities if it makes sense for the brand.

16.8. FAQs and pre –approved responses

Every brand should have pre –approved responses to known issues. This is a basic requirement from a customer service perspective. More mature organizations that have a dedicated customer service function will have answers to FAQs already in place, as well as more sophisticated response flowcharts for troubleshooting known issues. Take a page from the call –center playbook here, and help your team manage through the things you know and plan for the things you don't.

17. STRATEGY: THE FINAL WORD

It's important to note that this entire strategy process is all channel agnostic – we are not advising you to use a particular platform, channel or tool. It is content centric. Everything we have talked about here should be considered in the context of creating content and building audience. It applies to every single owned media channel. It doesn't matter which channel or platform or tool you use. It's more important that you know what you're saying and why, rather than where you say it.

By this point, you should have a great idea of how to make decisions and plan strategy around content and audience on a platform –agnostic basis. Get approval and buy in from the people you report to and the people they report to. Once your strategy is in place, use it! It is a living document. Go back to it, and change it when it needs to be changed, at least once a quarter if not once a month – especially early on.

Remember, we are dealing with a real –time media, and that is going to cause us to shift and pivot tactically on a regular basis. Luckily, we have our strategic framework – our guardrails – to keep us focused and on the road while still being flexible enough to swerve when we need to. That is how to use this strategic framework. There is no doubt some of the specifics here will be out of date by the time you read this, but the essential steps of this framework – and going through it in the order outlined – will always lead to a well –considered strategic approach to your owned media efforts.

Eventually you will need to change your destination or move your guardrails – so keep your strategy up to date and close at hand. Don't let it die a slow death in some folder somewhere. You put too much into it, and without it, your tactics will surely stray off course, crash through the guard-rails and explode in a fiery ball of disaster. Or, at the very worst, you'll have some dents you didn't need. Now let's get to the fun stuff. Execution!

Part III: Execution | The Newsroom Approach

3

18. ORGANIZING YOUR TEAM

Earlier in the book, we talked about the staff, operational structure, and resources you will need on your team. We also talked about all the external teams they will have to work with regularly – primarily, the paid and earned teams, but also other areas of the enterprise such as customer service and human resources. We decided in discovery who would be involved in the distribution process, and we know how that is going to work. At a high level, our team is looking well prepared from a strategy standpoint, but we need to help them organize themselves around a production and execution methodology, which we call the five M's.

To execute in real time, we will need to understand a couple of key concepts, such as story arcs, and challenge some pre –existing assumptions about content production best practices, like using content calendar spreadsheets to plan content. Additionally, we need to ensure the team has an agile, responsive production process to work within. We also need to make sure the team has the tools they need to make all the different types of content that may be required.

18.1. Understanding story arcs

The concept of story arcs is not new, but it is one that has not had a lot of focus in marketing in the past. The story arc, for our purposes, consists of three main areas – the introduction and development, the climax, and the resolution. The beginning, the peak point of interest and the end. Notice we are not saying the beginning, the middle and the end. Usually stories don't develop that way. There is much more focus on the front end, and they end fairly abruptly. Typically, a story arc's development takes some time, and the level of interest increases through about the first 75 percent or 85 percent of the story arc to its climax, then in the end, the resolution only takes about 25 percent of the arc or less.

In news, many stories are judged based on their story arc. Is this a new and developing story, or has the level of interest climaxed and this story is almost at its end? The audience's level of interest – oftentimes a subjective issue – is what drives the story arc and how the story gets prioritized. This level of interest determines what resources get allocated to it and how much time or space the publisher dedicates to the story and on which of its channels.

This is something to keep in mind as you are working with your owned media team. Remember our point about a 1,000 little ideas? This is how to evaluate those ideas. You can and should use your experience and evaluate story opportunities subjectively, but there are also lots of signals available from the audience – your version of the "ratings." You can leverage these "ratings" to help your team make decisions about how to prioritize resources. This works both for proactive content production and reactive content production. This plays into how you schedule your content, as well as how to monitor and evaluate engagement opportunities.

Because we are working in a fast –moving medium in real –time, the story arcs for our content, and the subjects that are relevant to our audience at any given moment are going to be fairly short. Weeks, maybe days, maybe even hours. Producing high –quality content in this environment quickly enough to be relevant can be a challenge, unless your team is structured purposefully to do this. This is why we think the electronic –news –gathering production style, the news room operational and production model, makes so much sense.

18.2 The rundown

Speaking of news rooms and how they operate, let's talk about scheduling content. We know companies that have tried scripting an entire month of Twitter. Some stuck with it to its tragically funny end, and others abandoned it after two days when they realized the rest of the world wasn't going to follow their script. There is a reason news organizations don't plan months in advance, or even weeks or days in advance, with the exception of stories that are going to have a longer story arc. A multi –package, in –depth story on a situation with a two – or three –month story arc warrants some advance planning and resources, but most of what is timely and relevant is going to be produced within a day or two or even within hours of publication, sometimes in real –time. Every time you see that little "LIVE" bug on your local news, you are witnessing real –time, somewhat unscripted storytelling based on a "right now" story arc. This is where we need to get your brand's owned media team.

Being able to accomplish this starts with flexible, adaptable, responsive content planning. We recommend weekly "rundown" meetings, similar to the meeting that a newsroom will have on a daily basis for each of its shows or editions.

A "rundown" is a loose agenda for a news program that purposefully accounts for the ability to re –prioritize and reschedule content – to move things around to best suit the audience's needs in real –time. The idea is to create a production process that can be flexible and fast when the rundown has to be changed.

These rundown meetings are typically led by the "producer" function on your team – the person ultimately responsible for the program's success. The producer uses his experience and knowledge of the audience and the business objectives he gained while he was leading the development of your strategy. All the documentation of all the advance decisions your team made in that process informs the producer's decision making about which stories to produce and how to prioritize them.

For instance, a typical rundown for a news program might include a review of 10 to 15 stories, or packages, that are pre –produced or "in the can." These are our known variables, the content we know we have to work with. In addition, that producer might be working with several "live shots," which are stories being told in real –time, locally via a microwave truck or coming from other sources nationally or internationally via satellite. These stories are less concrete and are typically stories that are early in the development of their story arc.

The producer will also want to identify gaps – important developing stories from outside sources that our audience might be interested in that we are not already covering. Depending on the importance of some of these developing story opportunities, the producer may shift additional resources to cover them and deliver a story by the time the program is on the air.

In the middle of planning for all of these stories being produced, even more new story opportunities will present themselves. We don't know how many or what kind, but we know the world doesn't stop because we made plans to publish content, and we already have resources assigned to cover other developing stories. Again, the producer will have to make decisions and prioritize resources in order to get the content to the audience that will be of most relevance and timeliness, at the highest quality level possible within the constraints of the resources at hand and the story arc. Producers who do this well get good ratings. In the world of owned media, our "ratings" are our audience metrics. Producers who do not do this well, and don't deliver good ratings, are not producers for very long.

So the rundown – and the producer, and the production process and methodology – has to accommodate for real –time story developments – breaking news. This can come from lots of sources, but typically an assignment editor (the listening and engagement function in owned media) finds new signals, trends, stories and other information and recommends to the producer that the team produce a story about it.

Some of these stories are more time sensitive than others, and some are more important to audiences than others. The producer's job is to take the created content, allocate resources to fill in the gaps, and prioritize publication, launch or broadcast according to the story arcs of each story – how interested the audience is likely to be based on where the story is in its arc.

18.3. Campaign calendars

When it comes to content planning, many companies will create a big spreadsheet or blueprint of all the content in advance – blog posts, press releases, special events, even down to the very tweets and Facebook updates – they are going to create over the year. While this seems to make sense at first glance, and does help keep things integrated and on track, a detailed content calendar is typically a bad idea.

It will either be broken as soon as something changes in product or services direction, upper management makes another of its unexpected, mind –boggling changes, or the first small crisis hits the media. The content calendar practice of producing or scheduling content by the month, sometimes quarterly or even annually, is great in theory. But it's horrible in the real world.

In Raidious' newsroom setting, content gets produced based on the rundown. Staffers discuss stories in the can from the previous week, they discuss developing stories, and they look at data and global trends that tell them what stories to start working on. Between the meeting and publication time, new stories and events will also break and develop that will also have to be addressed immediately. A calendar approach takes none of these audience signals into account.

This is the disadvantage of the annual blueprint: You can't turn on a dime and adapt to new trends and changes or the needs of your audience. You're stuck on the path you're on until you can turn that big aircraft carrier of a schedule in a new direction.

If you need to make a calendar, do it with campaigns, not content. It's OK to schedule some content production farther in advance if you know what's coming and what resources you will need from your owned media team to support the campaign. Better yet, if you have advance notice, bring the owned media team in to help you develop a campaign. But attempting to decide the specific content that is going to be produced more than a couple of weeks in advance almost always results in wasted time, effort and other resources because it is too difficult to predict what your audience is interested in that far out.

Your strategy, your team structure and your production methodology should be built to be responsive to the audience. Content calendars don't contribute much to this approach. Not having a plan, and letting your audience guide you, is all part of planning for what you can't plan for.

18.4. Agile tools and technology

You have your team in place, and they have developed a killer strategy. Now they're collaborating in rundown meetings about the audience data they are getting and what content they should create. They will need some tools to create the content. Lots of advancements have happened with tools and technology to enable agile production at extremely high –quality levels that were not possible even with experienced vertical specialists 10 – 15 years ago.

Let's use video production as an example.

The year is 1991. We want to make a 90 –second video to tell a story that is relevant to our brand. In 1991, this meant hiring a video or film production crew, booking editorial time at an edit suite, maybe blocking out a few days in a recording studio for the score and the voiceover, vetting talent with the talent agency, several steps of editing and mastering and mixing, a separate budget for visual effects and motion graphics, and fees for dubbing and distribution. In 1991, video was an expensive, time –consuming proposition, and for certain types of content, it still is. If you are investing millions in air time for a paid media campaign with a long shelf life (or story arc) or for some piece of important, evergreen content, there is absolutely nothing wrong with investing the appropriate resources to make it more awesome and to deliver the impact you want.

At the same time, in 2013, your team can produce high –quality video quickly with not much more than a laptop and a smart phone – or maybe even just a smart phone. The production tools and resources you supply to your team should be reflective of the quality of content you expect them to produce for your brand. If you are OK with the quality of video you get from a mobile phone, that might be the only investment you need to make. However, we would highly recommend looking at more profes-sional –grade tools for your professional content team. They are much more affordable than you might think.

For instance, in 2013, a good baseline video production package might include a nice digital camera that can shoot stills and video – something like the Canon 7D. You also will want to spring for some lavaliere mics for sound, a nice rugged but lightweight tripod, and some basic lighting essentials. Your team will also need the appropriate video editing software – something like Final Cut Pro – and a laptop or desk-top machine powerful enough to run it. Some other things to consider for your content team are the things you might not be worried about, but that play a big role in productivity – screen real estate, for instance. Give your owned media team some nice big monitors. They are going to be spending a lot of time looking at them. Also, invest some dollars in comfortable chairs. We are big fans of the venerable Herman Miller Aeron, but at the very least, find something they can sit in for long pe-riods of time and be comfortable. Finally, give them cases for their gear. Much of the hardware you invest in will be moved and transported a lot from one shoot to the next. Invest some dollars in keeping that gear safe and sound.

That's just for video production. What about tools for social media management, monitoring, email marketing, image editing, illustration, collaboration? There are many different tools available to help your team produce content and manage dialogue in real –time. In fact, there are so many, we do a rolling review of all of the tools in our space every six months to decide if there are any advantages we can gain from using new technology.

In addition to the video production tools we just mentioned, expect to provide the following tools for your owned media team:

- **Basic back office tools:** Basic office productivity, like email, calendar, contacts, etc.
- **Design tools:** Typically some combination of tools from the Adobe suite, like Photoshop, Illustrator, Fireworks.
- **Animation/editing tools:** Typically Final Cut Pro and Motion or Adobe's AfterEffects and Premiere.
- **Team collaboration tool:** We are big fans of 37Signals Basecamp for group collaboration, but there are dozens of great options here for production management. Please don't make them use Sharepoint.
- **Monitoring tool:** Software for off –channel monitoring. Sysomos, Radian6 and SocialRadar are some good examples here.
- **Social media/omnichannel publishing system:** This is an important one. We like Spredfast, Sprinklr, and Hootsuite Pro right now, but this space moves too fast and is too new for any company to be declared an industry standard at this stage.
- **Analytics platforms:** Google Analytics, Webtrends and Omniture are the big players here.
- **Email service provider:** ExactTarget, Constant Contact and Mail Chimp for smaller brands.
- **CRM systems:** Salesforce.com, Sugar CRM, Microsoft Dynamics.
- **Lifecycle/automation systems:** Marketo, Eloqua, ROI are all good tools here
- **Content management systems:** We love WordPress, but we are also fans of Drupal, Joomla, and Expression Engine. On the .NET front, Kentico and DotNetNuke are viable options, as are OpenText and Ektron. These are some of the more popular website for content management system products, but there are literally hundreds of these out there. This is one place where you may want to involve IT to help you narrow down your list.
- **External content resources:** Things like stock photography and stock video can become great assets for your team to quickly produce high –quality content. Also, developing a relationship with an external partner to help you scale your content production or developing relationships with freelance resources to fill in the gaps may be important, depending on the brand.

The most important thing to remember here is where we have put this chapter of the book. We did not even mention tools or technology until we had gone through a complete understanding of the approach, all of the strategic thinking, built out our team, and put them together for their first rundown meeting to talk about what content is getting produced. At this point, it is time to consider what tools and technology will best serve your needs.

Find the technology that fits your team. Don't build your team and your process around a tool. Let your strategy blueprint and your resources dictate the tools that need to be used. Let your team evaluate the tools that are available, and make the recommendations for what they think will provide the best value from a cost/benefit standpoint. Don't let your IT department or marketing or PR team dictate all of this. You wouldn't tell a master carpenter what kind of chisel and sandpaper to use. Let your team make the call about the tools they want to use, and own the decision. They will know better than anyone what is going to work best. Most importantly – get a live demo. We have found that while functionality is important, it is secondary to day –to –day usability. Don't make a decision until your team has had several weeks of "live" real world usage with your technology solution.

18.5. Getting started: subject, topic, type, channel

It is important conceptually to understand the difference between a subject, a topic and the actual content type. These things can be related but mutually independent.

A topic is a broad group of subjects. These are the things we identified in our subject topography – broad –based, topics –level story ideas that are relevant. A subject is the specific related entity to the topic. This is what the actual story is going to be about. For instance, if we want to sell more Air Jordans next quarter, maybe basketball is the topic we are focused on from our subject topography. Based on what our audience data is telling us, we might decide to create relevant content about the subjects Michael Jordan, the three –point shot, college basketball and the score of last night's varsity game because all those things are getting great engagement and there is an upward trend in the story arc. So now we have some relevant story ideas to pursue. But should these be delivered as text? Would video tell the story better? Maybe a photo gallery? Something else entirely? And what channels will we deliver them on?

We need to make a decision about what kind of content we are going to make first – and it is most efficient to create multiple types of content for each subject. Once you have a great angle on a subject, it is sometimes just as easy to write a video script as it is a blog post or an email. The story-telling – the actual creation – has to happen regardless. So create that story independently of the content type and channel.

When we find a subject that the audience responds to, we can quickly and easily repurpose it on other channels. Can you turn your blog post into a video? Your photo gallery into a presentation? Your video into a series of tweets? How can you leverage one of the "1,000 little ideas" that work into other channels and content types?

Thinking of the subject you are creating content about independently from the content type will help the team take a more channel –agnostic approach, and it will keep them focused on how best to tell the story. We use the term "content unit" to describe this at Raidious to keep us from thinking about channels and media types. How do we best tell the story in our content unit? Does it require a visual presentation? Are there a lot of details that need lots of explanation? What is the story arc of this subject for our audience?

First: Create the content. Write the story or an outline of the story. Then consider what types of content you could use to deliver that story in the most compelling way given the constraints of your production schedule and the story arc of the subject. This could be multiple different types of media – video, presentation and text. It could be presented independently or all together within a blog post or a landing page or an email. Links to the individual content elements could be shared on lots of different social channels. Let the content type dictate the channels where it is going to be published. For instance, if you choose to tell the story with video, it doesn't mean this is a YouTube story. That video can be posted to Facebook, Twitter, embedded on a website or a landing page, published to a blog, pushed to a mobile app, posted to Pinterest as a link or Instagram as a screen grab image. Stills from the story could be used to create a photo gallery, or it could be emailed to your audience. The content can still be distributed in any number of ways regardless of the actual channel or its capabilities.

This is what channel agnostic production looks like. We want to tell an amazing, compelling story with our content, and we want to put all our resources toward accomplishing that. We don't want to make content for

Facebook or Twitter or a blog. We want to make content for our audience, and let them decide where to engage with it. The content that works well in one channel is highly likely to work just as well in other channels.

Depending on your brand, you might have vastly different audiences on different channels. In this case, we come back to the voices, platforms, channels and accounts approach we discussed in strategy. Uniquely different audience segments around different platforms or accounts is something you will identify in discovery, and these segments should be part of your considerations as you are building personae and distribution approaches in the strategy process.

There are all kinds of different ways to tell your story and all kinds of different channels to tell it on. Here is a quick overview of the basic content types and some channels where you could leverage them. As you read through this, pick one subject, and try to imagine how you could deliver the story using all the different types of content, and on which channels that content could be leveraged to grow your audience.

19. CONTENT TYPES

We talk a lot about "content," and that usually means "writing" to us. We both come from backgrounds where the written word rules all, and everything else supports it. But say "content" to a photographer, and she thinks "photos." The video guy thinks "videos." So when we talk about "content," we're really referring to any and all information — written word, photos, videos, audio files — that can be read, seen, watched, or heard by your customers.

19.1. Text

Every platform online uses text. Let's start there. Words were being used online before photos and videos ever were. And they continue to be the best drawing power to a website. Search engine spiders index written content, and use that to determine what the content is about. And until YouTube perfects its ability to transcribe the words on videos, it won't be able to tell what a video is about, so it has to rely on the written descriptions that creators give it.

So words are going to be the most important form of content on any online platform. It's how visitors find out what your content is about. It's how they learn about your company. And it's how they're going to decide whether they want to connect with you and interact with you in the future. The words you use in your content mean everything.

The nice thing about text is that it can, and should, be used anywhere and everywhere. We've discussed most of these channels already – websites, blogs, news sites, forum discussions, social networks, white papers, ebooks, etc. In fact, there's really nowhere you can't use some kind of text, and that includes video, audio, and photo sharing sites. Make sure you take every advantage to use your global taxonomy to describe your rich media content with text when it's published.

Most of your written content is going to be in the long –form category of blogs, web pages, articles, press releases, and white papers. But it can also be in the short form – tweets, status updates, check –in's (140 characters), Tumblr posts (shorter blog posts), email newsletters, text messages and instant messages, and anything else containing the written word.

19.1.1 Text and search

One important thing to be aware of is that in the past, most of your written content needed to be written for two audiences: people and search engines. That is not necessarily the case anymore. Most algorithms take many different signals into account to determine content quality and relevance. On –page formatting still plays a role, as does categorization and labeling. However, the need to consider algorithms in content creation is always secondary to the need to present compelling stories to your readers. Remember, winning rank is not winning search.

The tendency for people who are still riding the SEO train is to over –optimize their site for the search engines, cramming as many keywords into a piece of content as they can and using it in awkward and ungainly ways. While that may help win rank, it will turn off the readers who see this kind of writing as such dreck, they quickly leave even if they click through on the search engine results page. That is not winning search. It is winning rank and losing search.

Remember, Google Panda and Penguin have essentially shattered the search engine optimization industry, forcing many SEO companies out of business, and the rest of them to become content marketers.

Google wants websites to have interesting, well –written copy. Every algorithm shift that has happened for the last two years has been about content quality. So the goal shouldn't be volume of content or checking off a list of search optimization best practices as you check off the list of keywords you're targeting. It needs to move someone. If you want to rank, then you want to produce the kind of content that people want to read, share and act upon.

This is not to say that search as a point of focus is completely useless. It's not, by any means. The search engines still have to provide useful results to people. They still turn to Google and Bing when they want answers to questions, so the search engines still have to know what the web pages and blog posts are about. So be sure to use your global taxonomy we created in strategic planning to know what terms people are searching for, and then have your writers create content about those subjects, using the keywords you identified to describe and categorize the content. Build it into your process. Don't make it a project or an initiative or a campaign. Increased rank and search metrics are a direct result of quality content and an engaged audience. Search rank is a side effect of great content, nothing more, nothing less.

19.1.2. Write for people

That brings us to our next audience you need to write for: the actual people who are going to read your work. Your whole reason for being online is to reach people. Whether you want people to read your news articles, comment on your blog posts, get answers from your FAQ or buy something based on the catalog descriptions, you want everything you do to be people –friendly first and search –engine friendly second.

Writing for both people and search engines actually takes some effort because you have to write copy that the search engines recognize but the readers won't. That is, the readers shouldn't trip over your keywords. The best approach is to write a great story, then leave it up to your editorial and optimization layer to find additional opportunities to gently sand and polish your words to help search engines understand the content without disrupting the flow of the story.

19.1.3 The value of a writer

When writing your content, it also helps to have people who are actually good writers. This is going to be rather difficult because everyone learned to write in school, and it's a basic skill we all possess. Anyone who can send a two –sentence email has the ability to write. But this does not mean they are writers.

As Erik likes to say, "Anyone can make a sandwich. That doesn't make you a chef."

This is the difference between an experienced, well –trained professional and someone who is functionally capable of typing words on a screen. Yes, everyone can write. No, not everyone is a writer. Learn to identify the difference, and stay away from using people who can write to make your content. Instead, hire writers.

In our jobs, we rarely meet anyone who says they don't like to write. We meet the occasional one or two, but they're rare. Rather, everyone fancies themselves a budding wordsmith, and everyone thinks that writing is something anyone can do. As a result, writing is a commodity that is not always valued very highly.

This is where you can gain a distinct competitive advantage. It's where you can race past your competition. By working with real writers – people who actually study the art and craft of writing – your copy will be read, appreciated and acted on by your customers. Real writers know how to tell stories, use compelling language and make complex information easy to understand. Real writers can punch up dreary copy, get people excited about their products and generate interest for some of the most boring, mundane tasks in the known world.

Invest in experienced content creators – especially great writers. How much is enough? How much is too much? It all depends on your available resources and goals. Your team should have at least one or two knock –your –socks –off writers and/or editors. Plan to make a significant investment here. If you are using freelance talent, the basement and the sky are the limit. You can find writers in India who will put words on a page for $7 or $8 an hour, or you can hire feature writers from the most well –known publishers in the world for hundreds or thousands of dollars, and everything in between. The average New York City creative director bills at around $950 an hour. Nine –hundred –fifty dollars an hour just to think about your brand and write words. That seems really expensive until that creative director comes back to you with "Just Do It," three little words that generated billions of dollars. That's a great example of the importance of investing more dollars into content that has a longer shelf life. Use your judgment to find the right writers for your text content. Don't use just anybody who can write because people who can write are not necessarily writers.

19.1.4. Typical uses of short –form text content

Short –form content can be used in lots of ways, both proactively (scheduled in advance) and reactively (in response to content others have posted). Here are some examples of short –form text content:

- **Status updates** – On almost every social platform, there is an opportunity to post short status updates. These are usually limited to 140 characters and can include a link. Facebook, Twitter and LinkedIn are the most common places for status updates to be published, but you can also update status on many other platforms.
- **Link shares** – Link sharing can happen as part of most status updates, but some platforms treat link shares differently. For instance, Facebook displays content pulled from the link itself when a link is shared.
- **Check ins** – These come from location –based platforms like Foursquare or Yelp. They show physical location and can sometimes link to other content as well. This form of content comes in handy for events, and it can be leveraged in lots of ways. As mobile devices continue to proliferate, it is important to understand how check –ins can be used and leveraged from an owned media perspective.
- **Text messaging** – Text messaging is an effective way to reach Generation Y because this is one of the primary ways they communicate with each other. A 2011 report on NielsenWire said the average teenager is texting 3,146 times per month[10]. They're used to receiving texts, so take advantage of that. Text promotions, special and free offers, and other short messages they would be interested in seeing. Whether it's an opt –in text club or ads as part of a service or app, like sports scores or news updates, people are more willing to accept promotional messages with that service. During the 2008 NFL draft, Coors Brewing sent updates about draft picks, complete with Coors branding on each message[11].
- **Instant messaging/live chat** – This form of content happens in real –time, usually one to one, but it can be leveraged in other ways. A great form of content to use at live events, webinars and in customer service applications.

---

10 http://blog.nielsen.com/nielsenwire/online_mobile/under–aged–texting–usage–and–actual–cost/

11 http://bits.blogs.nytimes.com/2009/01/22/start–up–raises–money–to–send–text–message–ads/

19.1.5. Typical uses of long –form text content

Long –form text content takes many forms online, the most common being your standard web page. For the purposes of this book, we are listing HTML based long –form content here under text content, and encapsulated files like PDFs under Rich Media because they are typically used in different ways. The most common uses of long –form text content in HTML include:

Information pages – There's not a lot of explanation required here. We all know what an informational webpage is. This is your basic, static, evergreen content, such as your address and contact info or your terms and conditions page – stuff that does not change very often and is found on just about every website.

Landing pages – This is a specific type of webpage that will be important for any owned media effort where capturing information is important. Landing pages usually include a form that gathers information, and in inbound marketing, it functions as a "firewall" for high –value, rich media content such as white papers or case studies. Entire books have been written on landing pages and conversion optimization. If lead generation or capturing specific user profiles is important to your business, we would suggest learning more about landing pages, split testing and multivariate testing, and conversion optimization.

Product pages – This is another type of webpage most commonly found on ecommerce sites that allows the user to navigate through and buy products. While these pages tend to be database –driven, usually dynamic and centered on moving product, there are opportunities here for the owned media team. Creating additional content around your products will help win rank, and from an ecommerce perspective, additional content can sometimes help drive additional sales, particularly for high –dollar items.

Articles/content pages – This type of general, long –form content webpage is your basic, standard webpage, but this content usually tells more of a story and needs to be updated more regularly than an evergreen informational page.

Posts – There is not much technical difference between a post and a page, except for one huge detail. A post usually includes real –time site syndication, where a page is usually a static page and not syndicated. Posts are often used for more time –sensitive information and usually include the ability for readers to comment. Posts are the easiest, most flexible way to publish content today – usually the content management system interface is built to make it easy for people to create and publish posts, and because they are syndicated, content published in post format is very easy to share and integrate with other platforms. For instance, many email programs allow you to pull in a real –time site syndication feed from your content management system's posts and automatically compose and send an email with that content. Like standard web pages, posts can include any form of media – video, audio, text, images – anything you can embed in a page can be embedded in a post and syndicated to other platforms.

Email – Many companies use email as a way to publish long –form text content. Probably not the best idea, given how much email everyone gets these days, and the limited amount of time they have to read it all. If you don't want to end up in someone's junk mail filter – or worse, have them unsubscribe – text content in email should be summary –level, directional messaging. Think in terms of getting your message across in the subject line and having maybe three to four seconds of the audience's attention if they happen to open the email. That is not the place for your 1,200 –word product pitch. It is the place for a quick summary of it.

19.2. Video

Video is becoming increasingly important in owned media. For one thing, it's gotten so much easier to view videos, thanks to mobile and high –speed broadband access. You can access videos on your mobile phone or tablet computer anywhere you can get a 4G phone signal or find a Wi –Fi access point. Also, thanks to television, lots of people are comfortable with and familiar with video content, and they love to see stories presented in this form. Because it can use words, pictures and sound, video is a highly flexible and highly engaging medium, regardless of the device or platform it is presented on.

Producing videos can be as easy or difficult, cheap or expensive as you want. You can use a film camera, or you can use the camera built in to your phone or laptop. The voiceover can be off the cuff, or it can be scripted with professional voice talent in a recording studio. You can buy royalty –free generic music, or you can hire someone to write and produce a custom soundtrack for you with a full orchestra.

The electronic –news –gathering (ENG) approach and the roles of your owned media team allow for lots of flexibility in quality, speed and cost of video production. If you are doing a lot of this work, you can always add a video specialist to your content team who can shoot and edit video, as well as write and edit copy. Or if you are really doing a lot of video, maybe it makes sense to hire an entire crew of video specialists – lighting grip, videographer and audio engineer – to work with your owned media team.

19.2.1. Other types of video content

Making video content doesn't always have to involve a big, elaborate production. In fact, it doesn't have to even involve a video camera. There are lots of ways to make video content without shooting video.

2D animation – It is easy to tell a story with words and pictures without shooting video. Simple 2D animation, using tools like Apple's Motion or Adobe's AfterEffects or Flash, or open source tools such as Pencil can be an effective way to create engaging video content without as many production costs. Also, HTML 5 now allows for some pretty sophisticated animation effects that are rendered right in the browser without downloading or executing any encapsulated files.

For some applications and storytelling methods, 2D animation, with or without a voiceover or music, can be even more effective than having a talking head or talent in a video. Check out the famous Social Media Revolution video on YouTube for a great example of using video without shooting video or using voiceover[12].

3D animation – While it is typically very expensive to produce high –quality 3D animation, like many technologies, the barriers to entry are dropping. This can be a very cool way to tell a story, but at this point, we would recommend finding a specialist to help you with this particular art form.

Screencasts – If you are producing instructional content, screencasts can be a great way to do this. There are plenty of applications out there that allow you to capture the video output of your monitor and create video content with it. It doesn't have to be demonstrative how –to video. It could be anything you can get on your screen!

Animated presentations – Did you know you can make video with Apple Keynote, Microsoft PowerPoint and other presentation tools? If you can build animations in your presentations, it is easy to export them as videos that can be used on YouTube, Vimeo and all your other platforms. Check your software help section to see how you can export your presentation as a movie.

---

12 http://www.youtube.com/watch?v=QUCfFcchw1w

Online animation and video sites – There are several sites out there that enable anyone to tell stories with animation. Online tools like Animoto and Masher allow you to upload your own images and video to create awesome video content. GoAnimate, Dvolver, Animasher, Xtranormal, Voki and several others can be used for creative storytelling in the form of animation and video.

Streaming live video – There are also lots of great options for streaming live video such as UStream, or hosting video conferences and live –video webinars like Fuze meeting or GoToMeeting. There are also services such as Google Hangout and Skype that can enable live group video chats. These video tools can be used in lots of creative ways beyond just publishing video. Some can also be used for capturing video, so it can be republished later in other platforms.

Video mash up/remix – This is one of the more fun approaches to video, which we have not seen a lot of brands do. However, lots of people online love to mash up and remix video content, especially music videos. Just go to YouTube and see how many versions of "Gangnam Style" you can find. Another interesting approach is Bad Lip Reader, which attempts to transcribe video with the audio turned off, simply by lipreading, usually with hilarious results. There are obvious issues for brands here as it relates to licensing and other issues, but we thought we should include this popular category of video content, just for the record. Plus, you'll have a lot of fun "researching" it. We did.

The rise of mobile video – Mobile video is becoming more and more important if your company is trying to reach Generation Y, people born between 1977 and 1994. Not only do they outnumber Baby Boomers, 81 million to 78 million, but in 2011, they were spending about $200 billion per year, and affecting another $300 to $400 billion in family spending (i.e. clothing, restaurants, and even family cars). This is great for marketers, right?

On the other hand, they tend to ignore or discredit traditional advertising and marketing – paid and earned media. They're skipping television, preferring to watch YouTube instead, on their phones, their tablets and their laptops. And when they do watch TV, they record it so they can fast forward through the commercials. Any newspaper articles they do read are read online, so they miss a lot of newspaper advertising. They don't listen to radio. They listen to iPods and iPhones and Pandora and Spotify, so they miss radio commercials as well. This behavior is most prevalent with Gen Y, but it is also spreading to other demographics. More and more people are spending more and more time online every day, and less time with traditional media. Your investment in owned media should reflect this new change in consumer behavior.

19.2.2. Video content hosting and distribution

In the past, it was difficult and expensive to host and stream video online. Today, it almost doesn't make sense to host your online video content in house, with all of the free and low –cost options that exist. Video hosting and sharing sites are typically going to be your best bet for placing your videos online for other people to watch. There's the video giant, YouTube, which gains more than 4 billion views per day.[13] There are also more vertically focused video sites, such as Vimeo, which is dedicated more toward well –made HD videos, perfect for people who take video seriously. There's Viddler, PhotoBucket, Flickr, the photosharing site that allows 90 –second videos, VideoJug for how –to videos, ScienceStage for science, teaching, and research, and even Blip.tv for independent TV shows and movies.

19.2.3. Beyond video sharing sites

Depending on how active you are with video in your owned media properties, and how many channels you are publishing to, the viewership, the depth and detail required for analytics reporting, and your unique corporate needs, you might want to look at video syndication and analytics services like Brightcove or TubeMogul. In fact, there are a few dozen video sharing sites that will let you upload videos, and embed them in other sites, like your blog or website. This can be a big timesaver as you only have to upload the video once and it can be shared across lots of different platforms and accounts with a mouse click instead of dozens of uploads.

Also, don't forget your other platforms can almost all deliver video. Have you tried video in email? What about on Twitter or Facebook? Video content – if it is compelling – works equally well on just about every online channel your brand owns or controls. Channel independence here – once your video has been posted to the video hosting site of your choice, you can still use that content in other non –video channels.

---

13 http://mashable.com/2012/01/23/youtube–4–billion/

19.3. Images

Image content is a great way to tell a story online. Remember, users don't really "read" online; they scan. The first and most obvious use of images we will cover is photography. Even when your story is a longer –form text piece, it is important to include an image or two or some other visual form of content to help break up the words and to help tell the story.

Your photos and images can be of anything you can imagine. We've seen companies that take accompanying custom photos for every story they produce. They publish product photos to go with marketing campaigns and product launches. They plaster photos of staff on their recruiting pages, and of course, photos of trade shows and special events. We have also seen memes storm the Internet, infographics take over inbound marketing and image mashups like Elf Yourself explode online. People just love images. It goes back to that old axiom, a picture's worth thousand words.

19.3.1 Photography

Thanks to the latest in photo and video technology, you can have photos of anything, taken anywhere, of anyone. And you can share it as soon as it's taken, via broadband and social networking tools.

In fact, one of the things we like about photos is that you can show in real –time the things that are happening at one of your events or campaigns. Mobile apps like Instagram and Hipstamatic have been purpose built around this activity, tying location to image. Beyond the camera app that comes standard on the iPhone, there are hundreds of "enhanced photography" apps available on the App Store. In fact, with the proliferation of smart phones with cameras, vast amounts of photos are shared every day by your audience. This can be a treasure trove of content to curate, engage with and share.

Photography is just like writing. It's something anyone with one good eye and a working index finger can do. But it takes someone with a lot of practice and experience to truly take beautiful photos. Handing your marketing manager a really fancy camera is probably not a good option. Even a good camera in the hands of an amateur still yields amateurish pictures. We'd rather put a cheap camera in the hands of a professional, than an expensive camera in the hands of a newbie. If you want some outstanding photos, hire a professional.

19.3.2. Memes, graphics, charts, infographics and other image types

You can't look at Facebook without being exposed to dozens and dozens of images. That's because Facebook knows its users engage more with images and video than they do with text and link shares. There is an important lesson here – one we will cover later when we talk about Facebook EdgeRank. Some of these images are photos, but there are lots of other types of static visual content types – images that are not just photos and don't include motion or interactivity – that work great to engage audiences.

Memes – Courage Wolf. Lolcats. This Is Sparta. ORLY? Philosoraptor. Condescending Wonka. Maybe you have seen these memes around the interwebs. A meme technically is an idea, behavior or style that spreads from person to person within a culture or community. The literal translation from the ancient Greek means "something imitated." Memes are the quick and dirty, high art of Internet mashup culture. Memes are difficult to explain without seeing them, so we would recommend visiting knowyourmeme. com to get a feel for what we are talking about here. These are usually images, sometimes videos, that typically poke fun at different cultural happenings.

Memes move fast. They tend to have fairly short story arcs, but some are much longer than others. These are a great example of the "mashup/ remix" culture of Internet content creators. As we write this, one popular meme is "McKayla is not impressed" (http://mckaylaisnotimpressed.tumblr.com), which uses U.S. gymnast McKayla Maroney's scowling expression during the 2012 Olympics, when she won a silver and not a gold medal. This meme is a mashup of an earlier meme, Spock is not impressed.[14]

This photo was taken by Bryan Snyder of Reuters news service, but it quickly started making the rounds in social media after BuzzFeed compiled a series of photos of McKayla making similar expressions. The Tumblr blog launched and started publishing Photoshop mashups of McKayla not being impressed about much of anything.

The timeline on this meme is very interesting. Buzzfeed published its series of photos Aug. 6. On Aug. 7, it made its way to QuickMeme and Reddit, where it was picked up by Mashable, What's Trending and The Examiner. By Aug. 8, it was on The Wall Street Journal. That's 48 hours from post to viral meme, folks.

---

14 http://spockisnotimpressed.tumblr.com

Memejacking – Brands can use developing and popular memes to help tell a story. It's also important to know that your brand – particularly if it has a successful marketing campaign that resonates with a lot of people – can and probably will eventually have people creating memes using the brand. This can be good and bad depending on the brand's understanding of Internet culture. If this is new stuff for your brand, your C –suite will probably freak out. If you have been doing this for awhile, your C –suite will probably high five you if you reach memejacking status with your marketing campaign. A great example of this is Dos Equis' "Most interesting man in the world" meme. Great example of likely unintended synchronicity of paid and owned media.

Are these silly? Usually, but they don't have to be. Are they clever? They should be at least interesting, if not downright clever. Are they funny? Usually, in a very dry or sarcastic way. Do they generate engaged audiences? In our experience, absolutely. Be creative with this approach, and figure out how to make it work for your brand, using cultural references your audience will understand and identify with. It doesn't necessarily have to be snarky or part of culture that is happening right now, but that usually helps.

Infographics – Infographics are a great way to tell a complicated story or give context to information in a more compelling way than a simple chart or graph. Infographics are about data visualization – how to tell a data –heavy story in a beautiful and compelling way. These are typically produced as fairly large graphic images, but lately we have been seeing a lot of interactive and animated infographics as well, which we will cover in Rich Media.

Over the last several years, the Internet has produced hundreds of thousands of beautifully produced infographics that cover everything under the sun. The best way to get an idea of all the different ways infographics can be used is to go to Pinterest and search for Infographics. Make sure you have plenty of time allocated for this.

Making great infographics is part art and part science – having a great data set to work with is a must, so gather your data first and decide what story it tells. This is the science part. Understanding how to visually represent it is the art part. You will need an artist with good illustration and layout skills who can understand the story and tell it in a visually compelling way. Infographics can be time consuming and difficult, and sometimes expensive to create, but good ones are very compelling, easy to share, and can usually be used in lots of different platforms.

Charts and graphs – Ahh, the "lowly" chart. The "basic" graph. These types of images can tell stories quickly and effectively – a more tame (and faster and easier –to –produce) version of the infographic. We have been using these to communicate visually for years in presentations. With a little graphic design love, a chart or graph can tell a great story all by itself or in combination with text content. Again, look at your story arc. Is this information we need to get out there right now, or can we spend some time and resources making a full –blown infographic out of this information? Can we tell the story with a quick chart? Or can we take this Excel spreadsheet we were given, and make a quick graph out of it? Excel has this feature built in, as does PowerPoint, and with a little work you can make charts look awesome in both of these programs. Apple's Numbers and Keynote do an even better job of making dry, boring information beautiful and compelling with their chart and graph functions.

Other edited images – A great way to make your text more compelling is to make it an image. Does your headline have to be text, or can you quickly create a graphic to tell the story with a stock image or some other image? What, visually, would say what you are trying to say with words? If you are asking a question on a social platform, can you do it visually with an edited image? Text doesn't always have to be typed. It can appear in an image and make a headline, statement or other content that would typically be text a lot more interesting to the user. When you are getting ready to add emphasis to text – in headlines, knockouts, block quotes, subheads or other similar applications – try to find ways to get your message across with an image or combination of an image and text instead.

19.3.3. Hosting and distributing image content

Some of the most popular applications built to host and distribute images are Flickr, Picasa and Photobucket. Flickr is owned by Yahoo. Picasa is owned by Google, and Photobucket is actually part of Rupert Murdoch's News Corp. Pinterest and Instagram are also very popular places for image hosting and sharing. These sites let you own and manage your own images, and they're an excellent place to store and manage your photos, rather than on a blog or website. Many of them allow you to create beautiful galleries that are easy to embed on your owned media platforms. For some,

Creative Commons licensing is built in, allowing you to select how people can borrow share and reuse your images while still maintaining credit for ownership. We named three of the most popular sites designed for photo management, but there are more than 30 different sites in operation. Photos and images are also shared regularly on Facebook, Twitter and lots of other sites as well. Make sure you understand the implications of each platform's terms and conditions. For instance, once your content is posted to Facebook, they own it, which means they can pretty much do what they like with it, including deleting it if it does not meet their terms and conditions. We would recommend finding a central place to host, manage and archive images that enables you to access and share those images however you like, whenever you like, on any platform.

19.4. Audio

Anyone with a microphone and a recording application can hit record and share their most interesting ideas with audio. Audio can be distributed on lots of different online platforms, but it has not been a popular way to tell a story online for laptop users. However, it is a different story when the audience is accessing your owned media on a mobile device. Audio content is what started the iPod revolution, which ultimately led to the iPhone and the smartphone revolution. Now mobile users are streaming audio content from Pandora and buying audio content over the air with their phones. Yes, the majority of this audio content is music. However, there are many other forms of audio content. Audio books are popular, and recorded lectures like TED Talks. But typically, if we are talking about audio content online, we are talking about podcasting.

Podcasting first became a way of sharing information back in 2000, pioneered by the likes of Adam Curry, one of MTV's first veejays. The first MP3 player, the i2Go had just been released, and in order to provide content, they created their digital news and entertainment category for people to find interesting stories and shows. That started more people figuring out how they could record audio files and radio shows and syndicate them so they could be heard. Once the first generation of iPods were released, and Curry released the RSS –to –iPod script, iPodder, broadcasting to iPods soon became podcasting, and the do –it –yourself radio show emerged as we know it today.

Thanks to mobile broadband, the explosive use of iPhones, which has iTunes on it, podcast aggregator and player Stitcher Radio, and Internet radio services like BlogTalkRadio.com and the Blubrry Network, we're now seeing – and hearing – more podcasts now than ever. And podcasting now can include video!

Don't expect to generate a huge audience of millions of people with podcasting. There are a devoted group of users, but this is not something people are doing as frequently as something like checking Facebook. Then again, a lot of this is not because of the medium – it is because of the content. Creating compelling audio content is not easy. That's why radio stations play music these days instead of producing shows the way they did back in the 1930s and 1940s before TV took over as the storytelling medium of choice.

Doug Karr has done the Marketing Tech Radio show on Friday afternoons at 3 p.m. for several years through Blog Talk Radio. He started it in October 2010 as a way to reinforce the content he was putting on the Marketing Tech Blog, where he also talks about marketing technology. The net result for his company has been growth from 2,100 listens in 2010 to 57,000 listens in 2012. For vertically focused brands such as Doug Karr's DK New Media, this can be huge.

Karr said, "The primary reason is to connect us with industry leaders and keep on their radar. We actively pursue leaders in the industry that we hope to build a relationship with. In turn, I believe that's grown our authority and the likelihood that folks will do business with us."

Pick up a book on podcasting, buy a microphone or two, learn how to operate the software and start producing podcasts that your target audience will be interested in. Go deep on topics you can't get information about anywhere else. Maybe it's an orthopedic joint replacement company talking about the latest surgical techniques, or maybe it's a human resources consultant talking about HR law. Perhaps it's a soft drink company doing a free music showcase where they play and interview up –and –coming bands. The content is what drives the success, not the medium.

19.4.1. Audio parodies, mashups and custom songs

This could really go into the video content section as well, since much of this type of content winds up being published as video, but most of the work goes into the audio. We have not seen a lot of brands do this, but audio parodies, mashups and custom songs are huge online. One of our favorites is Auto –Tune the News, where some very talented folks use an effect called AutoTune by Antares to remix and mashup audio and video clips from TV news to make hilarious, but incredibly well –produced custom songs.

19.4.2. Hosting and distributing audio content

iTunes, Blog Talk Radio (blogtalkradio.com), the Blubrry Network (blu-brry.com), and the Stitcher Radio app (stitcher.com) are all great places to distribute audio content. But iTunes is like the YouTube of the podcasting world. It's the biggest engine there is, and everyone knows it. If you want to be found, you need to be on iTunes. It's just a matter of submitting your podcast through the proper channels, and then waiting for approval from iTunes management, which isn't that hard to get.

Blog Talk Radio is more of a live Internet radio show, where you have to broadcast at the same time every week. Technical glitches are live, the sound quality is diminished, so it can be heard over even the slowest Internet connections, and if your guests don't show up or get cut off, you still have to go on.

The Blubrry Network is another distribution channel just like iTunes. But unlike iTunes, you can find podcasts of all kinds, not just ones that meet the approval of iTunes management. The problem they have is that they're not nearly as well known as iTunes or even Stitcher. But it's a way to get your content out there.

Stitcher Radio is a podcasting app that will pull in your favorite podcasts from its aggregation service. With categories such as New and Noteworthy, Comedy, News & Politics, and Business, you can find podcasts on nearly any topic. And you can contribute podcasts as well just by providing them with the RSS feed to your podcast.

19.5. Rich Media

The interactive, multimedia nature of the Internet has given birth to all kinds of media that include text, images, audio, video and animation in new and interesting ways from the basic PowerPoint presentation to cus-tom –built online "experiences."

19.5.1. Downloadable resources

While most of these types of content are going to be text driven, we have included them in the rich media category because they typically are used that way, and can include text, images and sometimes video and some level of interactivity. Also, they are usually delivered in an encapsulated file such as a PDF or a .doc rather than as HTML that is rendered in a browser. That's not to say you couldn't produce this kind of content as HTML, or that PDFs and .docs can't be rendered in a browser, but usually these downloadable resources are deployed as just that – a downloadable resource that can be easily printed or shared privately via email.

White Papers – Originating in academia and research, white papers started off as dry, typically multi –page documents outlining research findings and best practices. The white paper has become popular in inbound marketing and content marketing and is typically produced with a lot more graphic flair than in the past. White papers typically range from three to five pages and include text and graphics, and are usually delivered in PDF format online. That's not to say a white paper couldn't be longer. Especially in academic circles, the expectation for a white paper is a deep dive into the details of fairly complicated subject matter. Can it be shorter? Based on the expectations of most people about what they are going to get when they take the time to download a white paper, probably not. If you only have three pages of content on a topic, you are either not going deep enough or you need to present it in a different format (or call it something else to manage the audience's expectations).

Case Studies – Case studies can vary from simple one –page "situation/solution/outcome" overviews to in –depth descriptions and details. Like white papers, case studies came from academia and have become popular particularly in business –to –business content marketing and inbound marketing. Case studies are typically delivered as PDFs or sometimes in PowerPoint or Keynote files. At a minimum, a case study should include an overview of a situation, what steps were taken to impact the situation and how the situation changed.

Use Cases – Use cases are different than case studies. A case study typically goes into more depth, whereas a use case shows how a product or service has been applied to a specific problem. The audience expectations for the level of depth and detail in a use case versus a case study are different. Use cases typically are much shorter and more high –level than an in –depth case study, and use cases are also more demonstrative. Like case studies, a use case is typically delivered as a PDF or presentation, but video and animation can also be great ways to tell a story about how to use something.

Presentations – Presentations are usually delivered as a PowerPoint or Keynote file, or a PDF of a presentation file. Prezi files and other presentation tools would fall into this category as well. You can make a presentation about anything, but the information presented is typically not as text –heavy as you would find in a white paper or case study, or even a use case. Presentations were originally designed to accompany a speaker, so the use of bullet points and images and short sentences are hallmarks of presentations because they were designed to have a speaker filling in all the details verbally. Can you use presentations to present in –depth information? Sure, you can, but a better format for that would be a white paper. Presentations are great for concepts and big ideas, but not so much for the details behind them.

Guides – Guides are typically multipage "how –to" documents for learning about or accomplishing a task. These are typically presented as short eBooks in PDF format. This is different than a manual, which is usually built for a specific product, versus a guide which is typically more general. For instance, you might download the manual for Adobe Photoshop, which would show you what that specific software does, versus a guide to editing photos, which would be more broad and useful across multiple products.

Reports – Reports are usually in –depth and "just the facts, ma'am." A report might include some editorializing in certain sections, but typically the expectation with a report is a document that presents basic facts with little color. Research, financials, industry overviews, shootout –style comparisons and other similar data –heavy information are usually presented in a report. Reports can include summary charts and graphs, but users will expect to see the majority of the data in the actual report, or at the very least, references to where the details and raw numbers are publicly available.

Product Brochures – This is pretty self –explanatory. Product brochures at this point are almost all available online as a PDF. If you have a product brochure – or really any externally –facing print content – that is not available online, you may want to think about picking that low –hanging fruit. Product brochures don't have to just sit on your website. You might be surprised how they perform in other media.

eBooks – This is a form of content that is in a lot of flux right now. In the past, an eBook was a simple PDF version of the printed material. Now books and magazines are finding new life online, particularly with the ongoing evolution of the tablet. The iPad and other tablets have made viewing online content much more like the somewhat passive, "lean back" experience of television and print, rather than the more active "lean forward" experience a user has on a laptop or desktop machine. On a side note, smartphones tend to fall into both of those categories, depending on what you're doing with them.

eBooks and magazines are more rich media focused, although the writing is still the centerpiece of an eBook experience. Check out the iPad version of Wired or Esquire for a good idea of what eBooks are becoming.

19.6. The "Other" category

There are lots of ways to tell stories online that fall into the "other" category – things that are part application, part audio, video, images and text, and part something else altogether. Here are some examples of other ways to tell your story on the platforms you own and control, beyond the basic text, image, video, audio categories.

Interactive/Animated/Video Infographics – Static infographics, animated, video and interactive infographics are great at displaying lots of complicated information and data in a visually engaging way. Adding the "time" element of video and animation allows for more space to include content and more ways to tell the story with data. Adding interactivity allows for the audience to dig deeper into the data, or even adjust specific parts of the infographic, limited really only by the content that's included in it. You can see a great example of an interactive infographic from GE here: **http://visualization.geblogs.com/visualization/ renewableenergy**.

SlideShare – SlideShare makes your PowerPoint and Keynote presentations easy to share and repurpose as online content. After a talk, you can direct people to your SlideShare deck so they can download the deck. This saves you from having to email the deck to them. SlideShare decks can be embedded in other web pages as well. Another bonus: SlideShare decks are searchable by Google, and might pop up in Google search results.

Prezi – This is another presentation sharing site. Prezi's goal is to make presentations more visually appealing and interesting. Their approach looks more like a sophisticated animation than a typical presentation deck. Prezis also encourage brevity because you won't want to put a lot of text onto a Prezi slide. You can visit Prezi.com, set up a free account learn how to use the presentation service, create your own deck (also called a Prezi), and explore what other people have done.

Pinterest Boards – Pinterest has been a surprise social network to a lot of people because it's nothing more than finding images, "pinning" them to your own board and telling all your Pinterest friends, "I like this." You can even create different boards – food I want to make, favorite actors, or I want this!. This makes it easier to group your images. We've heard of people who created wedding gift registries, organized house decorating ideas and even planned vacations using Pinterest. Companies can get in on the action by encouraging visitors to pin their photos on their own boards. The pinned photos will then contain a link that takes viewers back to the original source of the photo, the company's own website.

Image Galleries – Flickr and some of the other photo sharing sites we mentioned in the Images section make it easy to create your own embeddable and shareable image galleries. In the past, you had to hand code image galleries into your site or use one of the many blog plugins.

Embedded Tweets – Embedded tweets are an interesting way to repurpose anyone's tweets. You can curate the best online comments about your brand, positive mentions from influencers and other testimonial –style content, or just find some tweets that are relevant to the topic you are creating content about, and include them in your content to help enhance the story. It's easy to do. Here is a link to the "how –to" from Twitter: https://dev.twitter.com/docs/embedded –tweets

Storify – This is a content curation site that lets you pull in other social media elements about a single topic or story. You leverage your own social networks – Twitter, YouTube, Flickr, Instagram, Google+, Facebook and even outside URLs – for the elements of the story. Then just drag and drop them to the Storify board, arrange them the way you'd like them, and publish it. While your content marketing strategy should be all about creating content, we like Storify as a unique way to curate and share it. You can gather all the elements you find from all of your channels, pull them into Storify, and share them again with your followers and fans.

19.7. Functional content

Can an application be content? It sure can. The majority of this book focuses on how to make content that is clearly just content. Lots of brands use functionality as content as well. For instance, creating a simple calculator application that people can use on your site to figure out what their mortgage should be. Creating simple, immersive games that users can play is an example of an application being used as content. Many brands are making mobile applications that help accomplish some task or provide some functional use. In a lot of cases, the branded mobile app delivers more content – which is awesome – but some brands go beyond just pushing content to their app, and use functionality to help a user solve a problem or accomplish a task.

There is also the emerging world of applications that can be built for Facebook, Chrome, Salesforce, and many other "platform –as –a –service" companies. Your owned media team should probably not be expected to be able to build these kinds of custom applications in –house. The "platforms" function of your team should be more of a support function, not so much a development and programming function. But if you have someone on your team who can create mobile apps, simple HTML 5 or Flash applications and experiences, or other code –heavy functional content, by all means, use their talent.

Creating simple online games, forms, surveys and other content the user can interact with is not as difficult as it once was. Lots of applications have emerged to help non –coders create this kind of immersive content.

Games – Gaming is a very big deal these days. It's no longer the sole province of hardcore console gamers mashing away on their XBOX or PS3. How many times has one of your Facebook friends invited you to Farmville? How many Angry Birds have you shot at pigs? Have you ever tried for a mayorship on Foursquare? Gaming is happening everywhere with every age group and demographic sector. Some brands have gotten involved here in interesting ways, but for many, the cost of entry – and figuring out how to make an awesome game – is a challenge.

You don't have to build the next version of Black Ops or Madden. Or even the next Angry Birds. How can you "gamify" your audience experience across all your platforms? In other words, can you reward them somehow for specific behaviors? This is becoming a big focus for many digital marketers.

Forms – The simple form. It is so important for gathering information. It used to take a good developer a couple of days to build, test and deploy even a simple form. Now, companies like Formstack make it easy to create forms, embed them anywhere, and tie them to about any data source you have in a matter of minutes, including many ecommerce functions. This kind of functional content is critical for landing pages or anywhere your team needs to gather information from users, including more content.

Surveys – Surveys can be fun and interesting if you approach them that way. They can also provide loads of great information, from in –depth research to simple yes/no polls. Formstack can also be used for quick polls and surveys. SurveyMonkey is also a popular tool for this, and Quipol is a great way to take the pulse of your audience. Don't underestimate the level of engagement you can get from simple polls and surveys on your platforms. Try it on your site. Try it in email. People want to share their thoughts and opinions, and if you make it easy for them, they will engage.

Contesting – It's a matter of time before someone on your marketing team wants to do some kind of contest with your owned media. This is a lot more difficult and high –risk than it sounds at first glance when you get into the nuts and bolts of how users enter, how a winner is chosen, etc. and would typically require lots of custom code and programming. The good news is there are several applications available that can make this very easy for you. One example is WildFire, which is an application built to help your brand run safe, legal online contests on Facebook and other platforms, without writing a line of code.

Your owned media team will still need to create content to support the application, but it makes life easy when it's time to run a contest. Keep in mind this can be a great way to generate awesome user content – photo contests, essay contests, art and design contests, video –based contests, contests where users have to get votes from friends to win. Contesting content can be a valuable way to quickly grow and engage your audience.

Coupons and rewards content – Online coupons and rewards content are usually generated by your ecommerce and merchandising team. However, it is important for your owned media team to know what programs are happening with this kind of content. These things are usually distributed via transactional, automated email, but if there is a way to leverage this content in other channels – for instance, asking rewards and loyalty customers to share with their network – you should discuss this internally to fully leverage the content opportunity that exists with your coupons/rewards/loyalty program audience.

The concept of "utility as marketing" is covered in –depth in Jay Behr's excellent "Youtility." We highly recommend picking up a copy of this breakthrough book next time you're on Amazon or in the book store.

19.8. Physical owned media

Does your brand have a storefront? Maybe some trucks? Digital signage? If you want to really stretch the boundaries of owned media, you should be thinking about how your physical structure could tell your story. Where some see delivery trucks, we see moving billboards. Where some see a lobby, we see a storytelling center. Where some see a door that says "Entrance," we see an opportunity to make a first impression with a great story.

This is always a fun exercise for brands. Look around your company's physical spaces and see how many different opportunities you can find for delivering a story. Some brands, like Walmart, have gone as far as installing their own network of video displays throughout all of its stores! How could you include physical (i.e. non –digital) assets in your owned media plan?

20. THE FIVE M'S: REAL –TIME EXECUTION

OK, we have rethought our philosophical approach to owned media. We have reconsidered its role in marketing, and we have reallocated resources to make it work with paid and earned media. We have our strategy in place. We learned about our needs in discovery, established a defensive perimeter in risk, defined our goals in our business case, defined our audience with personae. We know how we are going to distribute content, how it's going to be classified so people can find it and what we are going to create content about. We know how we will engage with our audience. We now understand how to structure our owned media team, and we have that team in place. They are well –organized around agile, ENG –style production methodology. They know what the audience wants, all the different ways to tell stories online, and they have the tools to tell the stories. They have made decisions about what content to produce for the next two weeks in their rundown meeting, and those stories have been assigned.

Now it's time to do the work.

As with the strategy process – which has eight steps to be performed in order, one more or less dependent on the next – there is a similar but non –linear process for execution. In other words, it's all happening all the time, not in a linear order.

There are five steps to this cyclical process, which we call the five M's – Make, Manage, Monitor, Moderate, and Measure. The five M's are necessary for every single owned media channel.

Make the content. Manage its distribution. Monitor the audience for reactions. Respond to those reactions through dialogue moderation, and measure the results to inform what content gets made next. The process is self –sustaining and ongoing, usually based on the production cycle timelines you outlined in your strategy.

Many would argue that monitoring should be step No. 1 in the production process, and we wouldn't totally disagree. But remember, this is not a linear process. These are not really "steps," as much as they are actions that need to always be taking place, proactively based on what the brand wants to say, and reactively in response to what the audience is saying.

Monitoring should always be happening, just like content creation – the "make" step – should always be happening, as should the next two parts of the process, moderation and measurement. It's all happening, all the time, with regular check –ins happening at the points you identified in the production timeline section of your strategic planning process. Here, we break it down into sections to make it easier to understand.

Just remember, each part of the production process is a constant. This is important to understand. The Internet is always on. That means your production cycle – your five M's – is always on. It functions on top of the strategic framework you developed with your team, and it is happening all the time, every day. It's not a linear campaign style that has a start and an end. In fact, there is no end. The cycle feeds itself, and campaign –style ideas are executed within this production framework.

This is another major departure from typical linear, project –oriented production methodology. No matter what the campaign idea is, on the owned media front, your team will have to go through this same process – which is already in place and always happening – to support the campaign. This makes it easy to integrate anything that is happening in earned and paid media. Campaigns simply "plug in" to the process that is always happening. These are all the things that need to happen to content in order for it to successfully impact your audience on all the platforms your brand owns and controls, including any efforts in paid and earned media. No additional work or production process is really required to support project efforts. They simply get put into the cycle in the rundown meeting, are assigned, and executed through the five M's.

Just like the strategy process, the execution process is platform and media agnostic. It doesn't matter where the content is being published, or what kind of content it is, it needs to go through these five steps. Social, email, blog, website, mobile, images, video, text, rich media … all of it must go through the five M's to fully leverage its value.

Let's go through what is included in each of these five steps, keeping in mind this process is nonlinear, and applies only to execution, and only works if a strategy is in place, and there is a properly equipped team in place to execute the process.

21. MAKE

21.1. Sharable storytelling

One of the things we talk about a lot at Raidious is the development of "shareable stories." We want to create content that is literally remarkable – meaning, it is so incredibly awesome, the user is compelled to share it. We want those stories constructed in a way that is quick and convenient to consume and because of the limitations around how they are shared (like the 140 –character limit on Twitter), we need to spend a lot more time on the headline than one might expect. The headline is what gets shared in many cases. We advise our team to spend about 25 percent of the time they have allocated to a content assignment focused on brainstorming a great headline for the content. This applies across the board – a great title for a video, a great caption for a photo, a great headline for an article. Not just great, but remarkable, in the most literal sense. We want to create a story that is not only remarkable and compelling, but is easy to share on lots of different platforms and is told in an engaging way. Video is a great medium for telling stories in a compelling way. Could it also be done with a presentation or an infographic? Or some other content medium? What is the best way to tell the story so that people want to share it, and it's easy for them to do so?

21.2. Signals to consider

Your audience will tell you, loud and clear, what they are interested in. Just look at the data. Your web analytics will tell you where they are spending time, and where they are bouncing. Your social media analytics will tell you what's compelling and what's not, what's remarkable and what's not. You don't get to choose. Your opinion is not a signal. Your audience metrics are.

Another signal to consider is topical search volume. This is a great way to generate story ideas or decide between two or three different stories. Google offers a free keyword tool that shows search volume. If you're planning ahead, look at several topics over a 12 –month period to determine when to create content about what. For instance, people are more interested in air –conditioning repair in July than in January.

A third signal to take into account is trending topics. There are dozens of social media tools that can tell you what is being discussed online in real –time. How can you make those topics relevant to the brand and your business objectives?

Figuring out "what" to create content about is always the hard part. We have the right tools to do this if you get stuck. The first is the "subject" –level content ideas from our discussion on subject topography. This gives you relevant, focused, broad direction on what to create content about. The next thing you need is a topic, and that comes from the signals in our audience and trend data. This is where you should be looking for "topic" –level story ideas. Now we are a little closer. We have a subject (Basketball) and a topic (Michael Jordan). Now we need a story angle. For that, we use the triangle of relevance.

21.3. Triangle of relevance

This is a simple, tactical, creative brainstorming exercise we invented at Raidious to help us leverage real –time signals to create content that will be relevant to our clients' brands.

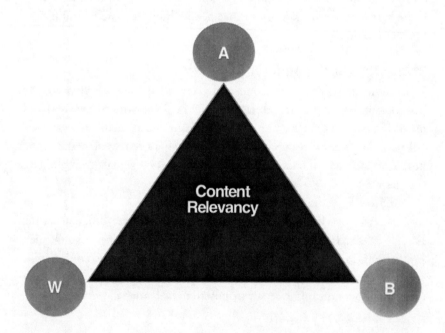

Imagine a triangle. At the right apex is the brand. At the left apex is the audience. At the top is the world. In order to find a subject with real –time relevance, our content team has to make a connection between all three elements: What the brand wants to communicate. What the audience is going to be interested in, and most importantly, what is happening in the world. It sounds harder than it is. For instance, if we are working on Nike, and there is a blizzard happening on the East Coast, we might want to create content about fun sports to do in the snow for our East Coast audience with a call to action to check out Nike's All Condition Gear line. Simple, right? It is relevant to the audience, it is relevant to what is happening in the world right now, and it is relevant to the brand.

21.4. Creation

There is a library full of books that can help you with physically "how" to create content – how to write, how to shoot video, edit images, create layouts. These are all skills your team should already possess. This is about the production process itself, and we don't think it's necessary to go into details on exactly how to create every type of content. It is important to know that this is the part of the process where creation happens, where the rubber meets the road and your content creators do their jobs. They do the one thing that no technology will ever replace. They create.

21.5. Editorial & optimization – QA

In traditional media they call it "editorial." In programming and developing, they call it "QA" (quality assurance). We prefer the latter term. The editorial process for digital goes way beyond just editorial. In fact, there are four things that need to happen to a piece of digital content before it goes live: search optimization, web readability, traditional editing, and browser testing.

Search – This is where all of the keyword editing takes place. While keywords might not be as important as they were in 2011, they're still important. And it's still possible to have too many or too few in a piece of written content. This requires more than a basic understanding of search engine optimization, and it takes a little practice to get right.

Google is not the only platform that uses an algorithm to make decisions about which content to show a user. YouTube is the world's second largest search engine, with totally different criteria than Google search.

Have you heard of EdgeRank? This is Facebook's algorithm for whether a piece of content will appear on a person's timeline or not. Given that the default setting for its news feed is top stories, content marketers need to pay attention to a few factors to help their stories rise to the top of their fans' and followers' news feeds. EdgeRank looks at the content connected with each user, and ranks it in importance to that user. By measuring the factors of affinity, weight, and time decay, Facebook knows whether and where to rank a particular piece of content.

Web Readability – People don't read websites. They scan them. Look at any eye tracking study and you'll most likely see a consistent E or F pattern of eye movement.[15]

This is how people consume information online. Let me say this again: They do not read websites. If they did Google would display search results in big paragraphs, not in an E shaped pattern of blocked headlines. Unlike the papers you wrote in college, web articles and blog posts don't need to be thick, dense blocks of text with nary a glimmer of white space showing. Instead, following the "short words, short sentences, short paragraphs" idea, there needs to be plenty of white space (also called "negative space") in articles. That white space makes your piece look like it's easily digestible. People will move from one paragraph to the next thinking, "Just one more. Just one more." Before they know it, they're at the end of the article. Use bullet points, block quotes, knockouts and other visual layout tactics to break up your "word walls."

Traditional Editing – This is just the basic editing every piece of written content should have. The editor is looking for typos, misspelled words, grammar and punctuation errors. Traditional editing. The editor needs to have a better –than –basic grasp of editorial grammar and rules, AP Style and Chicago Manual, but they also need to be willing to follow common day –to –day and colloquial usage, rather than making everything sound like we are paying attention to the strict rules we all learned in the seventh grade. That is not how most people talk, and in general, the language expectation online is grammatically correct, but conversational English (or whatever language you're working in for global and international brands).

Translation for International Brands – If you're working in multiple languages, this is where we would insert a cultural translator. With rich

---

15 http://www.squidoo.com/heat–map

media, translation should happen at the script stage. This need exists for more brands than you think, and like politics, all marketing is local. We won't spend a lot of time on this, but this is the point in your editorial process where translation should be inserted for text content.

Browser testing: Once your content has been optimized, edited and laid out for great web readability, it is critical to ensure it is going to render properly in multiple browsers. This becomes an issue especially when dealing with embedded content, like a YouTube video or a photo gallery or some other external media source within an article or post. Test your content to ensure it is rendering correctly in the major browsers (Chrome, Internet Explorer, Firefox, Safari) as well as in mobile browsers. There are lots of tools out there for this, like Adobe BrowserLab, Cross Browser Testing, and Litmus.

21.6. Leveraging external content sources

In addition to creating content, your team will want to look for opportunities to gather content from external sources. In fact, lots of brands rely on third -party and crowd -sourced content to help drive engagement with their owned media properties. This content should be treated no differently than if it came from one of your content creators. It should go through the same editorial and distribution process whenever possible.

Pepsi's recent "Live for Now" effort is a great example of leveraging external content sources to drive brand engagement. They have turned their main website presence, pepsi.com, into a beautiful display of content created mostly by consumers and other traditional news sources like Reuters and ABC News, as well as news sources more closely related to their brand and more relevant to their audience, like Complex and Buzzfeed.

What is important to understand when leveraging these sources – whether it's your audience, your employees or syndicated content resources – is that third -party content is not free. It still has to be curated and managed. Much of it can be automated, but your owned media team will still need to be involved with this content. Whether it's through editorial and optimization when dealing with content coming from your audience or internal content sources and subject matter experts, or by curating consumer generated content or content from other publishers.

Curated content has been all the rage for the last several years – finally, an endless supply of content! Everyone was so excited about finding and sharing interesting content that everyone forgot that brands still need someone to create content specific to the brand's business objectives. It was like everyone got so excited about museums, they forgot they needed the artists to paint and sculpt.

The main problem with using content from third –party sources is that they don't care about your business objectives. Remember, the whole reason you're doing this? Consumers and third –party generalist publishers don't have your business needs in mind when they are creating content. They are trying to accomplish the same thing you are – they are sharing or creating content that they think will be interesting to their audience, for their own specific benefit. You're going to grow audience and ultimately get people to buy from you, or even believe you or trust you, only if you're creating the content they're looking for. Curation of third –party sources can help in lots of ways, but it is still critical for the brand to make original content and participate in dialogue with customers if you want to influence your owned media in a way that delivers on the intended business objectives. You can't rely on these kinds of sources to get you where you want to be. You can only rely on them to accomplish the functional delivery of "some" content, not necessarily the "right" content for your business needs.

Third –party content sources can create great generalized content, but this should be considered another tool in the toolbox for your team, not a means to an end to provide endless amounts of content. It may be good, it may be relevant and it may drive some metrics for you. But alone, it will usually not lead to the outcome you're looking for because with much of the syndicated and curated content approaches that are easily available, at the end of the click path, the user is not landing on your owned media; they are landing on someone else's. Meaning, someone else's owned media strategy is working. Maybe you should consider syndicating your content, too?

22. MANAGE

Managing content is one of the messiest jobs on Earth. It will likely always be an exercise in chaos management because only humans can make content, and managing that content means also managing the humans making it. The function here is not just managing the content, but managing the resources and timelines of the people who are making it, internally and externally, and distributing it in the most effective way possible. We need to make sure we are going through all the appropriate governance channels and getting the appropriate approvals – including managing the revisions process – and we need to make decisions about which channels to publish it on and when. Without this step, content just sits there. We need to get the content in front of people. Let's get it out there!

22.1. Assignments, timelines, and resource management

At Raidious, we have one person in each of our pods who functions as a director and is responsible for task assignments and managing timelines and resources. Some organizations have dedicated project managers who oversee this part of the process. A big part of managing the content and the team is understanding your resources and how to apply those resources based on the audience metrics.

Depending on how your team is structured, it will be important to clarify how deliverables are assigned, and by whom. At Raidious, the producer would assign a deliverable based on the audience data (like a blog post or an infographic), and the director would assign related tasks to individual specialists in the pod based on their workload. Timelines – like due dates and where things are falling in the production cycle – are also taken into consideration when deliverables and tasks are assigned. It is also the director's responsibility to find additional resources to deliver the deliverable if resources are not available in house. Typically, the task would be assigned to someone in another pod who has availability, or if we have to, we go to our network of part –timers and freelancers.

Defining exactly how your team is going to manage the nuts and bolts of producing content and managing resources will be key to your success and your ability to hit deadlines at high levels of quality, and ultimately, to move the business outcome needle.

22.2. Governance, revisions and approval

Getting content through the governance, revisions, and approval stage is the most dangerous time for a piece of content. This is where your team must learn to "own" its product and learn to defend it. It is all too easy for external people in other areas of the organization to want to make changes that are either truly unnecessary or downright damaging to the content. It's OK for your team to push back on quality issues and content issues. They are the ones being held accountable to the success of the content.

If we have done the right due diligence in discovery and risk and distribution, we should be making content that will sail through this part of the process. More often than not, lawyers, public relations and marketing people want to play executive producer and make small and usually meaningless tweaks to content. Empower your team to squash that kind of behavior early, or your company will never be able to get out of its own way long enough to get to a real –time scenario. A three –day –old tweet is not helpful to anyone.

There are only two answers we want from people in the approval process – yes or no.

- Yes, it is approved.
- No, it is not approved. Here's why.

That's it. No editorializing, no rewrites, no markups. People in the approval path always want to help, but believe me, you do not want their help. You just want them to do their job – giving you one of those two answers – as quickly as possible, so you can keep the process moving.

There are a lot of good reasons approvals get hung up. It might be that the approver does not want to hurt anyone's feelings. It might be that the content is not written the way the approver would have written it. Maybe there's a political or relationship issue. To have a successful owned media program, these kinds of barriers must be removed. Make it brutally simple and as black and white as possible to approve content, and make sure the approvers understand the sense of urgency with which this needs to happen. We can't really overstate how important this is.

In some office cultures, this might be difficult to accomplish, but it is one area we would recommend pushing very hard on until you get the process to this level of simplicity. This is the one thing that absolutely kills agility and responsiveness across the board in every size of organization. It is a necessary step to take, however. Make sure you take the necessary steps to communicate with everyone in the approval path exactly what you need from them – two simple things, yes and no. Nothing else.

22.3. Distribution and optimization

In developing our strategy, we defined the voices and accounts we would use to publish content, as well as its distribution and governance path. We did not talk about "how much, what kind, where, or when" in strategy. This is done very purposefully to keep you from marketing by assumption or opinion. There is no right answer for these questions; there is only experimentation and optimization.

Based on the signals we are seeing and interpreting in our audience data, we will need to make decisions about which content to publish where and when. Optimizing distribution is all about understanding how to apply your audience data to making decisions about each piece of content. This also plays into decisions about future content assignments. Test. Optimize. Repeat.

This is one of the most difficult things in the book to really illustrate because the answers are going to be different for every brand, every channel and every piece of content. The best we can do here is help you understand what questions you should be asking in this stage of production. All the answers will come from your audience, and the data they are providing you in analytics. Your team's interpretation, insights and creative applications of those insights will drive not only how your content is distributed, but what content is made moving forward. It is, very literally, an ongoing science experiment. Here are some examples of questions to ask as your team is reviewing audience data and making decisions about where, when and how to publish each piece of content:

Voices – If you have a multi –voice approach as part of your strategy, start here: Which voices are doing well? Which ones are not and why? Which voices would this content work for?

Channels – Which channels can I use to distribute this content? Which channels <u>should</u> I use to distribute it? How will the formatting need to be adjusted for each? Will it work in email? Will it work as a blog post? Is this particular subject performing well in one specific channel? Is this particular content type performing well in one specific channel?

Platforms – Which specific social media platforms? Which specific email programs? Which specific blogs? Which video sharing sites?

Accounts – If you are working with multiple accounts within a given platform – multiple Twitter handles or multiple Facebook pages – which specific accounts should this content be published to?

Day and Time – When does my content typically perform best across all my channels, and specifically in the channels I am considering for this content? Is there a specific day or time where users are consistently more engaged? Keep in mind, this can become a self –fulfilling prophecy. If you get the best engagement on Wednesdays at 2 p.m. on Facebook, and you choose to publish your best content only then, guess what your best day and time will be the following week? Another approach would be to look at your lowest engagement days and times and use content then to help with those numbers. Make sure you test this variable regularly. Minutes matter.

Content Type – What types of content are moving the numbers best? Does video do better than images? Is there any relation to the type of channel it's being published on? Is the performance of the content because of the content type or the subject matter? (Hint: Usually it is the latter. A good story is a good story, regardless of how it's presented. If the story itself is compelling enough, you should be able to make it work in any form and in any channel).

Subject / Topic – Which subjects and topics are working best? This is more complicated than it sounds. Is my post about rubber bracelets getting traffic because it's also about bicycling, Lance Armstrong, the Tour de France, the LiveStrong Foundation, or the doping allegations? Understanding what is really driving the numbers at the subject level is going to be somewhat subjective and interpretive, but it's an important issue in optimizing both distribution and future content.

Frequency – How much content have I published to each channel, and how is that affecting the audience? Am I seeing any dips or gains in reach in different combinations of channels? Is that a frequency issue, or is it some other factor?

Author – In a multi –author environment, this is something to look at. Every content correspondent we have at Raidious has a specific analytics report attached to his performance. Looking at audience data by author can help you understand how your team is performing. Some may do better in certain channels than others, which is another consideration in optimizing distribution and future content assignments.

Real –Time Optimization – Technology recently has enabled content creators to automate their distribution through real –time optimization. Tools such as SocialFlow are a great example of this. SocialFlow uses real –time audience activity to determine the best time to publish content. Its findings have been interesting. For instance, with some platforms like Twitter, the available audience – people online and on Twitter at any given moment – can swing as much as 30,000 people from one minute to the next. This is what real –time optimization is all about. The difference between posting a tweet at 10:15 and 10:16 could be 30,000 people, which is worth about $1,500 at a $50 cost per thousand. The Internet is a constantly shifting audience of people logging in and out, checking in and checking out, surfing and shutting down. Understanding how to leverage the "tide" of your audience as it moves from high tide to low tide and back again on the fly can be powerful for your owned media program.

22.4. Understanding audience burn

We will discuss this in more detail in the Measure section, but it is important to touch on this in this section. Your audience is likely to see your content in more than one channel. That compounds its frequency. Frequency is the No. 1 killer of audiences. Our theory is that frequency is not the only driver. If the content quality is high enough and relevant enough, frequency will become a non –issue. But most brands, and even seasoned publishers, can't be relevant, compelling and remarkable to every single person in their audience every time they publish content, so the audience eventually gets some content that is not interesting to them. If this happens enough, they unfriend, unfollow and unsubscribe. They disengage. We don't want this to happen.

Many marketers who have some technical sense will look at this section of the book and wonder, "Why don't we just use a tool and publish everything to one place and push it everywhere automatically? That sounds a lot easier!"

NO! This is the worst thing you can do.

Don't be a one –click pony. If it worked, we would already be doing it. The reason why is audience burn – the compounding of frequency across multiple online channels. If I'm friends with you on Facebook, following you on Twitter and subscribing to your email, every time you publish something in your "one ring to rule them all" approach to distribution, I see that damn content three times. That is two more times than I need to see it. If you keep doing this, I am not only checking out of the relationship, I am probably going to publicly chastise you for spamming me, and then you'll have to make content just for me, when you respond and apologize.

Plus, every channel has its own set of rules – its own "dialect", let's call it – and content has to be adjusted to fit those rules. For instance, don't use @replies and #hashtags on LinkedIn. It does nothing but confuse people who are not Twitter users, and if they are Twitter users, they are going to be like "put that on Twitter, weirdo." (Having said that, the week we were editing this book, Facebook was discussing whether to start using hashtags in status updates.)

Customize your content to suit the dialect and best practices of the channels you choose. Don't just stuff it all in a fire hose and spray it all over everyone. It's not TV, people! It's a long –tail world of individual interests. Serve them and their needs, and don't be lazy about it by automatically cross posting everything to every channel. That can be one of the quickest ways to lose audience, especially if you equate volume with success. Getting content published is not success. Making something amazing that your audience values and tells their friends about, who all ultimately buy your product? That's success. It's not a one –click publishing solution, you have to do the hard work.

23. MONITOR

Now that your content has been published, we want to focus on monitoring that content and the content others are making about your brand. This is the part of production that enables your brand to respond in real –time. We can't be responsive unless we listen first.

23.1. Prioritizing your monitoring efforts

Monitoring is a fairly new art and science, and it is important to be empathetic to that. Monitoring will most likely not catch every single thing about your brand. Your monitoring team is likely to miss some things and to get "scooped" occasionally. It's a very big Internet. No matter how many queries and monitoring streams you have running, no matter how good your tools are, no matter how many bodies you have listening, you will not catch it all. Focus your resources on listening for what is most important to your brand. You can use your global taxonomy to help you prioritize.

- Your customers/your audience
- Influential sources from your watch list
- Other people talking about your brand
- Competitors
- Partners and vendors
- Category conversations (non –brand)

23.2. Off Channel vs. On Channel

Monitoring is an often misunderstood activity. Some people think check-ing your Facebook feed for comments is monitoring. It is, sort of. It is a version of monitoring. Others think creating a Google Reader feed full of search terms means you're monitoring your brand. You are, kind of. But there is a lot more to it than this. Let's start by understanding on –channel and off –channel monitoring.

23.2.1. On –channel monitoring

On –channel monitoring is monitoring for all the dialogue and responses that are happening **on** our owned media channels. We are only interested in our audience here, not the Internet at large. These are the online rela-tionships we have worked hard on and spent significant time and dollars to acquire, and many of them are probably going to be customers, or are on their way to becoming customers, if we are doing our jobs well.

Earlier in the book, we explained the relationship between voices, channels, platforms and accounts. We use the term "channel" instead of "platform" here because we want to apply our monitoring in an audi-ence –centric way, not in a platform –centric way. We want to monitor so-cial, email, web, mobile, and every other online channel we own or control, not just Facebook or Twitter. Most brands limit this function only to social, but someone should be looking at requests that come in from the website and all the forms you probably have there, as well as blog comments, re-plies to marketing emails (they should definitely be getting an unsubscribe and unread report, so those people in your email audience can be engaged with to find out what we missed, or what we are missing, from a content perspective), and any consumer dialogue coming from the mobile space, including things like location –based check ins. It's a central function for all owned media, not just your social media channels. Every digital medium is a two –way medium, and they all need to be monitored so they can be responded to.

23.2.2 Off –channel monitoring

Off –channel monitoring is monitoring for all the dialogue related to, ad-dressed to, or about your brand and other related topics you or your audi-ence might be interested in. This is a much bigger job than monitoring on channel. As with on –channel monitoring, we are not just interested in what people are saying on Twitter. We are interested in finding any content of any type that gets published anywhere on any online platform. This may sound impossible, and to some degree it is – like we said, there are going to be things that get missed, sooner or later. We can't drink the ocean, but we can take a few meaningful sips.

A big part of monitoring involves going beyond the tool you're using. Sitting in front of Radian6 or Sysomos MAP all day and generating a report once a week is not going to cut it. Good engagement team members will be constantly drilling down. They're drilling down into the conversation, into the users participating in the conversation. They are drilling down into the numbers to figure out what's moving where, and why, and drilling down into the content and how it is performing. It helps to get out of the tool and into the platform, or into the account level for a fresh look. It also helps to use multiple tools to cross reference your assumptions. For instance, if you see a rise in volume about a given topic in off –channel monitoring, check it against your on –channel metrics to see if this is interesting to your existing audience as well. Or conversely, check your community's trends against the Internet at large.

The engagement manager has to be able to step back to the macro view and be able to identify and escalate trend intelligence. Being able to identify a trend is a critical skill for engagement managers. Trend data is one of the things that drives content decisions that enable the brand to leverage time relevance and to stay current, and hopefully ahead of the conversations that are happening. A simple for instance: If we see an upward trend of people talking more about Product A, and nobody really talking about Product B, we can create some fresh new content about Product A, join the conversation, and use it to re –introduce some additional fresh new content about Product B. The tool and the basic reporting are not where the value is. The value is in finding actionable, real –time insights and establishing the ability to respond to those situations opportunistically on the fly.

It's also worth mentioning here that monitoring is not just about monitoring conversation metrics. Query metrics from search are a great tool to use for monitoring your audience, as are your email and website and mobile analytics. Having a good handle on what your audience is doing across all these platforms – every day, not just once a month or once a quarter – can lead to some great insights.

23.3. Refining your watch list

Your watch list is your directory of content sources that are relevant to your brand, but you don't own or control, including your influencers. We defined influencers in strategy, but as you monitor, you will most likely find additional influentials, both within the parameters established for an influencer and outside those parameters. Remember, these sources can be individuals or organizations or other traditional publishers. As part of your monitoring efforts, make sure you are updating your watch lists with new influencers, communities, and other relevant sources.

23.4. Refining queries

In the engagement portion of our strategy, we also built our first queries. We also mentioned that the strategy is a living document and should be updated regularly, particularly for query building. Your queries will constantly shift, like sand in the desert. It's important to take a science experiment approach to query building and constantly be testing them to see if there are any adjustments that can be made to allow for more signal (useful information) and less noise (irrelevant information).

Over time, you will develop your general queries to a fairly consistent point. These are the ones to spend the most time on early on so you can spend more time on developing situations you will need to watch. You will also be able to refine your watch lists over time – the most important and relevant sources for your monitoring efforts. Both of these activities – and documenting them – will lead to a more focused, efficient, and effective monitoring effort over time.

23.5. Filtering

In addition to refining your queries, you will also want to experiment with filtering to tweak the signal –to –noise ratio of content coming in through monitoring. The whole idea with monitoring is to identify threats and opportunities as quickly as possible, and get them escalated and responded to as quickly as possible. The clock is ticking, and filtering can help you find what you're looking for in your query results more quickly.

Recency is the first factor. How recently did they send their message? And how quickly do you have to respond? If you have messages that are 23 hours old, and you have a 24 –hour response time guarantee, then you know which ones you need to escalate first. But do we need to escalate and respond within the first two minutes of receiving a complaint? Not necessarily.

Regardless of all of these things, whenever possible, you should never <u>not</u> respond to a message from a customer whenever possible. Even if you were able to call that person directly, don't let anyone else who sees the message think you didn't do anything. Even if your message is "Thanks for talking with me on the phone today. I'm glad we could help," send it. That lets everyone else know that you're taking care of all your customers.

Here are some basic techniques to use:

Sentiment – Filtering by sentiment – positive, negative, and neutral – can help you find threats and opportunities faster, and it helps prioritize your escalations. Escalate negative first, then positive.

Geography – Limiting your scope to specific geographies can greatly improve your visibility. Don't monitor Europe and Asia and Africa if you're only concerned with the U.S. If your brand only has locations on the East Coast, we are probably not going to be as concerned with dialogue from California. If you have an event, focus on the city where the event is.

Keywords – Filtering out pesky keywords that show up in your queries when they shouldn't can vastly improve your results.

Reach – Filtering sources by level of reach is a good way to prioritize your monitoring and escalation efforts. Where are the biggest threats and opportunities with the biggest potential audiences?

Sources – Likewise, if you are getting lots of irrelevant content from a specific source, you can filter that as well. For off –channel monitoring, you may also want to filter out your owned media channels, so you are not seeing the same information twice. You should have already dealt with that content in on –channel monitoring.

Influence – Filtering by influence can also help you more quickly get to the stuff that matters most. This is particularly helpful in high –volume situations and crisis scenarios. Deal with the stuff that has the highest threat or opportunity level first.

Activity – You may notice some sources are way more active than others in your audience. If the content is frequent and relevant, but the source or user has a tiny audience, or gets no amplification from their audience, it is probably OK to filter this source out.

23.6. Alerts, reporting and intelligence

Much of your time spent in monitoring will be communicating what you find back to the team in the form of alerts, reports, and intelligence. We defined the parameters for these in planning, but expect this to become a moving target. As your brand becomes more comfortable with the idea of monitoring, more and more requests for specialized reporting – and more drill –down into the reports you have already provided – will be coming your way.

Engagement managers will often be called on to explain exactly "what this means" – either more detail on exactly what is being measured or what insights are available based on the data. Be prepared for this. Make sure you understand how your tool reports data, what the error factors are, and what the data sources are. Is it scanning Twitter, or are we looking at API (application programming interface) level data, or is it the "full Twitter firehose?" You may have to explain very complicated information to people who have never set up a Facebook account or have never even seen Twitter. They exist. Lots of them. Mostly in the C –suite.

As with any good content, ensure your reporting is right for the audience. The report you give your team or your boss, may need to be very different than the report you send to the C –suite. As with alerts, it is very helpful to define specific alert parameters, contents, metrics to include, framework and formatting in advance. What should this report include, and how will it be formatted/communicated in an easy –to –understand way?

23.7. Escalation parameters

The escalation parameters we set up in strategy should, tactically, be considered "guardrails," not a black and white guide to what to escalate. Your escalation parameters are another thing that will change over time as you become more familiar with your audience, and as your audience shifts and changes and grows. This is something to keep a close eye on the first year or two – as in, check it at least every week to make sure you are escalating the right information to the right people. You don't really have any control over the volume of the information that comes to you, but some people on your team may decide they don't need to see every single @reply and every single Facebook comment that comes through. They may finally decide that a Klout score of 50 does not necessarily make someone an influencer after reading through hundreds of Twitter posts from people with a Klout score of 50. Don't be afraid to play with your escalation parameters to dial them in over time, but keep your team in the loop about it. When you miss something (and you will), make sure everyone else is on board about changing the rules before you change them.

24. MODERATE

Moderation is the act of participating in or presiding over a debate or a dialogue. This is where the reactive content is made. Content is identified in monitoring and escalated for moderation. Content is produced in response that goes through the same production process – creation, editorial, governance and approval, additional moderation if needed and measurement. This is not always simple text responses to comments. We may want to respond to something with a video or an infographic or a white paper. If a member of our audience makes a fun video about us, maybe we want to make a fun response video. If someone publishes a disparaging infographic about our brand's ecological practices, maybe we should respond with an infographic about how green the brand really is. Proactive or reactive, regardless of content type or platform, the content follows the same process. Very simple.

Some people call this function community management, but in our experience, people think about managing specific communities on specific platforms when we say that – and ultimately, it is just another piece of content. But many people want to discuss how to manage their Facebook community, manage their Twitter community, manage the community on the message boards, the blog community, or the community on their custom –built branded social network. We don't really see it that way. We see it more like moderating the dialogue – not the channel. We are not managing a community. We are managing content within a community, being generated by members of the community. Communities exist with or without the technology that further enables their connections. We want to be responsive to content others create about the brand, regardless of where it "lives."

24.1. Moderating dialogue vs. community management

We have a platform agnostic worldview – the community exists. It can choose to engage with us on any number of online platforms, or it can engage without us on its own platforms. But the community – what we call the audience – exists with or without the technology.

Let's talk about social networks for a minute, while we are making our point. Community management, as a practice in corporate marketing, came about to satisfy the need for moderation and response in social media. The only problem is all these platforms like Facebook and Twitter and LinkedIn are not, technically, social networks. They are social network services. They enable communication between people with a common bond. They don't create that bond; they help people discover it exists.

Social networks are the people you went to elementary school with. They are the people you play softball with, or the people you maybe go to church with. If you play music, musicians are probably in your social network. If you play Dungeons and Dragons, that is your social network. A social network is a community of people with common interests. That community exists, with or without Facebook and Twitter and LinkedIn and all the other social network services. Let's not forget, at the end of every online interaction, there is not just content – there is a person. A human. That can be easy to forget with all the clicking and strategizing and data flying around.

24.2. The obligation of participation

When we talk about moderation, we are talking about participating as a leader – a moderator – in a community of common interest. The community is primarily an audience or a community built around a common thread – the core idea behind your brand. It's not your brand, but what your brand stands for. To go back to the example we used in our subject topography exercise, if you're Nike, your community is about athletic endeavor. That is the common bond. There are lots of sub –communities that exist within that, like people who play basketball, and people who play soccer. And beyond that, there are more sub –communities … and beyond that … and so on. That is the long tail; there is an audience or community for almost everything you can imagine – including your brand promise.

This has all kinds of tactical implications for our process. This means we are focused on the dialogue wherever it occurs – on channel or off channel. We should be participating in this community, with this audience, because the common thread that connects us is the most important thing to our organization – not our brand or products – our brand promise, the thing we have agreed to deliver to our customers and potential customers – our community, our audience.

The way that media has evolved has made this part of our process non –negotiable. Being a good shepherd for your brand – and at the executive level, having a fiduciary duty to protect it – means you are obligated to participate in the community around it. It is difficult to understand, more difficult to accept, and even more difficult to take action on for many marketers, but this is the way of the world. Just pushing out content is not enough. Just listening is not enough. Active participation is now a requirement for marketers. This is one of the reasons having an owned media function in place is so critical in the 21st century and beyond.

24.3. Influencing dialogue online

When we talk about moderating dialogue, we are just talking about another content problem. Dialogue is just more content, generated by the audience. It could be a comment on a blog post, or a tweet, or even an image, or a blog post or a video. It could happen on channel or off channel, with or without you, publicly or privately, but dialogue is going to happen.

User –generated content is usually outside your control. You can't always affect it, change it, avoid it, or edit it. User generated content is not just what your audience is saying on your platforms. It is what other people are saying about you on review sites like Yelp, through customer reviews like Google Reviews, and on their own blogs, tweets and Facebook updates. If you're doing a good job with your company, the content will be positive. If you're not, it won't be. But it's how you respond to this content that will make or break your efforts. Not responding is not an option.

24.4. Moderating negative content

Despite what your legal team may tell you, ignoring content others make about your brand – from the smallest tweet to the "yourbrandsucks.com" microsite – is rarely an option or a wise decision. This content is not just affecting you, it is affecting the entire community around your brand. Fighting back is also not typically a good option. That oftentimes makes you seem like an aggressive bully, rather than a fair and balanced participant in the community – especially if your legal team leads the charge and starts sending legal –sounding letters or posting very stern, legal –sounding responses. This rarely leads to anything good.

For negative content, the best response is usually to try and take the conversation offline, ideally via telephone. Email is another option, but that content is only private as long as the recipient decides it is. If they want to create a blog post or a video out of it, or quote it in a tweet, they will. Try to engage the other person in conversation, offer to fix any problems, apologize for any inconvenience, thank them for any compliments, and, regardless of whether they're complimenting or complaining, thank them for being a customer. Your responses to the user –generated content are also content, and it can be found and shared just as easily as everything else you publish. So be a good moderator. Be a good human. Even if you don't solve the problem, you will at least be creating content that shows you made an effort.

24.5. Moderating positive content

This is much easier and much more pleasant. Every piece of positive content about your company is an opportunity waiting to be fulfilled. At the basic level, at a minimum, you can amplify this content by sharing it with the rest of your audience, who might not have seen it. You can, with permission, reuse this content. Mash it up. Make a video out of it. Create an image gallery of positive user –generated content screen grabs. Link to it on Facebook and Twitter. This content is extremely powerful because it is coming from someone other than you. Marketers have understood the power of testimonials and endorsements for a long time, and that is what we have here – an implied endorsement or testimonial. Even if somebody just says "Brand X is awesome!" That is probably worth curating and sharing and amplifying.

24.6. Response flow charts

In strategy, your team may have built out response flowcharts for known issues and potential situations. As you participate in the dialogue on your owned media channels, and in external platforms and communities, you may find yourself posting and reposting the same responses. Make sure you track these and circulate them back to your team. New issues you uncover in your online conversations typically make great content ideas, and if there are issues you are repeatedly addressing, you may want to invest some resources in making some more in –depth or more high –quality content you can reference with a simple link during your moderation efforts. Then you can move the issue from a response flowchart to a FAQ, which is going to be more of a copy –and –paste affair than the discovery that might be necessary in a response flow chart.

If you've got a small business or your marketing department is more entrepreneurial and free, this can be much easier: Work under the guiding principle of "first, do no harm," and go from there. Apologize to the negative reviewer, and invite them to visit again. Apologize to the blogger, and send them a can cozy, t –shirt and commemorative gift. Answer the Twitter question. Respond to the forum comment. Be as helpful as you can, and make sure that the person who asked/commented/reviewed is happy, or at least satisfied with your response.

But if you have a larger organization or need more structure than this, then it's more than appropriate to have a series of frequently asked questions and response flowcharts. We always encourage clients to develop a FAQ page for their website, and then to delve into each of those questions more deeply as individual blog posts or other content. For one thing, it helps with search – meaning, it makes it easier for your users to find the answers they are looking for. For another, it can give a lot more detail on the topic than just the answer to a question, and oftentimes that is just what the person is looking for.

24.7. FAQs

Like the rest of your documentation, you will need to keep your FAQs updated as you identify recurring questions and issues. Again, if there are high volumes of the same questions over and over, you might want to consider investing in more compelling or interesting content – or content that is easier to find – to address those issues.

If you want to see a good FAQ/support operation in action, look at Apple's support page. Anytime someone has a topic, an individual page is generated where users can answer the question themselves, as well as representatives from Apple's support team. In some cases, the users are answering questions much faster than the support team can.

The net result of this: Apple is not only building content that boosts its search engine ranking (Google a question about syncing your iPad with your computer's iTunes, and see how high Apple.com's answer appears), but it also helps Apple build a community of enthusiastic users who will help defend the brand if the need ever arose.

24.8. Proactive Engagement

The idea of proactive engagement is difficult for many brands to get their heads around. This is part of the moderation process. The idea of being proactive about engagement means meeting the audience members on their terms, and sometimes on their platforms. Finding pre –existing communities and platforms online, and maintaining an active presence within them, is enabled by monitoring and moderation.

Let's say you work for Chevrolet. There are lots of die –hard loyalists for this brand, and many "splinter" communities around the products they have produced over the years. Camaro clubs, Corvette clubs and probably Volt clubs. These communities may stay in touch with their own online platforms – message boards, community websites or even specific social networks, which are really easy to build these days thanks to companies like Ning. Chevrolet should be finding ways to contribute to and participate in these communities, using their platforms. Just like these people can come to "Chevy's House" – your owned media properties – and participate, Chevy should be going to "their houses" – the platforms they use to stay connected.

This is easier on platforms like Twitter and Facebook, but many communities have built their own worlds, their own platforms, that are built just for their community. Finding ways to connect to these communities proactively is easier than it may seem, especially if you can add value to the community – like, for instance, with some high –value content. Whatever you do, don't go to these people's home and try to sell them something. Engage. Moderate the dialogue. Provide value. Your ROI on this kind of activity is going to come from all the positive content this community will generate on your behalf, your ability to amplify it and how it will impact your audience.

24.9. Scale

If your brand has a customer service department, the people in this department should be a part of the moderation effort for specific customer –service issues. Depending on what kinds of issues you have, and whether or not you knew about them before you started your owned media effort, you may need to create or scale up a customer service function to deal with the volume of dialogue. You want your owned media team focused on moving the marketing needle, and customer service is intrinsically tied to marketing and sales. But if it is taking up more than half of your moderation resources, it is probably time to move that function over to the customer service team, which is better equipped to handle those kinds of things.

Your owned media team should have oversight of this function and provide guidance to customer service (or any other areas of the enterprise involved in owned media), but if the volume of customer service escalations is extreme, it needs its own resources. (Or you could just fix whatever is broken, which is probably a better move.)

Moderation is the ultimate in real –time branding. You have all the tools and guidance you need to make it work for you, but make sure you use those tools. Don't let response time be the only driver of your next actions. Take the time to figure out the solution to the problem, refer to your script and process flow charts, and make sure you do it <u>right</u> before you do it <u>fast</u>.

25. MEASURE

25.1. Understanding what to measure

Understanding data across multiple channels is a challenge no matter how much technology you invest in or how smart your people are. It is a moving target in terms of how audience data is captured, the source, what it is actually measuring, how accurate the reporting is from one tool to the next, and how it is interpreted from one analyst to the next. The important thing to consider when measuring audience from an owned media perspective is all the different things the data can be used to measure. Your audience data will literally tell you everything you want to know about your brand if you understand how to apply it.

In planning, during our business case section, we identified our business goals. A 2011 research project by Altimeter Research, *A Framework for Social Analytics*, reported on how a number of brands tie their goals to audience metrics. Your goals will probably fall into one of these six categories, identified in Altimeter's research:

Innovation – How can the brand collaborate with or leverage its customers to drive innovation in future products or services?

Brand Health – What are the attitudes, perceptions, awareness levels, conversations and behaviors of our audience?

Customer Experience – How can we identify and understand opportunities and threats related to the customer's overall experience with the brand, and our products or services?

Operational Efficiency – How can we reduce expenses, labor time, shorten workflow cycles, and find other ways to drive operational efficiencies?

Revenue Generation – How can the brand generate more revenue through exisiting revenue sources or by discovering new ones?

Marketing Optimization – How can we use audience data to understand and positively impact the effectiveness of our marketing efforts?

In the measure portion of the five M's, we are looking for specific metrics to impact specific business objectives. These are the key performance indicators we identified in our business case, and as you can see, they will likely go well beyond the basic measurement of the audience itself. Tying your metrics back to the key performance indicators you identified in your business case is the answer to the most important question your company is sure to ask you, and one of the best questions to ask in business: So what?

Your audience is bigger. So what? It's more engaged. So what?

More people clicked through or converted or we showed up more in search. So what?

How can we connect these measurements of audience to how it impacts our business?

The measure part of the five M's should accomplish two things. The first and most important accomplishment is helping the organization understand how your efforts are impacting the business. The second is helping your team understand how your efforts are impacting the audience. Without an audience, there is not going to be any intelligence to share about your business. This is pretty profound – so let's repeat:

Without an audience, there is not going to be any intelligence to share about your business.

This means two very different areas of focus in your reporting – one focused on your business key performance indicators and one focused on the health of the audience itself.

25.2. Omnichannel publishing and audience burn

Your audience experiences content in multiple channels. Some people may spend more time with Facebook and email than with Twitter and text messaging. Others may spend a lot of time on multiple channels. Regardless, there is likely to be some channel overlap in your audience, so your publishing frequency is compounded. This results in audience burn – the No. 1

reason people unfriend, unfollow, unsubscribe or otherwise opt out of your audience is too much frequency. When the net loss of audience exceeds the net gain, you have audience burn.

Are you over publishing or under publishing? Are you losing people because you're posting too much or not enough? What is the half –life of your of content? What does the engagement level look like – an hour before it drops off? Or a few minutes? Is it getting buried because you published too late in the day, or is not not being seen at all because you published it while everyone was in bed?

Frequency is the total number of times you publish content across all your platforms, not just your blog or website. If a person in your audience is a fan on Facebook, the odds are higher they're also following you on Twitter, receiving your text messages, and subscribed to your email newsletter. So if the frequency of messaging on Facebook is 4.5 times a day, texting is 1 and Twitter is 10, your frequency – the number of times this person has potentially seen content from you – is 15.5 times. The No. 1 reason people unsubscribe on email, unfriend on Facebook, and unfollow on Twitter is because the other person is over publishing. This is what we mean by audience burn.

There's no magic number for what is too much or not enough, so you have to keep track of what the audience is doing. You can see them react to it because when the frequency gets too high, the audience starts unsubscribing, and the half life of your content goes down (the immediate levels of engagement over time, right after publication).

It goes beyond just losing a certain number of people. For example, if you lose enough people on Facebook, EdgeRank will hide your content from your fans because too many people have unfriended or unliked your page. This can be especially bad because if your fans don't engage with you, EdgeRank will also stop showing your content to other people in that channel because of your poor engagement levels and declining audience. Like us, Facebook uses the signals from its audience to determine what content to show its users.

But this is not just a Facebook problem. It is a multichannel problem. We need to measure the total audience across all channels for this reason, as well as understanding and comparing similar metrics across channels. Frequency is an important issue, but it is just one small piece of the puzzle. In order to understand how our audience is responding across all channels and to gain the intelligence we need to inform our production process, we need to find metric commonalities across all platforms.

25.3. Total audience analytics

Total Audience Analytics is a framework designed to help you understand how your metrics apply across the entire audience, in addition to the channel, platform, account and content level – and to minimize the No. 1 driver of audience burn.

This is the framework we use to measure our audience in a omnichannel way. These are broad roll ups in the most important metrics categories to review, with short definitions of each. Using the same language across all of your metrics reporting will help your team understand how their efforts are impacting the audience.

25.3.1. Direct reach

Direct reach simply measures your owned media audience size. This is a measurement of the number of people you reach, or have the potential to reach, in a given time period (daily, weekly, monthly, whatever time frame is most applicable to the brand's situation). This number represents your total audience across all your owned media platforms. Specific metrics may include:

- Facebook fans
- Twitter followers
- YouTube subscribers
- Flickr followers
- Unique visits (website/blog)
- Logged –in visits (website)
- Mobile subscribers (Text)
- Total app downloads (apps)

25.3.2. Amplified reach

Amplified reach measures the total number of impressions delivered by your content across all your owned media. Here we are looking for an indication of passalong from your core audience. How is our core audience amplifying our content? How many total people potentially saw our content?

- Facebook newsfeed impressions
- Twitter retweets and mention audience
- Emails delivered
- Total page views
- Website shares
- Syndication views

25.3.3. Activity

Activity is publishing related activity – measures proactive volume and frequency of published content across all of your channels. How much and how often are we publishing content? What impact is that having on reach and amplification?

- Facebook posts
- Twitter tweets
- YouTube videos published
- Flickr uploads
- Email sends
- Blog posts
- Content pushes to mobile app
- Text sends

25.3.4. Engagement

Engagement is a measurement of active audience response to published content. This is going to be a point of discussion and debate, as engagement is seen differently by lots of different people, and there are a lot of opinions on what is and is not engagement. Our recommendation is to choose the metrics that are common across as many channels as you're using that would indicate the user has taken an action – any action – in response to content you have posted – that is not an amplification action. From our perspective, engagement and amplification mean two very different things. When a user is engaged, it doesn't mean they are interested enough or find the content compelling enough to share it with others. It also means they are comfortable with the implied personal endorsement that comes with the action of amplifying or sharing content. Engagement metrics could include:

- Facebook comments
- Twitter mentions
- YouTube comments
- Flickr comments
- Click –throughs

25.3.5. Amplification

Amplification is a measurement of how often your audience members actively retransmit your message to their audience. This is different than amplified reach. This is how often your audience finds your content to be literally remarkable. They have made a conscious decision to share it, to amplify your content to your audience. This is also different than engagement, which indicates the content has moved the audience to take an action in response to your content. Engagement is inward –facing, and amplification is outward facing. Some amplification metrics might include:

- Facebook likes
- Facebook shares
- Twitter retweets
- YouTube favorites
- YouTube shares
- Flickr reposts
- Email forwards

25.4 Conversion

Conversion is measured whenever the audience takes a specific, predefined action. This can be anything we can measure online. It does not necessarily mean conversion to a customer. It means we can confirm the audience took a specific desired action.

- Providing contact information
- Making a specific purchase
- Visiting a specific page
- Completing a series of actions on a website
- Signing up for an email list
- Taking a poll

25.4.1. Sentiment

Sentiment measures the positive and negative connotations of online dialogue about your brand. It is important to measure this metric on channel (our audience) and off channel (the rest of the world). Sentiment analysis should be taken with a grain of salt, as it is typically based on machine language processing. Computers and algorithms do a fairly good job – particularly with large sample sizes – of understanding whether comments are positive, negative or neutral, and in some cases, to what degree. However, a "fairly good job" does not always mean a completely 100 percent accurate view of your audience sentiment. You will need to use humans to verify the data, and clarify what is inaccurate.

- Content is machine classified as positive, negative, neutral and no sentiment.
- Key content is reviewed by humans to ensure accuracy of information.
- Sentiment ratio can be expressed as a ratio of positive to negative sentiment, minus neutral sentiment.
- Make sure you establish a baseline sentiment measure before you launch into any new efforts so you can understand how you are moving the needle.

25.4.2. Passion

The degree to which sentiment is considered positive, negative or neutral is often referred to as a measurement of "passion" about the given topic. The idea here is that it's one thing to say, "I like Product X." while it's another thing to say, "I LOVE Product X! I can't live without it! Everyone should use it! It's AMAZING!" Understanding this metric is important, but as we mentioned above with sentiment, take it with a grain of salt and make sure you use human analysis to verify and clarify.

- Passion can be expressed from neutral to extreme in lots of different ways depending on your software tool of choice and its capabilities.
- Make sure you spend time talking to your software vendor to get clarity on the parameters and methodology for measuring sentiment before you buy.
- If you choose to measure passion, make sure you establish a baseline of this metric.

25.4.3. Dialogue volume

Volume is different than reach. Volume is the total amount of dialogue about a topic, both on channel and off channel. This is the total number of mentions about a topic, regardless of its source. This would include your direct reach, your amplified reach, and every other mention found online about the keyword or query. This is a quantitative indicator of "how much" people are talking about a given query or keyword.

- As with sentiment and passion, it is a good idea to have a human verify and clarify your dialogue volume data.
- Make sure you spend time talking to your software vendor to get clarity on the parameters and methodology for measuring volume before you buy – particularly with regards to duplicative data.
- Establishing an early baseline for dialogue volume so you have norms to compare to will be very helpful in the long run.

25.4.3. Share of voice

Share of voice is an expression of how much of the dialogue volume is about your brand. For instance, if we wanted to see share of voice for Audi, we might use the query "cars" and break down by competitor brand mentions AND cars to see what Audi's share of voice is in the dialogue around cars. Or you could do car subsegments like SUVs, luxury cars, or similar sub –segmentation. This is a great metric to help brands understand "softer" metrics like awareness and perception.

25.4.4. Query volume

Query volume is a search metric. How many queries were performed in a given time period for a given keyword or phrase? This gives us an understanding of the level of interest in a topic. This can change a lot over time – sometimes from one hour to the next for breaking news and developing situations. Don't assume that because query volume for snow boots is low that you should stop tracking it. If it's July, there is a reason.

25.4.5. Influence

Influence measures the overall online influence of a given voice. Keep in mind that just because a person does not have a high influence score doesn't mean they aren't influential. They just may not be a strong social media user – but that doesn't mean they don't influence a lot of people. Check out your favorite reporter. What is his or her Klout score? Did they even break 30? While many journalists use social media, many more do not. Or they don't use it very well. That does not mean they are not influential.

How much influence do they have offline? How many people read their stories or their columns? How many thousands of readers do they have? And what happens if that reporter decides to write something less than flattering about your company or pay closer attention to the CEO's implication in the bribery scandal, or even writes an entire column about their experience. (Yes, it happens.) Our point is this: Social media influence scores are important, but that doesn't mean you should ignore someone who has a lower score. You kind of have to use your human brain to identify your influencers.

Influence is another metric that requires machine interpretation of human dialogue. This means it is an easy metric to "game" and its accuracy should be verified and clarified by other humans. Like with sentiment, share of voice and passion, this requires some interpretive nuance and is not always going to be as accurate as we would like. That being said, it is worth measuring and having a baseline to start from will give you accurate context to understand how your influence and the influence of others is moving.

25.5. Apples –to –apples metrics

There are lots of new ways to measure audience. However, much of the marketing world is focused on one or two metrics, primarily reach and frequency. After decades of buying audience through paid media, marketers have a very good understanding of how many dollars it takes to reach enough of the right people enough times to accomplish their business goals. In fact, with many retailers, they have it down to a level of science where they can accurately predict how many more units of product will move off the shelf with minor changes in their weekly ad – front –page billing in the upper right –hand corner with a quarter –page minimum means a 200 percent increase in sales of canned corn. This isn't because they're using a fancy algorithm. They just have decades of historical information they can use to make fairly accurate predictions.

The same is true in paid media, which is the basis for measurement in earned media as well – the cost per thousand metric. How much does it cost us to deliver 1,000 impressions to our target? This can be a very valuable thing to understand and measure, especially when you are entering the owned media space for the first time. This is a great way to show and communicate value in a universal language that marketers understand. We have had varying degrees of success with using cost per thousand in owned media. Much of this has to do with the level of sophistication of the person to whom the metrics data is being delivered.

Those who understand the methodology behind Nielsen, Arbitron and other similar metrics know the data is *projected*. Meaning, the information is not "real" in the way that digital data represents actual, real things, not a guesstimate of actual, real things. In digital, reach is reach. It is not an estimate of reach. Knowing this, it's apparent that digital metrics are actually far more accurate than what you would get from offline methodology. For more on this, check out the methodology of Arbitron or Nielsen or the Audit Bureau of Circulation (ABC). In comparison to how we measure digital audience, the methodology is arcane and almost laughable. Nevertheless, brands have used this data for decades to spend untold billions of dollars to reach untold projected audiences.

Establishing a comparison cost per thousand for owned, paid and earned gives us common ground. Your owned media reach should include ALL of your owned media channels. Email. Social. Website. Microsites. Blog. Mobile. Everything. How many impressions did you deliver? Divide that by 1,000 and multiply it by the cost per thousand (CPM) you're paying for your offline media. This gives you a good indication of what it would have cost you to deliver the same number of impressions in paid media. Earned media works the same way. Figure out the reach of the publications where you got a hit, add it all up, divide by 1,000 and multiply by your paid media cost per thousand. This at least gives you reach potential, which is really the same thing you are getting in your offline paid media metrics. Nielsen, Arbitron and the ABC are all saying "this is our best estimate of audience size" in paid media. In earned media, we are using that same data to determine reach. In owned media, reach is reach. There is no real estimating. It is what it is. Being able to show its value in a language that everyone in marketing can easily understand will be an important consideration in the continued funding of your efforts.

25.6. Measuring content quality

High –quality content is somewhat subjective. What is "good" or "bad"? It is different to different people. This is something every brand struggles with. What is "good" to one person is "bad" to another on your team. One of the challenges is the language we use to talk about content quality. We use a lot of very subjective words. Some common ones are relevant, compelling, engaging, remarkable. These are the words most often used to describe "what kind of content your brand should be producing." Of course those things hold different meanings to different people, but the only people who really matter are the people in your audience.

What do metrics tell us about the quality of our content? To help your team and its stakeholders translate from subjective human analysis to empirical metric analysis, find out what the words they are using really mean – what is their literal definition. Then find a metric equivalent. Here's an example of how to translate subjective descriptions of content quality to empirical measurements:

Relevant – reach metrics. The audience has made a decision to view the content. It is relvant to them.

Compelling – conversion metrics. The audience was compelled to take the action we want.

Engaging – engagement metrics. The audience has displayed an action that indicates they have experienced the content.

Remarkable – amplification metrics. Literally, the audience remarked to someone else about the content.

25.7. The impact of algorithms

In addition to all the care you take to measure the success of your content and your audience's reaction to it, many other companies are doing the same. They are measuring your content, and the audience, and making decisions for the end user about whether or not your content will be relevant and engaging to them.

In fact, almost every digital platform has an associated algorithm or filtering methodology that makes decisions for the user about what content they get, and what content they don't get. This is why the practice of search engine optimization became so popular. It was the most obvious of all the algorithms. But today, "search" happens everywhere, in different ways but with the same outcome – a curated presentation of content that is most relevant to the end user, usually on an individual basis.

We are talking about algorithms and filters, the gate keepers that exist between your content and your audience. The most common one everyone thinks about is the Google algorithm and other algorithms from search engines. These are just the tip of the spear in the war for audience.

While they use different signals, algorithms determine what content is going to be displayed to your users and are employed in lots of different platforms. Facebook's EdgeRank algorithm is one example. The spam filter is another. These are essentially algorithms or sets of rules that impact whether or not the application is going to share your content with the user. Many of the "reader" style and "my news" applications employ algorithms to find what's relevant to the user, and algorithms help them prioritize it. This can have a big impact on how your content is consumed and shared, and an even bigger impact on your reach and other metrics.

25.7.1. Google and other search algorithms

Google is just another platform that displays content. The whole point of a search engine is to find relevant content. Not relevant web pages, relevant content. Search algorithms are at this point fairly agnostic about what the content "is." They show web pages in search results, but they also show results from social media, from map applications, from location –based mobile apps, and lots of other online sources.

Nobody really knows how search engines make decisions about what content to show users, but the search engine optimization industry has made some good guesses over the years, and through testing, we know two things that matter. You will not be surprised to find out what they are: Quality content and engagement.

Google and other search engines want to show users the best, not the most. That's why the first search engine results page only displays 10 or so of the hundreds of thousands of results that a given query turns up. Search engines want to give the user the best content for their query. So it makes sense that the best way to win search is to make incredibly engaging and compelling content, and make sure your audience interacts with it regularly. This is not brain surgery. You can spend a lot of time and effort on this, and for some brands, it makes sense to be more granular in your approach to search. But what it will always boil down to at the end of the day is this: You must earn your rank.

25.7.2. EdgeRank

Not unlike search algorithms, Facebook's EdgeRank examines your Facebook content and determines whether it shows up in users' news feeds or not. EdgeRank looks at three major factors:

Affinity – Whether people have engaged with the content or not in the past.

Weight – Weight is a description of the content type. Some types of content get more engagement than others. Video has more weight than a photo. Photos have more weight than a link share. A link share has more weight than a status update.

Recency – All things being equal, content that is newer has a better chance of showing up in the news feed. Recency – how old the content is – is a big driver of EdgeRank.

EdgeRank is extremely sophisticated because of the number of factors that are taken into account and how they relate to each other. The algorithm makes different decisions about what to show in the feed (their proactive version of the search engine results page) based on each individual user. For more information on EdgeRank, check out our introductory presentation from 2011, EdgeRankNinja, on SlideShare.

25.7.3. EdgeRank outside of Facebook

We've already discussed EdgeRank as it applies to Facebook content. But it also applies to your website and blog because that content uses Facebook's application programming interface to share and like content. Leveraging Facebook data to customize other applications like websites and mobile apps and other social media apps is a very popular practice. Depending on how it's used, EdgeRank could determine what shows up on your website or what dynamic content is being displayed to the user.

The short of it is: If you want your content to appear on more fans' pages, it needs to be remarkable, high –quality content that resonates with the audience. You can find this out using Facebook's paid media tool. For example, if a sports apparel marketer wanted to know everyone's favorite sports team, Facebook can tell them based on the different likes they've all made. If you like the Cincinnati Reds, then the apparel marketer will put a Reds jersey into the ad that appears on the side of your page.

You can use this data for owned media as well. You can ask Facebook to show you the people who "like" your content or your page, and then cross tab it to examine the trends of your followers. You then produce and promote content based on the information you're able to find.

25.7.4. Spam filters

While not nearly as sophisticated as Google's search algorithm or Facebook EdgeRank, spam filters are the grandfathers of content quality algorithms. Don't forget that every time you send an email, there is a spam filter somewhere making a decision about whether or not to put that content in the user's inbox.

25.8. Content quality is all that matters

The only way to break through the plethora of algorithms and filters standing between your content and your audience is with quality content. If you haven't gotten this throughout the rest of the book, let this be your one takeaway – digital marketing does not work without content. Not just content for content's sake – high –quality content, as defined by your audience. This doesn't mean just technically well –executed content, with all of the i's dotted and t's crossed, with all of the proper metadata and link structures, with the right compression settings to increase page speed. Those things matter, but what matters more is delivering to your audience relevant, engaging, compelling, remarkable content and engaging with that audience and the content they are producing. If you do that well, you will overcome the limits of algorithms and filters, as well as the limits of success.

Epilogue: Getting Started

26. MAKING CHANGE HAPPEN

Well, there you have it. All the thinking, strategy and execution you need to get rolling with owned media. Your C –suite should have no problem totally reinventing how the marketing function works in your organization. Right? Rigggghhhhhttt. Change is always difficult, and we have a few tips here to help you enable change in your company.

26.1. The sixth M

We talked about the five M's earlier, and these are absolutely all the steps you need in your production cycle to manage your audience. There is a sixth M we implemented at Raidious to help remind us to communicate to our internal audience – in our case, the client team, but in the case of an internal team, it would be your stakeholders. The sixth M is merchandising. Not "merchandising," as in part of the marketing function, but merchandising your success internally. You need to continue to sell this concept internally and your team needs to continue to get credit for its success. Building in a sixth step – the merchandising step – to the five M's can help accomplish that.

Make this a step in your process. Treat it just like you would treat content development for your external audiences. One way we do this at Raidious is with a monthly "greatest hits" report. This is a list of the highlights from all of our clients each month, which we use to help our team understand the impact Raidious is having on our clients' business. We post it publicly in our office and share it with our team. Find a way to tell everyone in your company about the work your team is doing, and how it is helping move the needle. Even small wins are worth sharing. This could be done in a number of different ways – as simple as a piece of paper you hang outside your office with your list of wins for the month or an email that gets sent out monthly to give a status update. You could even use a real –time dashboard or command center where you can help your company visualize what it is that you're doing. While you're at it, ask for their feedback, input and questions, just like you would for any other audience. Merchandise, merchandise, merchandise.

26.2. Executive buy in

Everything becomes magically easier when you have executive buy in. Someone at the top level of the company needs to champion your efforts. You are going to need their help to communicate internally, as well as to shake loose the dust of complacency and habit across multiple areas of your company. We would include someone from the executive team as an official "sponsor" of your owned media initiative beyond just the chief marketing officer. If you can get the CEO, or other senior team member to put their thumbprint of approval on your approach and actively participate in it and advocate for it, you will have a much easier time getting cooperation and collaboration from your colleagues.

26.3. Resource allocation

You need to rethink your marketing budget in light of your new owned media operation. This will be your bloodiest battlefield. Everyone in the company wants resources – money, people, space, technology and attention. It's critical that you get the right resources, or like any project, it will fail. The good news is your budget already exists, it is just being classified differently. The bad news is your budget already exists, it is just being classified differently. That means it is likely under someone else's control. This is where we have found executive buy in and support to come in handy.

Here is a rough guideline of what you should be looking for and where you could find it:

Currently, we have found that most enterprise companies are spending between 30 percent and 40 percent of their marketing budget on digital efforts. This is where the majority of your owned media spend should come from. Look at pay –per –click budgets, organic search budgets, web design and development budgets, email marketing, and paid online media like banner ads and Facebook ads and retargeting. Also, look at application development budgets, money being spent on tools and technology. How much of your paid spend is in digital? How much of your earned spend is in digital? How many people in your marketing department have been put into digital –only roles, or platform –specific roles like social media roles, email marketing roles and website –specific roles?

We think 50 percent or more of that money should go toward content development. Erik has a client who was spending $60,000 per month on pay –per –click advertising. After one year of content marketing, the client dropped his pay –per –click advertising and put his focus and energy solely on the content development side of his marketing.

Let's say a company has a $3 million marketing budget. They are currently spending 40 percent of that on their digital marketing – or $1.2 million. Half of that should be devoted to content development – or $600,000.

If you're spending $250,000 on your in –house staff's salaries, that leaves you:

- $40,000 to $60,000 for software, tools, and training.
- $150,000 for additional outside assistance, scalability and specialized projects.
- $100,000 for other opportunistic spending.

Your marketing and public relations agencies should be involved in your owned media efforts. This is not a time to play one against the other or keep them from communicating with each other. Encourage collaboration. Let them learn how they can all contribute to this new campaign. If it all goes well, this will soon mean more work and more business for everyone involved. Rather than jealously guarding their territories, this is a chance for them to work in a truly integrated way across paid, owned and earned to help each area maximize its performance.

26.4. Tiny victories

Don't try to win every battle at once. Don't expect to grow your site's viewership to 100,000 readers in six weeks. Don't try to grow your Twitter follower count to 50,000 in three months. There are social media professionals and companies in this world that have been at it a lot longer and doing it better than you, and they're barely breaking 100,000 readers and 50,000 followers.

Everyone is going to ask you about audience size. It's an easy way to gauge success, and is an important metric, for sure, but it's not the only one that tells a story, and you need to merchandise your victories immediately. Audience growth takes time. It does not happen overnight. Expect at least six months to a year to start seeing significant organic growth, unless you plan on leveraging paid and earned media as a catalyst.

Instead, stay laser –focused on the key performance indicators you identified in planning. Figure out what you'd like your long –term goals to be – 12, 24 and 60 months, and then set milestones along the way. Make some semi –educated guesses, but don't set them in stone. You're either going to be disappointed or wildly surprised with them.

Remember this is a science experiment. Just be flexible, and adjust as necessary. If your first goal was to get 1,000 visitors to your blog in the first month, and you got 100, reassess and adjust your goals. If instead, you got 10,000 visitors, figure out what you did right, figure out how to repeat it, and then adjust accordingly.

Don't shoot for the moon and then quit when you don't hit it. Instead, start small, aim low, and win the battles you know you can win. Show the decision makers, the nay –sayers, and the bean counters your tiny victories and plot your growth from there.

27. GETTING OUTSIDE HELP

We touched on this earlier in the book. It's likely you have some outside partners you already work with who are doing parts of what we have outlined in this book. As you introduce this concept to them, keep in mind the difference between functional capability, and experience and expertise. It is a fact that 99.9 percent of marketing firms were never designed to grow audiences for brands. They are simply not staffed or structured for it, and their strategic process does not account for it. Just because they can design and build websites, or make a 30 –second spot, or illustrate a great ad, or write press releases and ad copy, or create a compelling strategic message does not mean they can deliver all of the real –time, always –on, audience –centric, content –driven deliverables your owned media needs to be successful. They just were not built to do that. If your company is not already working with any outside agencies, and you feel this is a direction you'd like to go, or there are some services that you would like to add to your team, there are some pros and cons for each type of outside company.

27.1. Managing your partners

The most important thing you can do as a leader of an owned media initiative is manage your resources, including your outside partners. Set the appropriate boundaries for your partners, and communicate those boundaries. If they want to contribute across the multiple disciplines of owned, earned and paid media, by all means, collaborate with them, but don't ask your public relations firm to buy your media, or ask your agency to pitch stories for you, or ask your owned media team to develop your brand strategy. Use the right tool for the right job, and keep those tools in their respective tool boxes if they won't stay there of their own accord.

One of the best clients Raidious has ever worked with included outside partners from an SEO firm, a media buying firm, a web design firm, a branding agency, as well as a large internal PR department, all on the same initiative.

Right before our first collaborative meeting, our client sent an email to all of us: "Please check your business card at the door. This is not the place to pitch your services. You are here as an extension of our team."

It was simple, direct and to the point – and highly effective. It's OK to set some ground rules for your internal and external partners, so everyone knows they are there to work for you within their area of expertise. Make no mistake, every marketing services firm is in business to make money. They do that by making you successful, but if opportunities arise on the fringes of their scope of work, they are going to ask for the business. And if they don't arise organically, these firms will bring them to your attention. This is not a bad thing by any means, but being aware of your team's limits, experience and expertise – and using the right tool for the right job – will make your owned media efforts more focused, easier to manage and ultimately more successful.

27.2. Marketing agencies

Marketing agencies might understand your whole goal of owned media, and many of them are making a move in this direction. Good marketing agencies understand the new relationship –based marketing era social media has ushered in. They understand word –of –mouth marketing; they know where social media fits into the mix and can make it part of a larger strategy.

Their writers tend to be focused more on writing marketing copy than the kind of compelling stories you will be looking for, although many of them can easily make the switch with a little rethinking. Occasionally, they will have a writer who has some journalistic experience, whether they came from the newsroom or public relations, and can write the kinds of stories you need for an owned media campaign.

However, not all marketing agencies have embraced social media. Some of them recognize that it's not their strength, and so they won't offer it at all. Still others have added it to their service offering, but their solution is usually to hire a couple of coordinator –level staff members to actually do the social media work.

We know a few agencies that "offer" social media services, but their strategy has been to sell it through their account executives, who have no social media experience, short of the Twitter account they set up two years ago, and haven't used since. The account execs typically have the coordinators actually do the work. What ends up happening is the coordinators come up with a passable channel –specific approach, but it is not the fully integrated strategy that a seasoned pro could create, and it is usually an afterthought from strategic perspective.

The best agencies have fully embraced social media. They use it as a regular part of their strategy, and they see it as one more tool in the marketing toolbox, not just an afterthought.

27.3. PR agencies

Public relations agencies actually come in a multitude of flavors and areas of expertise. Some of them are great at media relations, promotion and writing press releases. Others are more suited to event planning and organizing. Still others are great at "PR 2.0" and do blogger/new media outreach, and identify online influencers as a way to guide conversations within social media. If you work with a PR agency, find the right one to do the part you need. Don't work with an event planner when you need traditional media relations, and so on.

We do like some PR agencies for content creation. Depending on the shop, many PR pros are former journalists and news writers who left the newspaper business and went to work for the other side, going from "hack to flak." If anyone is suited to writing long –form copy, it's the former journalists. If they've been doing it long enough, their muscle memory kicks in, and you can see the old reporter instincts flare up. They'll hammer out a top –notch story as quickly as you need it. The problem is, that's only one kind of content; most PR firms do not have the multimedia production chops or structure to make effective use of most owned –media channels.

The one thing to be wary of is that while many PR agencies are well –suited to writing press releases, or ghost writing articles, that's not necessarily the kind of content you're going to be looking for. Many press releases look like they were written by someone from the "hyperbolic adjective" school of journalism. This is not the kind of writing you need. You want real –sounding stories, not something that sounds phony. Public relations firms are typically more agile than agencies, but it is rare to find PR firms that understand how to leverage real –time audience insights to create real –time content. Also, many PR agencies are way short on understanding how audiences use the web. Some firms are getting there, but most are not quite there yet when it comes to building audience in the digital space.

27.4. Digital shops

Digital shops make digital platforms, not digital content. They're web designers and web architects. They're great at design, user interface and code, but they're short on content creation. We've seen many instances where both the digital shop and the client are expecting the other to write all the copy for the new website launch, and with no other option, the "old milk gets poured into the new carton" at the last minute.

Or in some cases, the client figures they'll "throw something together" when the time comes. Then they pass it off to their most junior staffer who wrote college papers thick enough to stun an ox and is current on all the latest industry jargon, and by the time the staffer is finished, he has written something that actually doubles the size of the Internet.

Digital shops are useful for creating your web presence, sites, portals, microsites, online applications and designing your blog, but that's where their involvement should stop.

27.5. Production shops

These guys make content, right? Well, sort of. Most production studios are highly creative storytellers. They're perfect for video creation, animation, interactive platform creation, and creating a user experience, but they can be rather expensive and usually take months, not hours, to produce anything. Again, these shops were designed and built to tell different kinds of stories – ones with very long story arcs or shelf lives, ones that need to be produced at extreme levels of quality to have an impact.

Depending on your needs, your budget and your timeline, a production shop can be a valuable partner for your more high –end content, and for rethinking how your digital experience can play out from a platform perspective.

27.6. SEO companies

Search engine optimization companies are a dying breed. After Google Panda and Penguin, many SEO companies took a serious hit. Their techniques and tactics were no longer effective, and some of them were even harmful to their clients. Many of the small SEO firms shut down completely, while the larger ones have been forced to retool themselves, abandoning the techniques that made them a lot of money. They've become "content companies." Beware of quality issues here. Most most SEO companies are data –driven, which is good, but they tend to have a very dim understanding of the more irrational, emotional side of marketing and storytelling – not to mention a dim understanding of what it takes to produce quality content from a technical perspective.

To be sure, there are still successful SEO companies out there, but there is no such thing as a "white hat" SEO company. At the end of the day, if they are intentionally gaming the Google algorithm in order to generate higher rank, they are technically breaking Google's best practices, and thus a "black hat" operation. At the very least, a gray hat.

They're not all bad. The best companies not only survived Panda and Penguin, but were doing all of the right things in the first place that they didn't even see a drop in their results after both algorithm changes were rolled out. Be very cautious when working with an SEO company. While they can help you with keyword optimization, and can do some on –site optimization, which is still important, they need to be kept on a very short leash, especially when it comes to back linking strategies. Much of the work a SEO company would have done in the past would, if used today, potentially damage your brand and cost you millions of dollars.

27.7. Social media agencies

Social media agencies are a good source for social media strategy and execution. If you're building your owned media division, but don't have any social media people – or you work for a company with an IT department that has decreed that no one, including the people who will use it to make money for the company, can use social media – then you may want to work with a social media agency.

You may have the staff on hand already, but don't want to hire a social media director. Instead, outsource that function to the social media consultant, engage the consultant for 10 to 40 hours per month, and have the consultant spend time with your social media coordinators to make sure the strategy is working.

27.8. Content companies

Although few and far between, there are a few content companies that can help you with a content –marketing campaign. Two of them are owned by the authors writing this book. But that doesn't mean that out of all these agencies, we're the only ones who can do it. (Although you should call us first, just in case.)

On the one hand, content companies know content marketing. It's what they study, practice, and do on a regular basis. They hire real, professional writers who know their way around the written word. They work with people who have mastered the English language and know – and can execute – in several different writing styles.

On the other hand, many content companies don't do the other things we named. They don't do public relations; they don't do web design, and they don't do marketing or social media campaigns. They write content. As we know, content just sits there. So you will need to make sure your team or one of your other partners is hard at work on the manage, monitor, moderate and measure pieces of the puzzle.

28. CONCLUSION

While what we've said is not an absolute statement about each and every company on Earth, it has been our experience that the services firms we described often fit these descriptions. There are exceptions to every rule, but they're a little harder to find. For example, we know content companies that are good at SEO. We know digital shops that actually do great marketing strategy. And social media agencies that are good at web design.

So we're not saying you should avoid any and all of these companies when looking for an outside agency, or a place to recruit talent from, but rather keep a strong eye out for the company that can do the things you want. Don't automatically reject a company just because they fall within one category or another. Use the right partner for the right job.

The important thing to know is that each of these agencies and firms are all part of a larger puzzle. If you don't have a piece of the puzzle, hire it out. Or if you don't have the budget to bring on a new staff member, outsource the work to the appropriate agency. It is pretty rare to see either extreme – all in –house or all outsourced. In almost every case, it is some combination of the two. And, in any case, just remember that developing an owned media program is a process and involves lots of different moving parts. Keep at it until you find the parts of the puzzle you need to be successful.

28.1. Where it's going

Here are some emerging trends we see coming around the bend that we think will impact and enhance your owned media efforts. The good news is that if you have followed this doctrine, you don't have to change a thing. When you have a content –driven, audience –centric strategy for your owned media properties, the landscape changes and evolves around you.

28.2. Technology that uses you

This is the next area of marketing we think will change things significantly. Many brands and applications are already getting into this, and we think it is pretty thrilling. The idea of "technology that uses you" is applications that use signals you generate to proactively serve up content, in a dynamic, real –time nature, that you will find useful, informative, entertaining, compelling, engaging. And these signals, thanks to mobile devices, can be context –based around your location.

Apple's Passbook is a great example of this. Show up to an airport, and Passbook knows, so it gives you an alert with your boarding pass. Show up at a concert venue… and bam, your tickets pop up. Grocery shopping? Here are some coupons and your store loyalty card. Highlight is another example that shows you which of your friends are nearby – so you can connect (or avoid them if you still owe them $20 bucks from that bet last week).

This is a pretty simplistic use of location context, but it gives you an idea of what could be around the corner for smart marketers who are prepared. What are the implications for owned media? None, really. Owned media is still going to be some form of content and engagement in any case. Remember your strategy is platform agnostic, so if Highlight becomes the next big thing, or some other context –aware application takes the world by storm, all it really means is you need to add it to your list of channels and determine what the best practices are. You will still need content to drive it, and you will still need to listen in real –time to leverage audience data to drive your next piece of content.

28.3. The customer relationship management movement

Remember, social media is about building and growing relationships with specific customers. Just like you wouldn't introduce yourself to someone at a party and then assume they're lifelong customers, you have to nurture your owned media program and your audience in order for them to pay off.

We talked earlier in the persona section about an "audience of one" being the right segmentation strategy, and many brands are taking this CRM –driven approach to social. This is one of the fastest –developing spaces as we complete this book.

A few companies worth mentioning here are Nimble, which is an omni –channel CRM tool that allows for users to see opportunities for unique interactions with everyone on their list.

Another interesting tool is Newsle, which shows information about your contacts and alerts you when they or their company is featured in a news article. These tools are both great at being opportunistic and developing and showcasing engagement opportunities for brands that want to take a more data –centric, CRM –oriented approach to their owned media channels.

What are the implications for owned media? Again, there really are none, outside of the potential need to scale. All of the strategy steps we went through in this book will still apply with this approach. All five M's are still going to be needed, and really nothing more. You will need to make content, manage its distribution, monitor the dialogue, moderate and re-spond to the audience, and measure the results.

28.4. Automation and dynamic owned media

As a result of a more singular customer relationship management driven, lead and conversion focused approach (some call this inbound market-ing) to owned media, companies like Marketo and Eloqua have sprung up to help companies automate their owned media efforts based on the actions and behaviors of each individual person in your audience. ROI, an Indianapolis –based company a block away from Raidious, calls this Customer Lifecycle Marketing. Once the users have been identified, based on their behaviors, ROI dynamically sends content to the user, and the content is especially targeted to his or her situation and is delivered on any of the owned media properties your brand owns or controls. The idea is to move the client through its lifecycle, from awareness, to prefer-ence, to customer, to advocate, on an individual, one –on –one basis.

Being able to do this without some form of automation would be nearly impossible from a scale perspective. But automation tools can make this easy for your team.

As automation and more CRM –focused approaches are deployed, how does that impact your owned media strategy, and the way it is executed? Once again – there is no impact. Every step of the strategy process is still needed. Every one of the five M's is still a requirement. Tactically, you might spend more time developing more proactive content based on triggered events for more segments, but it is still the same execution process – make, manage, monitor, moderate and measure, regardless if the content is automated (proactive or reactive).

29. CREDITS

A quick note to everyone out there looking for more discussion and debate: Neither of the authors have said, ever, that they are experts. Are we experienced? Yes, but we are always learning. If there is someone out there who deserves some credit for their contributions to the owned media concept that we did not mention in this edition, please let us know and we will work it into the next edition. If there are some points in this book that you don't agree with, we would love to hear about your experiences so we can share them with others. If we are flat out wrong about something (it has happened before), we want to know about it. You'll find us at ownedmediabook.com, or just Google our names, Erik Deckers and Taulbee Jackson, to engage in the platform of your choice.

29.1. Acknowledgements and props

Taulbee

I've spent the last six years preparing for this book, and there are a lot of people I would like to thank for their involvement and influence.

Our clients: Everything you have read in this book was enabled by a group of brave, visionary companies and people we at Raidious are proud to call our clients. They took a chance on a young firm with a lot of new and promising ideas, that operated very differently from their other marketing partners, and it paid off. We are so grateful for the opportunity to work with all of the wonderful people we get to work with day in and day out. Thank you so much for having the courage and fortitude to think different about marketing.

The Raidious Family: Joel Read, our co –founding partner. You made this all possible. Brian Wyrick, another founding partner and our CTO. Your vision and level –headedness have made our business thrive. Bob Bourgeois, a stakeholder in our company and its chairman. Without Bob, there would be no Taulbee Jackson. His influence on my thinking and the owned media doctrine is unmatched. Ryan Smith, my business partner and a hugely influential part of what you've read here. Ryan's leadership of our team day to day has lead to dozens of operational, strategic and tactical insights, all of which informed this book. Jim Hyslop, our president and fearless leader. Understanding how to talk about all this came straight from Jim and our work together trying to figure out how to explain all this in a 10 –slide sales deck. (We've done it if you want to see it.) PJ Gindling and Matt Chandler, Brian Conradt – Raidious stakeholders, business partners and hires No. 4, No. 5 and No. 6, respectively. Thank you for all you have done for the company, especially in its early days (and its early nights!). We would never have gotten anywhere without you, and your efforts will always be valued, never taken for granted. Thanks for your continued support.

Our staff, each of whom has contributed greatly to this book – Senior Producer Craig Lile, Director of Content Dan Dark, Director of Strategy Topher Howden, Senior Engagement Managers Kaitlin Coons and Ruby Kohler, Special Projects Manager Kira Peavely, Producers Kelly Simon and Andrew Gouty, Content Correspondents Natasha O'Neill, Kris Davidson, Ashleigh Lay, and Adam Wren, Production Specialist Lisa Manthei, Sales andMarketing Assistant Jennifer Love, and of course Brix the office dog. You guys have no idea how amazing you really are, and I am honored to be working for you.

My previous coworkers and managers: I have had the good fortune of having a career's worth of excellent management and leadership by some true legends in broadcast, marketing, and audience development. Thank you, Wally Leavitt, for all you have done for me throughout my career from the time I took my first job in radio. I bet you didn't see this coming, huh? Thank you, Harry McGinity, for being patient with me and teaching me the ropes of broadcast and audio production, audience development, how the agency world works, as well as how to value my own work. I wanted to work for you for free just for the experience, but you lectured me about it and forced me to take payment. I never forgot that. The entire team at WRTV –6, the Indianapolis ABC affiliate. I learned everything about broadcast news and how to make an incredible story – fast, and in response to what the audience wants – working here. Jeff Smulyan, Kim Moore, Mary Young, Chris Woodward –Duncan, Donna Pitz, and the rest of the awesome people at Emmis Indianapolis –thank you for putting up with me. I learned so much from all of you about broadcast, audience development, and marketing, but mostly about being patient, managing myself, and learning to be a good follower so I could become a good leader. Jeff, you are a model CEO and an inspiration to your people (and they will always be your people, even long after they leave). Thank you, Roger Ingram, for the funnest job I ever had besides this one, and for giving me enough rope to hang myself. Brad Holtz, Laura Duncan, and everyone else there, what I learned about audience development at WTTS lead straight to this book. Bob Meyer and Tim Wallis, thank you for giving me a shot in the agency business at a truly legendary agency. I am proud to have worked with you both, and the opportunity there was incredible. Jason Zickler, Jason Bales, Matt Mays, Dave Lucas and Jim Eiteljorg – it did not turn out how we planned, but I really appreciate the opportunity to have worked with all of you at Boost.

Indianapolis Measured Marketing Family and Partners: It takes a village, and we have one helluva village here in Indianapolis – the Measured Marketing Capital of the World. All kinds of Indiana companies influenced Raidious and the ideas in this book, including Doug Karr at DK New Media, Kristian Anderson, Scott Dorsey and the folks at ExactTarget, Chris Baggot and Ali Sales and the team at Compendium, Kevin Bailey, Aaron Aders, and Jeremy Dearringer at Slingshot SEO, Jacob Leffler, Brian Phillips and the team at The Basement, Jeb Banner and company at SmallBox, Mitch Lindle, John Heur, Jeff Reynolds, and John Reynolds at Cogent Media Group, Troy Burke and team at Right On Interactive, Tom Hirons and everyone at Hirons and Company, the entire Delivra team, and the teams at Aprimo, Marketpath, Imavex, Formstack, Modal Logix, MyJibe, Cantaloupe, Tinderbox, 12 Stars, WebLink, Quipol, SmarterRemarketer, MailBots, iGoDigital, ChaCha.com, AngiesList.com, AutoBase, Candido, PatronPath, Proposable, KA+A, and Denver at The SpeakEasy. #NaptownReprazent.

Special thanks to Chris Dittoe and the entire team at Dittoe PR. Extra special thanks to The Center for Media Design and the rest of the team at Ball State University. Joshua Hall, Jim Jay, Mike Langellier, and the rest of the Techpoint group, and all of the other measured marketing companies we may have missed who have made Indianapolis <u>the</u> place to be for any company in owned media, inbound marketing, content marketing, media, and measured marketing.

Also, to my fearless partner in this endeavor, Mr. Erik Deckers. Man, this was a lot harder than we thought it was going to be, but well worth it. Thanks for agreeing to put up with me on this project. It has been an absolute pleasure working with you.

Influencers: This will be a familiar list to many of you, but I think it is important to give credit where credit is due, even if (especially if) the person has no idea who you are, but they influenced you anyway. Let's start with Seth Godin. Everything in this book, and everything my company is about, was hugely influenced by Mr. Godin's writings and thinking, from permission marketing to "The Purple Cow" and beyond. Morville and Rosenfeld's "Information Architecture for the World Wide Web" is a book everyone involved with online marketing should read and was hugely influential. Tom Peters – highly influential, highly recommend reading "Circle of Innovation and The Pursuit of Wow." The classics – David Meerman Scott's "Inbound Marketing," Jay Conrad Levinson's "Guerilla Marketing," "Marketing in the Age of Google" by Vanessa Fox, "Positioning" by Al Ries, "The Fall of Advertising" by Al and Laura Ries, "Truth, Lies and Advertising" by Jon Steel, "The Art of Client Service" by Robert Solomon, "Content Strategy for the Web" by Kristina Halvorson, "Don't Make Me Think" by Steve Krug, "Letting Go of the Words" by Janice Redish, "Content Rules" by CC Chapman and Ann Handley, Ogilvy's "Confessions of an Ad Man" and "Ogilvy on Advertising", "Managing Enterprise Content" by Ann Rockley, "Blue Ocean Strategy" by W. Chan Kim, and Guy Kawasaki's "Art of the Start" and "Rules for Revolutionaries."

We also were influenced by research and white papers from Sean Corcoran (at the time, of Forrester Research), Jeremiah Owyang of Altimeter Research, The Pew Internet Research group, Society for New Communications Research, the Interactive Advertising Bureau, marketing trade groups including the Chicago Interactive Marketing Association, the American Association of Ad Agencies, the Public Relations Society of America, and the American Marketing Association.

We got real –time education with data, research and findings from the teams at eMarketer, ExactTarget, Compendium, Razorfish, Radian6, Hubspot, Spredfast, Awareness Networks, Sysomos, HootSuite, Alterian SM2, EdgeRank Checker, Crispin Porter + Bogusky, Stamen Design, Big Spaceship, and a multitude of public posts, thinking and tweets from Doug Karr, Jay Behr, David Armano, Boxes and Arrows, Rachel Lovinger, Steve Rubel, and probably a whole slew of other people I have overlooked. To you, I apologize in advance. To everyone else I have listed here, thank you so much for sharing your wisdom and experience with me and with the world. We all appreciate it.

Last but not least, I would like to thank my very patient and under-standing family. Wendy, Taulbee (not me, there's actually another one), Tyce, Tayton - thanks for putting up with me. You're the most amazing family anyone could ask for, thanks for being you.

Erik

This is the fourth book I've contributed to, and the third I've been able to stick my name on (don't ask; long story). It's also one I'm very proud of. And everything I've learned over the last six years has been because of some very smart and special people. So, thank you to my business partner Paul Lorinczi, past co –authors Kyle Lacy and Jason Falls, Douglas Karr, Jay Baer, Darrin Gray, Sarah Robbins (the fairy godmother of Indianapolis social media), Lorraine Ball, fellow word nerds Allison Carter and Ryan Brock, Duncan Alney, and the guy who gave me my social media start professionally, Mike Seidle.

There are quite literally hundreds, if not thousands, of people I have met who have shared some piece of knowledge that imprinted on my brain, made connections with other pieces of knowledge, and they all got amassed into, well, this book. If you have read this book and said to yourself, "Hey, I know that dude! He's following me on Twitter!" then you're one of the hundreds, if not thousands, of people I'm thinking of. And while I can't thank everyone personally, let me thank you now.

Finally I would especially love to thank my loving wife, Toni, and my three children, Madison, Emmalie, and Benjamin. Family always comes first, unless you put them last in the credits so they're set apart typographically.

30. PREQUEL TO THE OWNED MEDIA DOCTRINE

This concept, like most good ideas, was built on the shoulders of giants. It has been a group effort. Lots of people have contributed their thinking and influenced both authors. If we could trace it all back, we would probably find the DNA of this idea – the "prequel" to The Owned Media Doctrine – in Bill Gates' famous "Content Is King" essay from 1996. That was Taulbee's first year working in radio and TV, and in 1996, Erik was working for an international export company, marketing poultry feeding equipment overseas. Way before either of us considered the ramifications of the changes in today's media environment, and how to solve all the new problems that exist.

More recently, Taulbee wrote an article for Digiday about how the concept of owned media was at the core of ideas like Real –Time Marketing, Brand Newsrooms, and other related concepts. This article does a really good job of introducing these concepts, and giving marketers some things to think about as they move in this direction. The Digiday article was limited to 1,000 words, but here is the rest of the article in its entirety.

30.1. Ten Reasons Your Brand Newsroom Will Fail: Real –Time Marketing in The Real World

by: Taulbee Jackson

Is the brand newsroom approach the right operational approach for managing real –time owned media? Absolutely, without a doubt. Nobody is a bigger proponent of this idea than I am. The marketing operations model has not changed significantly since DDB paired up writers and art directors in the 60s. Agencies, PR firms, and client –side teams have not evolved operationally with media habits over the years. It's way past time for change, people. . . but the concept of the "brand news room" is just the tip of the iceberg.

Just because this is the right operational approach for owned media doesn't necessarily mean it's a good idea for brands to attempt to do it in –house. Nor does it mean it's a bad idea. There are lots of good arguments both ways. Like most questions in marketing, it depends on the brand. Clearly the companies that are doing this well in house are very successful with it. They are an inspiration, and they are helping marketers think different. So, here's to you, Coke. Thank you, Red Bull. There are a handful of other companies that have similar efforts going on, and there is a lot of good work starting to happen in this space with those brands. That only leaves. . . well, the rest of the marketing world. But, just like video edit suites and TV production studios and animation workstations and social media command centers, brand news rooms and the operational approach and real world requirements associated with them are not the right in –house solution for every brand.

First of all, the "brand news room" approach popularized at the 2012 Super Bowl that everyone is now so excited about was not groundbreaking, it was just high profile, and marketers were ready to understand it. The most truly interesting thing about it is that it has inspired marketers to take the next step down their maturity path to fully understanding the new realities of marketing ops in the real world.

After all this buzz about social media and content marketing and in-bound marketing, we are finally starting to understand which questions to ask. We've matured from "what's social media" to "how do I handle monitoring" to "how do I drive conversion" to "wow, it's *really* just about content" to "oh, it needs to be in real –time," in about three years. That is fast for our business. Now, we are finally considering the operational im-plications of all this … because the operational methodology of agencies, PR firms and in house marketing teams is failing to fulfill the real world requirements.

They're not staffed or structured to handle it. The newsroom approach was built for it, and gone through a lot of evolution and refinement as media has evolved, for the last several decades. Soon, marketers will mature even further and get to the deeper issues, like the long term implications for traditional marketing theory, the need to totally rethink integrated mar-keting strategy, and the implications for spend allocation. . . but let's deal with the operational issues first, since that is where the conversation's at in today's reality. The answers will come soon.

So, you may be asking, "why should I listen to this guy about real –time marketing and brand news rooms?" You probably have no idea who I am. Let me introduce myself. My background and experience is in marketing and audience development for broadcast, broadcast news and production, and I spent some time as an account planner, moving into a VP, digital role on the agency side for a large regional firm. Everywhere I have been, I was always the "digital guy." Agency people know the guy I'm talking about, you've all had one. The go –to person for "websites and email and interactive stuff." That was me.

Instead of spending the last decade becoming an "influencer" on the topic of content and real –time marketing and brand newsrooms, like Armano and Rubel and those kinds of folks, I started a company – I tend to learn faster by doing, rather than discussing. I asked the right question, and solved the right problem. I spent all my time testing and optimizing it in the real world with real clients, and delivering real world business results. My company has a 100% success rate growing audiences for brands. We are structured, staffed, and operate exactly like. . . an embedded brand news team. And we have been operating like this, by implicit design, for years.

I'm the CEO of a real –time owned media services company called Raidious. We found the answers marketers have been searching for. . . even if they didn't know they were, even though it was right in front of them the whole time. How do we handle digital? How do we handle social? How do we staff for this? What skills do we need? All good questions in their time, and tough problems to solve. But Raidious was purpose built to solve the only problem that matters in digital marketing – creating and converting audiences on brand owned media channels. Every online channel is real –time. Every medium is social. None of them work without content. All of them are dependent on audience development to work. So the tactical problem is a content problem, because the strategic implications revolve around audience development and motivation. By definition, because media (all media) is an always on, non –linear, place –shifting, time –shifting multichannel multi –device environment — the solution, strategically, operationally and tactically — has to be functional in real –time.

We were the first agency specifically created from scratch to take the newsroom approach to real –time marketing. In fact, we've been working on solving real –time content problems using the newsroom approach since 2006. We created the concept of the Content Correspondent, a cross –functional role based on how reporters work in 2007.

I was one of the of the first to use the term "owned media," helping define its integrated relationship with Earned and Paid months before Forrester's popular early research on the topic in 2009. We developed the first comprehensive strategic methodology built to address owned media strategy, creating and refining best practices around real –time marketing theory, strategy, and operations in 2010. Raidious was the first agency to create our own real –time brand news room, which we have used for client work every day since it launched in 2011.

Everyone is familiar with the real –time marketing efforts for the 2012 Super Bowl, and how brand news rooms were used to accomplish it. My company created and ran the "brand news room" for the Super Bowl. We developed the strategy and designed and built the command center. We also executed all of the real –time marketing – including all content development, social media monitoring and moderation, email, blog content, web video.

Did we do the Oreo work? Uhh. . . no, that was a different shop. I'm not talking about the Super Bowl everyone's talking about right now, with the iconic Oreo interaction. I'm talking about one that happened the year before — Super Bowl XLVI in February of 2012.

We've spent the last six years creating and optimizing everything from strategic process to production process to technology all the way down to the psychographics of the perfect employee. We literally wrote the book on this stuff, it's coming out this summer. We've helped organizations like Walmart, the U.S. Government, Turner Sports, Finish Line, Klipsch, and over 40 other brands figure out real –time marketing. Along the way, we learned a few things here and there about what it really takes to do this well, both within our company and on the client side. I would like to share those things with you here. Not to scare you off, or discourage you from building your own brand news room – just to make sure you know what you're getting into – in the real world, it is not as easy as it looks.

If you want to take your company in this direction, there are several things you need to consider before you start building out a brand newsroom, and addressing your company's real –time marketing needs with tactics, tools and resources. Considering these real world implications will, I hope, ultimately lead you to the new marketing reality you've been searching for. But it can be a rough trip getting there. You have to forget a lot about what you think is reality, and unlearning what you currently know to be true is always harder than learning something new. Some can't or won't do this, and will cling to historical operations best practices, and that is okay. There will always be a need for great brand strategy, great TV spots, great relationships with traditional media. . . there is nothing wrong with taking the blue pill. At the same time, if you're going to take the red pill, you won't be sorry – but you should know how far the rabbit hole goes.

Here are some current realities that may be a challenge to you and your company as you move to a real –time newsroom model in the real world:

1) You believe you're in the content business. Actually, brands are *not* in the content business. Neither are agencies or PR firms or digital shops. More importantly, they are not in the audience development business. That is what news rooms are about — not creating content in real –time, but creating audience that can be monetized. Be focused on the end, not the means. Audience development is the newsroom's sole reason for being. Everything about news organizations, from culture to employee compensation is built around moving the audience needle. If you're building a brand news room to enable real –time content production, instead of enabling audience development across all your owned media properties, you're looking through the wrong end of the telescope.

2) You think you can just dive in with tactics. It's not just about using the production process real newsrooms employ to produce content in real –time. Yes, it's true: digital marketing does not work without content. Content is the fuel that drives every single online interaction on the Internet, regardless of channel. Every digital marketing problem is a content problem, and brands do need to be able to get content produced in real –time. But building a brand newsroom is a tactical answer to much deeper strategy, operations, culture and marketing theory problems. "Change the corporate org chart" kinds of problems.

If you don't have an understanding of how your owned media strategy is going to integrate with your paid and earned strategy, do not pass go, do not collect $200 ... stop what you're doing, and handle that. If you think a content audit and that crazy spreadsheet you call an editorial calendar is a real –time content strategy, go straight to jail. You don't know what you don't know, and you're not ready yet for real –time. If you do have a firm understanding of how owned, earned and paid media are going to work together to produce a business outcome, and you're appropriately allocating dollars and resources, and you've gone through the basics of owned media strategy ... like risk assessment, developing a business case with measurable KPI's, creating personae, developing taxonomy, building a subject topography, working through all the governance and distribution issues, creating the appropriate engagement, monitoring and moderation strategy ... then you can have your newsroom.

3) You think your company is agile. The internal communications structure for many brands will not allow for reasonable real –time governance because that has never been a requirement until recently. Again, having the nicest newsroom in the world doesn't matter if governance issues cause a roadblock to real –time response. It also doesn't matter if you have to put all the right people in the same physical room to achieve real –time governance. That might work for one –off events, but it is not a sustainable operations model, and if you do it right, you won't need everyone in the same room ever. The large majority of brands don't do anything in real –time, and most people work 9 –5. Real –Time marketing is a 24/7 proposition, and getting people to think and work that way is harder than you think. It's a cultural issue. You're most likely not fast enough culturally to do this well. This is where we see most brands fail with real –time marketing. It's not as much about how newsrooms make content as it is their entire cultural orientation toward real –time audience development.

4) You think someone should "own" creative. Your marketing team most likely can't deal with the creative process requirements for real –time owned media. It probably took them five years to get control of the website from the IT department, and PR and Advertising are probably still fighting over "who owns social media." Your team probably has at least three to five levels of approval for most marketing efforts, all of which ultimately roll up to a CMO or VP of Marketing person who has the final say over all things creative, and tends to either have the ideas, or control the ideas.

On the agency side, the creative director has the ideas. Yes, there is collaborative brainstorming, but at the end of the day, someone makes the call on creative. Decentralizing the creative function – for real – will be the most incredibly painful thing for clients and agencies alike. The best ideas and executions will come from the team that is interacting with the audience and seeing the data and feeling the flow, every day. There is also scalability and localization to think about. . . a Creative Director doesn't really fit in this operational equation. That role was designed to create The Big Idea based on creative interpretation and expression of consumer perceptions – not a thousand little ideas based on empirical data. Are they related? Yes. Same thing? No way. In a newsroom, storytelling and creativity is a decentralized, individual effort where the people telling the story are expected to research, develop and execute the story, without the guidance (some would say constraints) of an overarching creative role. Trusting lots of people to make creative decisions is not easy, but it's a real world requirement for every day always –on media.

5) You think you can judge what "good" content is. Sorry, nobody on your team gets to do that anymore. That is now in the job description of your audience. This hugely subjective topic may be one of the most difficult issues to deal with, and most difficult behavior and mindset to change ... but in a way it is also the easiest, because your audience is telling you, right now, what content is good and bad. In fact, they are screaming it so loudly from the rooftops that entire industries have been spawned to understand what it is that they're saying.

We're talking about analytics. Audience metrics. Social media metrics, email analytics, website metrics ... every measurement we look at online is a measurement of content quality, not the effectiveness of the platform. We're not measuring whether or not Facebook works, or email works, or mobile works ... we know those platforms can technically accomplish the delivery of content. What we actually are measuring is not the platform, it's the content, and your audience will tell you loud and clear what "good" content is based on these metrics.

In the real world, there is room for subjective interpretation and creativity ... you can and should experiment freely. Let your gut guide you, by all means. But understand, no matter what you or anyone else on your team thinks, in the world of the newsroom, the ratings always make the final decisions for you on content quality – and digital metrics are your version of the ratings. You get a report card back every day (or every minute!) on the quality of your work product. That is the reality of judging content quality, and it can be overwhelming and intimidating for people who believe they are making good content to learn that that audience is telling them ... ahhh, not so much. Which they will. Early and often, sometimes through comments, more likely through silence, but always through data.

6) You think marketing and PR people can make content. Most brands and agencies and PR firms don't have a team in house that understands audience development. They understand PR, they understand marketing, they understand technical production requirements, and are skilled at delivering high quality output with industry standard tools, but that is not what a Brand Newsroom is about.

It is not about the "how do I get you to buy something" mindset, but thinking in the "how do I deliver content to you that is relevant, interesting, compelling, and remarkable consistently, so you stay engaged with me?" way. Much different proposition, this is not a marketing problem, it is an entertainment problem that takes a much different mindset.

You should also examine the difference between functional capability, and experience and expertise. Everyone can type. Very few can write. Everyone can shoot video on their cell phone. Very few can tell a compelling story with video. Everyone can draw a picture. Few are illustrators. Everyone can take photos. Very few can compose a compelling image. Everyone can sing. Everyone can dance. Everyone can act. But very few are good at it in a way that would cause an audience to consistently pay attention and engage. The ability to make a :30 second spot and write a press release or a great headline is a transferable technical skill set, but it's a totally different mindset and approach to use those skills to develop your own audience, rather than just influence or sell to someone else's audience.

7) You think technology can solve the problem. Owning a hammer does not make you a carpenter. It definitely does not make you an architect. Yet, the first thing most brands do when faced with the problem of how to deal with real –time marketing is look to technology. This is a hard and expensive lesson to learn in the real world, but I imagine almost every brand has some tool or software or technology somewhere that they thought would solve all their problems that is currently gathering dust.

Leveraging technology is a crucial component to making this work, especially if you don't want your entire marketing team standing in a room waiting to approve content in two or three shifts a day, and on weekends. But the tech is truly the very last thing you should be worried about. Too many brands are letting the technology they have invested in drive their strategy, instead of letting their strategy drive their technology decisions. We have seen this with literally every brand we have worked with.

Doing "real –time" well requires more than just addressing content and social media tools for creation, management and measurement. It often has implications for enterprise systems, from office productivity suites to CRM to customer service tools. It all has to work together, and there is no one tool or system in existence that does it all well. Even if there was, without the appropriate strategic, cultural, philosophical, tactical, monetary and human resources, investing in technology is like burning money you could be using to create great content, which is the only thing that makes it work in the first place. So invest there before you buy that shiny new software tool with all the cool charts and dashboards.

8) You're afraid to fail. In a lot of company cultures, failure is a bad thing. It is highly unlikely that your first efforts will be successful. Don't let the deafening silence of zero engagement on your first real –time content sway you. To do this well, you have to be a scientist with your right hand and an artist with your left.

There are only six things you need to do to make a failure a success: Test. Optimize. Test. Optimize. Test. Optimize. Do not be afraid to experiment. There are so many variables for every piece of content, even minor modifications to today's failures can lead to major future wins, but you have to develop a culture of measuring, testing, experimenting — and failing — all the time, at the cultural level.

A lot of what you do won't work well. Some of it will. A tiny portion of it will be absolutely mind –blowingly successful. This is not just about split testing and multivariate and what color a button is. At the subject level, having a good handle on what's failing and what's not — again, the subject, not the content type, or the platform — will be crucial to moving your brand newsroom from early failure to wild success. In the real world, real –time failure is a requirement, and so is the cultural, strategic and operational capacity to learn from real –time failure. In real –time.

9) You think you have a content strategy. You probably think an audit and an editorial calendar are enough. If there is one thing we have learned for sure, it's that editorial calendars are a huge waste of time when you're dealing with real –time marketing, and they actually take you in the opposite direction you should be heading. Editorial calendars — which everybody spends a lot of time on, and nobody ever uses — are great at helping the brand decide what *they* want to publish, which is the exact opposite of what they should be using for guidance on content production.

Generally, the editorial calendar is all about what the brand wants to talk about, and it is tied to some kind of product launch or campaign or other marketing calendar item or campaign. You know what your audience wants to talk about? What ever they're interested in right now. Depends on what's happening in the world right now. Something that is relevant to them and helps them somehow. Right now.

Good luck getting content produced that your audience cares about with your editorial calendar. Magazines use editorial calendars. They publish once a month. Broadcast Newsrooms use rundowns. They publish when it's relevant to do so, often in real –time, and often across multiple channels. Think about that, and what it takes just operationally to make that work. That is newsroom methodology.

Now, if you really want to bake your noodle, think about the strategic implications — not only must you now plan for what you can't plan for, but real –time marketing goes beyond simple content strategy – how do you deal with the reactive content piece of the puzzle? What are the customer service and HR implications? How will your organization deal with that? You will need to understand a little bit about a lot of things, from search to crisis management to library science to in –depth cross platform analytics to really get to a usable strategic approach. You will have to not just rethink marketing strategy, but marketing theory, operations and execution – we are talking wholesale reinvention of almost everything you've been taught. That's the reality of real –time content strategy.

10) You think it's all about The Big Idea. I am a huge proponent of the Big Idea. Agencies have gotten extremely good at developing and communicating the brand promise through highly creative campaigns. But real –time marketing does not only require The Big Idea (which is absolutely critical), it requires a thousand little ideas. It requires that those little ideas support and extend and activate The Big Idea. It requires that those little ideas, even when not directly related to The Big Idea, convey the essence of it. It requires that those little ideas find a contextually relevant relationship at the subject level between your Big Idea and whatever is happening in the world right now, and what ever is relevant to your audience right now.

How those thousand little ideas are going to work with all those re-quirements has to be understood by your Brand Newsroom team. The Newsroom only solves the production issue, you still have to answer the "what" questions — what should we be creating content about, right now, to support the Big Idea, and everything else? Or better yet, how do we le-verage our audience to get to the next Big Idea, and how does it play out in real –time? Well, that changes things, doesn't it?

The idea of a brand news room is similar to all the buzz that happened around social media command centers awhile back. It is a super –sexy, easy to understand, tactile, real –world representation of a new and complex idea. But for the most part, it's merchandising, it's not mission critical. Ask any social media manager if they could do their job without a command center. If you have a social media team, does it help to have a big wall of screens with data? Absolutely. Do they spend most of their time with their eyes on their computer monitors instead of the wall? Well, yeah. Could they do most of their work from a cell phone anywhere there's 4G? Yep. Does that make their work any less valuable? No, it doesn't. Would the company have funded their position without seeing it all happen in a command center environment? Probably not. Would the level of internal awareness about real –time and social media issues suffer without a command center? Sure it would. Is it, then, a good investment? Yes. Does it matter without the appropriate strategy, staff, structure, and tools? No. It does not make any impact on business without those things. In the real world, a brand newsroom – like a command center, and like all those software tools everyone buys – only matters if there is strategy and experienced, expert human resources behind it, making it deliver value. Only humans can make content. Not tech. Not process. Not hardware. Not software. Only humans.

As innovators in this space, it has been great to see the rest of the world catch up over the last six months. Not only on the client side with all the Super Bowl and Oscar stuff, but lots of digital agencies have entered the fray in early 2013. PR firm Golan Harris has restructured to help address real –time. After visiting with Raidious, another PR firm, Edelman, rolled out their SICC with thought leader David Armano in their Chicago office, and a few short weeks ago, finally created their first executive content role, for the visionary Steve Rubel. Deep Focus is starting to take a newsroom approach. Even big agency holding companies are getting into it: Publicis rolled out their take on our approach, with their Digitas Brandlive experiment (full disclosure: Publicis has been a Raidious client since 2010).

The tide has finally turned. What has been interesting over the years is we kept waiting for someone to shoot holes through this concept, and nobody did. Nobody told us we were crazy. Once you think about it, it is, like most good insights, incredibly simple and obvious. We explained it, the light bulb came on, and everybody just nodded. And not only has it worked incredibly well, but it is now being embraced by the companies who live and die by marketing operations. It is exciting and vindicating to see major global forces come to our way of thinking on this. It's a major, historical shift in the way people think about marketing.

Even SEO companies like 360i are moving this direction. They obviously made a big splash with Oreo, but their solution wasn't really a new solution at all, was it? Do things the old way, but faster, and in the same room? Really? And why only on Super Bowl Sunday, or Oscar Day? You know, your audience shows up every day, and to do this well, it takes everyday commitment. If your agency's solution to establishing real –time governance is to put all the client stakeholders in the same physical room with the art directors producing the content, you have a problem. Your agency missed recent developments like instant messaging, email, file sharing, cloud services, and the evolution of the social media management system. Plus, I am pretty sure client side marketers have lots of other things to do besides stand around and wait for the lights to go out.

I know a lot of what I've written here is challenging – but it's reality, not theory. If you disagreed with each of the points above, and said with conviction, "No, I don't!" then by all means, create your Brand News Room. You should open it right next to your Social Media Command Center. Welcome to the Matrix.

Or, if you really want to do it right, and make it work in the real world, you can start by rethinking what marketing theory and strategy should accomplish in today's media environment, by examining how you're allocating your spend to rent eyeballs, or pitch and pray, instead of owning the audience, and what needs to change operationally to support that.

Marketers have been talking for years about 360 degree holistic integrated marketing strategy but they are completely missing a full third of the equation, and with the way media has evolved, the first two thirds are backward. Customers only come from audiences. Marketers can only access audiences three ways: they can buy their attention with paid media, they can borrow their attention with earned media, or they can build relationships directly with owned media. All of it needs to work together in real –time, with a unified strategy that addresses paid, earned and owned, and allocates the right resources to each of those areas, and the only way it works is with content.

But instead of looking at owned media as a support mechanism for earned and paid, think about the implications of what happens when you use paid and earned to support owned media. Why are you still letting other organizations charge you to have a relationship with your potential customers, when you have the means to reach them directly? It makes no sense, but it's the way things have always been, until now. Start with that, and the function of the newsroom concept will make a lot more sense in the bigger scheme of things.

References

http://tess2.uspto.gov/bin/showfield?f=doc&state=4006:p4wq4q.2.5

http://www.raidious.com/owned-media/

http://www.raidious.com/content-marketing/earned-media-vs-paid-media-vs-owned-media/

http://blogs.forrester.com/interactive_marketing/2009/12/defining-earned-owned-and-paid-media.html

http://darmano.typepad.com/logic_emotion/2009/02/thoughts-on-bought-earned.html

http://www.flickr.com/photos/raidious/sets/72157626169817923/show/

https://docs.google.com/file/d/0B8qZfMHgtHnKMUFvT3l4TnlUY1NjO UJKaUdrZjZ1UQ/edit?usp=sharing

http://adage.com/article/viewpoint-editorial/time-brand-invested-a-creative-newsroom/237225/

http://www.digiday.com/brands/should-brands-have-newsrooms/

http://adage.com/article/cmo-strategy/super-bowl-oscars-ads-show-marketers-fascinated-rtm/240035/

http://www.prdaily.com/Main/Articles/The_essential_ingredients_of_a_brand_newsroom_13970.aspx#

http://www.digiday.com/brands/can-brands-build-newsrooms/

http://contently.com/blog/2013/02/27/why-rethinking-the-brand-newsroom-is-a-smart-move/

http://www.clickz.com/clickz/news/2251142/brands-move-to-newsroom-model

http://www.digiday.com/brands/brands-need-a-new-type-of-newsroom/

http://darmano.typepad.com/logic_emotion/2012/11/brand_media.html

http://www.thedrum.com/opinion/2012/04/13/do-you-have-brand-newsroom

http://adage.com/article/digital/oreo-s-daily-twist-campaign-puts-cookie-conversation/237104/

CPSIA information can be obtained at www.ICGtesting.com
Printed in the USA
LVOW13s1135230114

370665LV00003B/4/P